CW01510141

PSYCHOLOGY AND PRIMITIVE CULTURE

PSYCHOLOGY AND PRIMITIVE CULTURE

Bartlett,f.c.

www.General-Books.net

Publication Data:

Title: Psychology and Primitive Culture
Author: Bartlett,f.c.
Reprinted: 2010, General Books, Memphis, Tennessee, USA
Publisher: At The University Press.
Publication date: 1923
Subjects: PHILOSOPHY. PSYCHOLOGY
Philosophy of mind

How We Made This Book for You
We made this book exclusively for you using patented Print on Demand technology.
First we scanned the original rare book using a robot which automatically flipped and photographed each page.
We automated the typing, proof reading and design of this book using Optical Character Recognition (OCR) software on the scanned copy. That let us keep your cost as low as possible.
If a book is very old, worn and the type is faded, this can result in numerous typos or missing text. This is also why our books don't have illustrations; the OCR software can't distinguish between an illustration and a smudge.
We understand how annoying typos, missing text or illustrations, foot notes in the text or an index that doesn't work, can be. That's why we provide a free digital copy of most books exactly as they were originally published. You can also use this PDF edition to read the book on the go. Simply go to our website (www.general-books.net) to check availability. And we provide a free trial membership in our book club so you can get free copies of other editions or related books.
OCR is not a perfect solution but we feel it's more important to make books available for a low price than not at all. So we warn readers on our website and in the descriptions we provide to book sellers that our books don't have illustrations and may have numerous typos or missing text. We also provide excerpts from each book to book sellers and on our website so you can preview the quality of the book before buying it.
If you would prefer that we manually type, proof read and design your book so that it's perfect, simply contact us for the cost. We would be happy to do as much work as you would be like to pay for.

Limit of Liability/Disclaimer of Warranty:
The publisher and author make no representations or warranties with respect to the accuracy or completeness of the book. The advice and strategies in the book may not be suitable for your situation. You should consult with a professional where appropriate. The publisher is not liable for any damages resulting from the book.
Please keep in mind that the book was written long ago; the information is not current. Furthermore, there may be typos, missing text or illustration and explained above.

1

PSYCHOLOGY AND PRIMITIVE CULTURE

PRINTED IN GREAT BRITAIN

MY WIFE

PREFACE r OR the psychologist the unity of primitive and modern society is as important as their differences. In primitive society the groups are smaller, more localised, and less diversified; and individual initiative is probably less prominent. The underlying psychological mechanisms, however, remain much the same at all stages of social development. Since these mechanisms stand out more clearly in the early stages, and are there, on the whole, less intricately intermingled, the psychological study of primitive culture forms the best introduction to the psychology of contemporary social life. This is the position which is adopted and maintained in the present book.

The book falls naturally into three parts. First the principles which the psychologist should use in his attempt to understand the behaviour of man in society are set forth; secondly these principles are applied to the psychological treatment of certain outstanding problems of primitive culture; and in the third place it is shown how the use of the principles must be modified as the psychologist passes from the study of the social life of remote times, or peoples, to that of modern civilised society.

Throughout I have tried to keep closely in touch with concrete problems, and, except in the chapter on the formation of folk tales, I have chosen to consider questions which have so far been dealt with by the ethnologist, rather than by the psychologist. Thus I have discussed the psychology of the contact of peoples; of how elements of culture are "borrowed," and so transferred from one group to another; and of the psychological mechanisms of the diffusion of culture within a group, and its consequent elaboration or simplification. All of these I have tried to put in terms of the psychological tendencies which they express. In modern life precisely the same tendencies are at work. I have shown, for example, how they help to produce the "broken contracts" which are a noteworthy feature of much modern political and econonic bargaining. What is peculiar to contemporary society, I have urged, is not the tendencies, but their arrangement.

The book is based on some lectures which I delivered in 1922 at the Bedford College for Women in the University of London. It was mainly on the advice of the late Dr W. H. R. Rivers that I undertook these lectures. He died before the book was completed, but I many times discussed its subject-matter with him, and owe more to him for his friendship and interest than I can ever adequately express. To Dr C. S. Myers I am as deeply indebted. He has helped, criticised, and encouraged me throughout. He read the book in type and improved it in many ways. A similar kindness in reading the typescript was shown me by Dr Paul Radin, to whom I am particularly indebted for help in regard to the discussion on "borrowing."

It will be obvious that I have profited greatly from the writings of various American anthropologists. In particular the ethnological and anthropological publications of the Smithsonian Institution appear to me to be mines from which the psychologist may quarry a great quantity of treasure. I desire to thank the Smithsonian Institution for permission to reproduce the drawings which appear on p. 233, and to make numerous quotations from various publications.

And most of all I wish here to acknowledge gratefully the constant help which has been given to me by my wife.

F. C. BARTLETT.

CAMBRIDGE, April, 1923

CONTENTS

CHAPTER I

THE APPROACH TO THE PROBLEM

The Argument: The psychologist, in dealing with primitive culture, must first try to discover the fundamental tendencies which find expression in human social behaviour. I Some of these the instinctive tendencies are common to all people, others the individual difference tendencies differentiate one person from another. Both alike are expressed in the course of education, but are independent of its particular details. Characteristics of the external environment, and of social structure, affect human behaviour through their relations to these tendencies, and to others which are derived from them.

The tendencies must be distinguished and described; their relations one to another in the primitive community must be discussed; we must show how they act upon and are themselves influenced by their material and social environment; how they persist, and aid in the formation of new tendencies; and how some of them may become overlaid and weakened as the complexity of culture increases.

In all our explanations we must guard against the temptation to separate the individual entirely from his group, and to seek a pre-social origin for social behaviour. There are certain problems as to the beginnings of things which can always be raised, no matter what social community is being investigated. To deal with these inevitably leads to speculation. In other cases, questions arise concerning the origin of modes of behaviour which have become stabilised as conventions during a period preceding that which we have selected for study. We are justified in accepting such modes of behaviour without further investigation into the manner of their growth. But changes in social behaviour which have arisen in a group during the period which we have selected for study must be explained.

Throughout the whole of our investigation we shall be dealing, not with the nature of human beliefs, ideas and attitudes, but with the determination of behaviour in the primitive group, and with how such behaviour is affected by facts of social structure and by cultural possessions.

It is insufficient merely to make lists and classifications of the tendencies which issue in types of behaviour. The ways in which these tendencies are related to one another in primitive society must also be considered. For it is not the response alone, but the person who makes the response, that we wish to understand. A study of material environment is often of great help in the elucidation of the inter-relations of different forms of response.

Into our psychological explanations we may frequently, as a matter of method, admit social facts which have not been analysed into their ultimate psychological elements. Accordingly, the psychological study of the primitive group is not to be treated as if it were independent of sociology.

It is curious to reflect that anyone who desires to write about psychology is still forced to enter into a preliminary exposition of his point of view. Psychology may be concerned with almost anything that has any connexion whatever with human beings, from a study of the movements of muscles, and the secretions of glands, to speculation about personality, free-will, and the Deity. At least such an impression may well be conveyed by a study of current discussion. When a topic containing the word psychology is proposed, nobody can be quite sure what field of fact or of fable is going to be explored, or what method of treatment is going to be adopted.

The inquiry which I am about to undertake professes to be a psychological study of certain problems of primitive culture. It is my first duty, therefore, to state as definitely as possible the main features of the treatment which will be adopted.

Everybody now recognises that human beings begin the: r lives with certain tendencies to action and to feeling ready to come into operation the moment appropriate conditions are established. Some of these tendencies are common to all men, or, at least, are very widely shared indeed, and these we call instinctive 1. Others possess a more individual character. From the first they are the tendencies which distinguish one person from another. In the course of their development they play a large part in building up those interests and specialised abilities which constitute a man's personality, and are the most ready means of differentiating him from others. On account of their main function, the tendencies belonging to this second group are best known as "individual difference tendencies

Flight, for example, is an instinctive tendency. It is one of the several modes of response to a danger situation which no human being needs to learn by gradual process of education. No doubt in many cases we learn only by repeated experience that a particular situation is dangerous. But once the dangerous situation is presented, and its dangerous nature is, however dimly, perceived, response by way of flight may follow immediately in much the same way at all ages provided of course the necessary physiological mechanisms are 1 No doubt this is to apply the term "instinctive" in a very wide sense, but the characterisation given is sufficient for the purposes of the present argument.

sufficiently developed in all climes, and at all stages of human development. If, on the other hand, we take the outstanding artistic, mathematical, practical, or religious ability of particular individuals, and attempt to show how it has been built up, we are apt to be led back to the very beginnings of the life of the individual with whom we are concerned. When we have accourted for everything we possibly can in terms of education, there still often remains something left over, a group of temperamental characteristics distinguishing our individual from others. As he gives way to his tendency to flee from danger he is at one with all other people; as he expresses the tendencies upon which are built his peculiar abilities he is marking himself off from others. How great a variety of individual differences thus have their parts to play from the dawn of life, and by what subtleties they are distinguished from one another, we cannot yet with certainty say. That they exist and are important seems more certain the further psychological research advances.

Both of these sets of tendencies the instinctive and the individual difference tendencies are ready to come into operation apart from the precise character of experience which is subsequent to birth. They are revealed in varying degrees during the process of education, but they do not appear to be dependent upon the particular course of education to which an individual may be subjected.

Throughout our lives, then, our behaviour is constantly being determined by these tendencies, and by others which are derived from them. They are not however the only factors that help to decide what we do. Clearly facts belonging to the external material environ- ment have a part to play, and, in a large number of cases, facts of social structure. Yet these do not at first operate in quite as direct a manner. They affect human behaviour because they are related to already existing tendencies in the individual or group that is responding to them.

For example, certain of the Eskimo forbid the use of caribou and seal flesh on the same day 1. Boas suggests that this may ultimately be traced to an alternating inland and coast life of the Eskimo among whom the prohibition holds good. When they hunt inland there are no seals to be had; when they hunt on the coast there are no deer. These facts, repeated many times over, at length give rise to a rule. Under normal circumstances a diet of seal flesh cannot possibly be accompanied by one of deer, and when deer is available no seal can be found. It may, however, occasionally happen that both kinds of meat can be provided. Nevertheless, to eat both is odd and abnormal, and is hence regarded with great disfavour.

If we accept this explanation, we must admit that into the Eskimo taboo there enter facts belonging to the external environment. That there are no seals inland, and no caribou on the coast are important. But these facts are important only because they are intimately related to a pre-existing hunting tendency, to that deep-seated organic need which produces hunger, and to the whole group of derived tendencies which have conspired to produce an alternating inland and coast life. Moreover should we attempt a complete analysis of the prohibition, we should find that these tendencies also come 1 See " Psychological Problems in Anthropology," by F. Boas, Amer. Jour, of Psychol. xxi, 371-84.

to produce their full effect only by relation to that potent impulse towards conservation which Haddon calls: 44 The sheet anchor of the ethnographer 1."

What is true in this instance is true in all. When we set out to explain human behaviour of any kind we must be prepared to take into account facts of the external world, and facts of social structure. At the same x ime all such facts must be considered in their relation to tendencies towards thought, feeling, and action expressed in the individuals who are being studied 2. This applies just as much, and in precisely the same sense, to human behaviour in the primitive group, as to that of the person who enters a laboratory and submits to a modern psychological experiment.

I shall begin, then, by trying to say what are the most important and fundamental tendencies, both active and affective, which find expression in human behaviour. I shall next consider how these tendencies act and react one upon another, enquire which of them are dominant at certain stages of development, and study how they may be affected by the external environment in which they are called upon to work. These will be our typical problems throughout. They are not the only problems which a study of primitive culture thrusts upon us. They are, however, the problems which, if we desire to understand the behaviour of primitive people, must be attacked first. Were we indeed concerned with modern, instead of with primitive, social life the general type of 1 "The Decorative Art of New Guinea," Royal Irish Academy Memoirs, No. x, p. 179.

2 Compare, however, the treatment adopted throughout this volume of the "group difference tendencies." Not all psychological analyses need or can, for that matter be pushed to their last terms.

our problem would remain the same, and some of the answers themselves would have to be made in very much the same terms 1. In certain respects, however, the differences between primitive and modern culture are more important than the likenesses, and it is a part of our aim to understand where and why this is the case. The first striking characteristic about the tendencies which have just been referred to is their relative permanence. The child's pugnacity, and the man's are apt to be called forth in widely different circumstances, but essentially they express the same type of reaction tendency. All through his life a man will show the same set of temperamental capacities and abilities. They may be set to work upon constantly changing materials, they may be called into play at periods of time that may be separated by long intervals, but they, more than anything else, are what we take to be the distinguishing marks of the man. They are what we rely upon when we want to picture to ourselves how the man will behave when he is face to face with some new situation. This is true, whether the tendencies are individual, in the sense that they do not require a social group for their expression, or whether, as is the case with those that will be our main interest in this book, they are social, in the sense that they depend upon society for their occurrence. Undoubtedly, through the interplay of the fundamental tendencies, new ones may be produced, and these may persist, or they may be transient. But the root tendencies remain. Only their inter-relations vary, together with the constantly changing external environment. Students who have their eyes fixed upon the fundamental tendencies say that human nature never changes; those 1 For a discussion of this point see chapters ix and x.

who concentrate upon the ways in which the tendencies are related to one another, and upon the ever-shifting play of external nature, assert that man moves endlessly towards the novel. Both views are, in fact, true.

So far, then, we may say that, selecting human behaviour in the primitive group as our field of study, we are going to try to account for such behaviour in te v ms of the tendencies, fundamental and acquired, which human beings possess, the ways in which those tendencies are affected by their working relationships one with another, and the influence of all forms of external environment, including that of the social structure itself. At this point an important question arises: Are we, in our search for explanations, always to go back to the individual as he may be pictured to exist outside of any particular social group? Shall we endeavour to find an origin for all forms of social behaviour at some pre-social stage?

At first sight it may seem as if we are bound to do this, if our study is legitimately to be called psychological. For psychology is generally regarded as dealing essentially with the individual. Suppose we find, for instance, that the members of some particular primitive group are in the habit of meeting together to practise certain ceremonial rites. Here is a fact which we must try to explain. We study the features of the ceremonial, and it seems to us that the practice must spring from, or at least be accompanied by, certain beliefs. Now we picture some individual, setting him, for the time being, entirely outside his special group. Some striking occurrence in his life leads him to associate an animal, let us say, with the birth of a child, or with the securing of food. By the inevitable laws of association, acting upon him just as they might conceivably act on any other individual in any other natural environment, he connects the animal with the child, or the food, and may come to regard the first as the cause of the second. More than this he persuades others of the connexion. The spreading belief, also by a common psychological process, finds dramatic expression in a form of ritual. Thus, by simply considering the laws of the individual mental life, and without supposing any special form of social grouping, we may seem to have arrived at a satisfactory explanation of the origin of the ceremonial we set out to investigate.

As a matter of fact it is exactly this type of argument which has, in the past, been regarded as a specifically psychological way of dealing with the problems of primitive culture. This method of explanation was employed frequently by Tylor 1, and has been adopted by most of his followers. Particularly the brilliant researches of Professor Sir J. G. Frazer yield constant attempts to account for the absolute origin of rites and ceremonies in terms of individual experience, the individual not being considered specifically as a member of any social group. Religious rites and ceremonies, for example, are held to be mainly interesting because of the underlying beliefs which they express. The origin of these is then traced to the savage's attitude towards his dreams 2. Totemism is explained as arising from a connexion by association between a child and an animal, which follows when the animal has been seen by a woman at the moment of quickening 3. Initiation ceremonies are traced to a desire for food which in itself has no 1 See particularly in Primitive Culture, London, 1873.

2 Tylor, op. cit. vol. i, ch. xi.

3 Frazer, Totemism and Exogamy, London, 1910, vol. i, pp. 156 ff.

necessary social significance 1. Agriculture, again, is supposed to have had its birth when the primitive man noticed the natural effects of digging the soil for roots or seeds 2. We might go on to give many more illustrations. It is as though the problem which makes primitive culture really worth investigating is to find out how everything began. And in our search for beginnings we n ust always, if we possibly can do so, go back to the individual mental life, since everything social must ultimately have been built up by a combination of individual characteristics.

To many investigators this method appears to be a great mistake. They think that it is bound to lead to pure speculation. Looking upon it as distinctively psychological, they propose to banish psychology from the study of primitive culture. Of Frazer's explanations, for example, it has been urged that: " In the last analysis they are psychology, and as history only a pleasing fabrication." "Ethnology," we are told, "like every other branch of science, is work, and not a game in which lucky guesses score 3."

Now there is no good reason for regarding either Sir James Frazer's work, or psychology, as a game of lucky guesses. But there is equally no good reason for regarding Frazer's type of explanation as the only type which can be called psychological. The psychologist, as much as any other scientist, is concerned with the immediate conditions of those observable results which he has elected to make his field of study. His explanations of 1 Frazer, The Golden Bough, 3rd ed. London, 1911, Part i, vol. i, p. 106.

2 Frazer, op. cit. Part v, vol. i, p. 128.

8 The quotation is from Kroeber, Amer. Anthropol N. S. 22, p. 55.

behaviour undoubtedly take the form of endeavouring to connect what he has observed with its antecedents. But he is not forced to consider only very remote antecedents, and with the curious exception of his studies in the realm of primitive culture, he never has agreed to do so.

As a matter of fact if we consider carefully the implications of that method of approach which has already been outlined, we shall see that the attempt to find the beginning of social customs and institutions in purely individual experience may be essentially a mistaken one. In general terms our problem is to account for a response made by an individual to a given set of circumstances of which the group itself may always be one. It is very easy indeed to forget this possible determining influence of the group. If we do this we fall into the temptation to study the individual as he might conceivably be at a pre-social stage, and we ignore all those influences which arise directly from membership of a group. Probably we do this on the ground that to consider such influences is not strictly relevant to the individual standpoint. It is not difficult, however, to show that such a view is based upon error.

The individual who is considered in psychological theory, in fact, is never an individual pure and simple. The statements made about him always have reference to a particular set of conditions. The individual with whom we deal may be the-individual-in-the-laboratory, or the-individual-in-his-everyday-working-environment, or and in social psychology this is always the case the-individual-in-a-given-social-group.

The point may be illustrated from any department of social activity. Take the influence of a certain set of artistic conventions.

In vain (remarks W. D. Wallas) does the Dahomey artist convince himself that he is following a new design, in the execution of which he is merely following momentary promptings. Though he believes himself to start and to continue without any conception of the figure which he is able to produce, an examination of the procedure of such a native artist is a demonstration of the existence of "determinants." When "turning in his free-hand design he must not make smooth curves, but put a characteristic kink in each. Moreover having started his design the rest of the figure must fall into a certain harmony of outline and balance of parts which of course limit individual choice. These characteristics are imposed by the culture, the artist merely varying the prescribed form, and never deviating from the general rules laid down by the convention of the group 1.

Suppose we were to watch the Dahomey artist at his work. We should see him, perhaps, making his peculiar kink in a free-hand curve, and building up a design possessing harmony of outline and balance of parts. We might well ask from whence he obtains these characteristics of his art. But if we should imagine that, in order to preserve an individualist point of view, we must separate the artist from his social group, and explain his work wholly by reference to the laws of his own mental life and his relations to his material environment, we should miss the most important of the influences that are being brought to bear upon him. The outstanding peculiarities of his art are derived directly from his membership of a particular social community.

It is only if we interpret individual to mean pre-social that we can take psychology to be prehistoric. The truth is that there are some individual responses which 1

"Individual Initiative and Social Control," Amer. Anthropol. N. S. 17, 1915, pp. 647-68.

simply do not occur outside a social group. To look for these outside such a group is to court failure, and leads inevitably to speculation and guess-work.

We can see, then, that in all our explanations of the behaviour of man in the primitive community, we may have to assume the existence of some specific group possessing certain institutions and customs which have already become relatively stabilised. No doubt such customs and institutions themselves have a history, and we could very well try to show how they have grown up out of simpler beginnings. But we are not in all cases bound to attempt this further task. Moreover should we endeavour to go back to a yet more remote stage, and to build up social customs out of a combination of purely individual responses, we should lay ourselves open to the charge that we were running beyond any known facts. There are some matters the beginnings of which cannot be discussed without speculation; some the starting-points of which may be shown, but need not be demonstrated for the purposes of an immediate argument; and some of which we both can and must discuss the origin.

How, then, may we discriminate between these three cases? The clearest illustration of the principle involved may be obtained from the realm of psychological experiment. I will take the case of certain investigations which have recently been carried out in order to obtain an answer to the question: When two sounds of like, and known, pitch, quality, and intensity are conveyed separately, one after the other, to the two ears, what is the smallest period of time at which the normal individual can tell that two sounds, and not one, are being presented to him? The answer to this question has an important bearing on certain theories of the localisation of sound.

In the experiments the record of the time interval presented was accompanied by an account given by the person examined of his own experience. Every account contained reference to the varying affective character of the experience. It was stated that as the experiment proceeded the task became increasingly disagreeable. Or again a slight variation of the procedure made a given trial more pleasing than the others. Undoubtedly the record of changing feelings was relevant from the point of view of the experiment. The results did actually vary to some extent with the variation in the affective state of the observer. The record of feelings, then, was undoubtedly of psychological interest.

But, as every psychologist knows perfectly well, experiments of this general type are always accompanied by variable feelings on the part of the observer. No doubt we could enquire, with some chance of finding a solution, why, in general this is so. Moreover the enquiry would be of interest. The answer would not in the least further the particular purpose of the given set of experiments however.

Similarly we could, if we pleased, ask why it was that affective disturbance ever came to arise in the first place. But an investigation of this point would not only take us beyond the limits of usefulness in regard to any particular experimental problem on which we might be working, but would lead us into a realm beyond the fields of observable fact.

Another illustration may be taken from the same experiment. An observer's delicacy of discrimination of single from double sounds depends largely upoi the "attitude" which he adopts towards the test. Sometimes a record shows a sudden marked improvement. It is found that at this point the observer's attitude changed. Perhaps instead of attempting to count and characterise each sound "first right," "second left" he hit upon the device of attempting definitely to determine only "first" or "last."

Now a question with which the experimentalist must deal is: What is the origin of this sudden improvement within the course of the experiment! A question with which he may legitimately deal, though the answer will not serve his immediate purpose is: How, in general, must we explain the occurrence of changing attitudes during the course of psychological experiments calling for repeated observations? A question which would immediately plunge the experimenter into speculation is: How do attitudes arise at all in the mental life? What is their absolute origin?

The analogy between the position of the experimentalist and that of the student of primitive culture is, in this respect, a perfect one. There are certain problems of origin I have indicated two which can be propounded by the experimentalist, no matter what special experiment he has on hand. Their solution involves him in psychological speculation. Similarly, no matter what specific point in primitive culture is being considered, there are certain problems about beginnings that might be attacked. For example, as we shall see in detail later on, the solution of every one of our questions involves some reference to deep-lying social instincts. These can certainly be distinguished and described; their functions and their mode of operation can be discussed; but it is futile to attempt to display their origin.

Again, analysis of the results of any psychological experiment always reveals factors at work which have their rise certainly within the life history of the individual concerned, but outside the limits of the particular experiments involved; and the consideration of any problem in primitive culture is apt to reveal an analogous situation. For there is no known social group which does not possess certain stabilised conventions finding expression in individual behaviour. These conventions may often be shown to have a perfectly definite history in that group, arising from the inter-play of the fundamental instinctive tendencies, the contact of the group in question with other groups, and the influence of a certain material environment. But we are justified in treating the stable conventions as starting-points for the purpose of enquiry, and are no more forced to investigate their origin than, in the case of the individual, we are forced to investigate the origin of modes of response which he brings, already formed, to an experiment.

Finally, just as we must attempt to account for modifications of response which have their origin within the course of a psychological experiment, so we must deal with the origin of changes in social response which come into the social setting that we are studying within the limits of the period with which we are concerned.

We can now see clearly the principle which ought to guide us in our search for psychological explanations of behaviour in the primitive group. Our attempt in general is to understand the antecedent conditions of response, and we want to know how far back we must go in our enquiry. If we try to deal with problems of beginnings which might be asked of all social groups whatsoever, their discussion is bound to be speculative; if our questions have to do with common modes of response that have become stabilised before the period with which we are concerned, we may accept those stable modes of response without enquiring further into the manner of their growth; modifications of response arising within a given social group during the period under consideration must be explained.

I have laid stress upon this matter because commonly one or other of two extreme positions is adopted. On the one hand, in dealing with social customs and institutions, and with the modes of human behaviour which they involve, we may be told that only questions of origin are worth study; or, on the other hand, that no questions of origin are worth study. I have attempted to suggest a principle by which we may know when to attempt, and when to avoid problems of this nature.

The distinction between the method of approach to the study of primitive culture which I am proposing to adopt, and that which has, in the past, been most generally regarded as "psychological," is probably, however, more fundamental than has yet been indicated. The psychologist has commonly been regarded as solely interested in experience. By the psychologist a social custom has generally been considered less as a mode of human behaviour than as a way in which certain underlying ideas or beliefs are exhibited. It is the ideas, the beliefs, which he strives to describe and explain. He does so because they seem to be the materials of experience. We are urged to study the primitive man in action only for the light which this may throw upon what he thinks and believes.

Now once we admit that we can be psychological only in so far as we get behind the behaviour to the belief or if, as commonly occurs, there is nothing definite enough to be called a belief to the attitudes which the behaviour expresses, we lay up for ourselves a store of trouble. As we shall frequently have to remind ourselves 1, a group of individuals may unite in common or harmonious behaviour, although the attitudes of the individuals concerned may vary very considerably. In fact to split social behaviour into individual attitudes is an endless business, and to construct social behaviour out of individual attitudes is at present a hopeless task. The investigator who wishes to show how the group custom grows out of the individual belief simply takes some outstanding belief as typical, and assumes that everybody in the group experiences this. His explanation is pure fiction. At no stage are human beings as unanimous in their ideas, beliefs and attitudes as he supposes. I do not for one moment wish to deny that it is important to discover the belief that is behind the institution, the attitude that accompanies the practice of the social custom; but as I shall urge more fully later, this is the last step, and not the first in the psychological study of society.

Throughout this book very little will be said about the beliefs, ideas, or attitudes of the individual savage. Our attempt is, first to show the main determining conditions of behaviour in the primitive group, and second to indicate the ways in which these influence the development of customs, institutions and social structure. That such treatment is fairly regarded as psychological can be better shown at the end than at the beginning of our discussions. I propose, therefore, to consider this question 1 See further pp. 266 ff.

again at a later stage, and to turn now to another point of considerable methodological importance which is consequent upon the general position already adopted.

If we look at any ordinary text-book of psychology, we find that the different, broadly distinguishable, mental responses are as a rule given separate treatment. Thvs we are offered a section on perception, another on sensation, another on memory, others on imagination, thinking and reasoning, and yet others, particularly if the text-book is a fairly recent one, on instinct, and the varied types of affect. Very much as the physiologist may tend to lose sight of the organism in his pre-occupa-tion with the ways in which varied parts of the organism react, so the psychologist may tend to lose sight of the individual responding in his pre-occupation with the different types of partial response of the individual. It is possible to know a large amount about the particular response, and at the same time to know strikingly little about the man as he makes the particular response.

So much has this traditional mode of approach to our subject become a part of the accepted attitude of the psychologist, that the treatment of a particular stage of mental development is often made to follow precisely the same line. Thus we talk about primitive emotions, primitive belief, primitive imagination, primitive memory and the like. An example of this may be seen in the extremely interesting book by Dr Carveth Read entitled The Origin of Man and of his Superstitions' 1. This book is definitely intended as a study of the psychology of primitive peoples. A part of its aim is to explain the "mental changes" which "our race has undergone" in the course of its history. The first portion of the book 1 Cambridge, 1920.

is concerned with an attempt to account for the actual origin of man's life in a group, and is, I think, open to some of the criticisms which have been urged already with regard to the study of origins. This attempted, however, Dr Read adopts the usual psychological method of dealing more or less separately with the various mental responses of the individual, and of iis-cussing the nature of beliefs and attitudes rather than the determination of behaviour. He thus enters into a detailed discussion of primitive imagination, belief and reasoning. But he makes no case it may be said, indeed, that he does not even attempt to make a case for the assumption that these mental processes are, as mental processes, markedly different in the primitive from what they are in the civilised mind. The psychological analysis of the varied types of response we call imagining, or remembering, is, in fact, precisely the same whether our concern is with the savage or the contemporary. What Dr Read really finds himself driven to discuss are the differences of the material dealt with in these responses, by the primitive, as contrasted with the civilised man. Thus we get long chapters on Magic, Animism, the relations between Magic and Animism, Omens, Totemism, and the striking change in the material dealt with by the mind as advance is made from the magic to the scientific stage.

There is one exception to this general mode of treatment. In the chapter entitled " The Mind of the Wizard," Dr Read, although still to some extent concerned with the characteristic type of material with which the mental responses of the wizard are in the main occupied, does definitely attempt to show the balance and combination of tendencies which the wizard exhibits. Without in the least supposing, that is to say, that the psychological characteristics of the wizard's mental processes are different from those of his modern counterpart the priest, he does strive to demonstrate the characteristic combination of responses which the wizard illustrates.

Let us consider two questions which are suggested by a s+udy of Dr Read's book. There are some people who would urge that a consideration of the material dealt with by mental responses ought not to be included in a specifically psychological discussion. With this view, as should be clear from what I have said at the beginning of the chapter, I most emphatically disagree. My main reason for this disagreement is that psychology should deal not merely with the response, but with the person who responds. Certain efforts of primitive imagining are pre-occupied with what we call omens, and certain attempts of highly developed imagining are equally pre-occupied with what we call scientific constructions. The material dealt with differs enormously, but the response itself, the imagining, undoubtedly involves the same kind of mental processes in both instances. An analysis of the one will serve for the other. And supposing that our sole aim was to understand the character of the response, that is as far as we need go.

Our business, however, is not merely to treat of imagining, but to deal with the individual as he imagines. Directly we realise this we see that a consideration of the material dealt with by a specific response may be of immense importance. It is, for example, often a study of the material that best shows the relation of one type of response to others, and that helps us to disentangle those responses that are dominant at a given stage from those that are in a subordinate position.

Often, again, we can most readily appreciate how responses change in their relation one to another by noting changes in the type of material dealt with. The imagining that is chiefly concerned with omens, for instance, leads to certain practical adjustments which are widely different from those initiated by the imagining that is pre-occupied with "scientific constructions." 3"he Australian native, exercising his imagination and belief upon the securing of food and the continuance of life, develops a mass of complicated ceremonial. The modern plant, or animal breeder, starting with very similar general aims, sets to work upon exceedingly different material, and in the result arrives at practices in no respect similar. The difference in the materials dealt with thus carries with it an important difference in the relation of imaginative and practical responses.

But though a study of the material dealt with by the various types of human response is relevant to psychology, its interest is always subordinate to a more important question. What we chiefly want to understand are the inter-relations of the responses at a given stage; which are dominant, and why they are dominant; what occurs when they conflict, and what when they unite; and what are the broad lines of change in their inter-relations which they have undergone in the course of history. We need not, then, speak of primitive imagining, belief, thinking, and so on, as if these, considered as psychological responses were any different in the primitive as contrasted with the modern mind. But what we must do is to study how imagining, thinking, believing, or other typical human responses, may vary in the position of dominance which they occupy at different stages of culture. Moreover we must try to show precisely what follows from this varying exercise of different outstanding psychological reactions.

These reflections immediately bring to mind a further objection which is often urged against a psychological study of periods long gone by. We are apt to approach primitive psychology as if it were something strange and far off, remote from our understanding. If the view which I have just put forward is correct, there is no real need for this timidity, save in so far as it should apply to all psychological study whatsoever. It is both significant and interesting that there is no law of necessity connecting the keenest psychological insight with the widest worldly experience. The man who knows intimately but one mental life will the sooner enter into others, than the man whose observation has grasped the external form and movements of thousands of people, but has gone no farther.

The difficulty of psychological interpretation is just as great, and has precisely the same character, whether we are concerned with primitive or with modern social life. In both cases psychological analysis is difficult, not because the responses of the human beings whom we are studying are very different from our own, but because the conditions of the responses are often different, and because the relations of one mode of behaviour to others may vary in important respects. The conditions which may stimulate uncontrolled laughter, or fury, in one group may perhaps leave us untouched or merely scornful. We, in our turn, however, may be roused to fury or to laughter, though by other means. We have that basis in our own lives which enables us to enter into and to understand the lives of others.

Thus the study of special groups in contemporary society offers precisely the same type of problem as that of the primitive community. If we shrink from the latter, we ought similarly to hesitate before the former. Undoubtedly the psychological analysis of primitive behaviour may in certain respects be peculiarly difficult. The conditions of the responses we study are often different from those which excite similar response in ourselves, and particularly the various modes of behaviour that combine to make up the complete life in the community may be very differently related one to another. But the difficulties must not be exaggerated, as they are apt to be, whenever we assume that the mental processes of the primitive man are, in any remarkable way, different from our own.

Seeing that this chapter is an attempt to state a point of view and elaborate a method for our subsequent study, it is perhaps fitting that I should bring it to a conclusion by a very brief consideration of the time-honoured question of the relation between sociology and psychology. Of all the writers who, in this country, have dealt with this problem, by far the clearest and most definite statements have been made by the late Dr W. H. R. Rivers. Writing as a sociologist and dealing with sociological problems he rejects a psychological method, not because it is inapplicable, or even irrelevant, but because it is less immediately fruitful. In his lectures on Kinship and Social Organisation 1 he says: "In social, as in all other kinds of human activity psychological factors must have an essential part. These psychological elements are, however, only concomitants of social processes with which it is possible to deal apart from their psychological aspect." Sociological argu-1 London, 1914, p. 92.

merits may, indeed, be supported often by a consideration of psychological motives, but "this is a process very different from the interpolation of psychological facts as links in a chain of causation connecting social antecedents with social consequences." The sociologist should at present, Dr Rivers maintains, rigorously confine his attention to purely social determination. And the position which he states thus, and illustrates in these lectures on Social Organisation, he reiterates, and further exemplifies with a success that is truly impressive in his monumental History of Melanesian Society 1.

Now the question before us may be stated quite simply in the form: "Can we reverse this position?" Can we, for our part, state our explanations in the form of causal series within which only the responses and relations of responses of the individual find a place? Or rather is it desirable that we should attempt to do so? As I have already urged, it is frequently necessary to take established social conventions and institutions as facts determining the character and relations of individual response. Such institutions and conventions are legitimately regarded as group responses. They are social facts, but they exercise a direct and important determining influence upon varied series of individual reactions. If we refuse to admit the psychological significance of this determination, we have to resolve all such group responses into their individual components. Theoretically, no doubt, this might be regarded as possible, but it would in practice resolve itself into an endless, and indeed in many instances a hopeless, task.

Thus while I agree entirely with Dr Rivers in his 1 Cambridge, 1914.

exposition of the limitations of sound sociological method, the case for the psychologist appears to be different. In his study of the conditions and relations of individual response he will find it necessary over and over again to admit, as possessing critical importance, the influence of social conventions and institutions. And he will be perfectly justified in introducing these social facts, without any further detailed analysis, into his account of the determination of the developing processes of human motives, feelings, belief and knowledge. At least this is the position which I propose to adopt for the purposes of the present discussion.

A brief summary of the argument of this chapter may now be given: 1. The first problem is to determine what are the main tendencies towards behaviour, feeling and cognition, as these find expression in primitive society.

2. Next the relations one to another of these tendencies have to be discussed, the main changes of relation which they undergo in the course of development have to be traced, and the ways in which new tendencies are derived must be shown.

3. No absolute, pre-social origin of social facts need be sought. Problems of origin may be either futile, as when they attempt to display the beginnings of factors present throughout the whole of our field of study; or irrelevant, as when they are concerned with factors arising beyond the limits of the particular period which we are studying; or necessary, as when they come into the stream of events we are discussing during the period dealt with.

4. Special emphasis must be placed upon the ways in which the tendencies leading to human behaviour in the primitive group are related one to another, and upon how certain of these may be dominant at particular stages of development. Study of the material with which the responses have to do often throws an interesting light upon these questions.

5. There is no need to assume a necessary ignorance of primitive psychology simply because of the remoteness in time of the mental processes studied. It is in their conditions and inter-relations, rather than in their chrracter, that primitive mental processes differ from our own.

6. Social facts may be legitimately accepted as among the determining conditions of response with which we have to deal.

CHAPTER II

THE FUNDAMENTAL FORMS OF MANS SOCIAL REACTIONS

The Argument: If we consider those forms of human response which are generally classed as instinctive, we find that some of them are immediately social, whereas others are not. For example, in Macdougall's list the directly social forms are: gregariousness, self-assertion, self-abasement; in a narrow sense the sexual and parental instincts; and perhaps pugnacity, and a social form of constructiveness. Similarly of what Macuougall has called "general innate tendencies," sympathetic induction of the emotions, suggestibility, imitation, and probably play are all immediately social.

These reactions, however, display varied relations of independence one to another, and lead to different results according to their inter-relations. Particularly important, if we wish to understand the effects and character of social reactions, is it to know what is the prevailing form of social relationship among the persons by whom the behaviour is exhibited. There are three fundamental forms of social relationship expressed in: (a) the tendency towards primitive comradeship, (b) the tendency of assertiveness, (c) the tendency of sub-missiveness. Each of the last two involves a relationship of superiors and inferiors, but no such inequality is required by the first.

In the next place, as distinctively social, both of them of immense importance to the psychological study of the primitive community, are the tendencies towards conservation, and a variety of that tendency towards constructiveness which is at the basis of all social organisation.

The other specific tendencies may best be termed individual since, in so far as they are possible at all except on a basis of the forms already discriminated, they can find expression as well outside the social group as within it. In their social expression they have different results according to the fundamental social relationship forms which are prevalent in the com-mibiity. Fear, for instance, and the avoidance reaction, produce very different results in a "primitive comradeship" group from its effects in a group displaying assertiveness on the one hand or submissiveness on the other.

In addition to these fundamental forms of social reaction, every community displays certain more specialised social tendencies. These are what distinguish one group from another, and they are best called "group difference tendencies." They cluster about a group's established institutions and act directly as determining factors of individual social behaviour. It will be our duty, not to provide complete lists of such specialised tendencies an endless task but to show in specific cases how they come into operation, and to discuss the common modes in which they may enter into relations one to another. Our basic scheme thus consists of:

A. Fundamental forms of social relationship responses: those of primitive comradeship, assertion, and submission.

B. Other responses of a fundamental nature having a specifically social reference: the two most important being the tendencies towards conservation, and the social form of constructiveness, or that tendency which produces new modes of social organisation.

C. Individual instinct responses the social effects of which are very largely dependent upon their relations to the A group.

D. Group difference tendencies which cluster about the social institutions and conventions of a particular community, and exercise a relatively direct influence upon the social behaviour of the individual.

We shall, in succeeding chapters, proceed to the concrete exposition and illustration of the scheme proposed.

The first problem before us in this chapter is to discuss the underlying human responses which are to be found wherever there is any social group. We have to decide, so far as may be possible, what these are, and how they find expression at those primitive stages of development which are our main concern.

The most convenient starting-place for our discussion will be to take the well-known list of instinctive tendencies which Professor Macdougall put forward at the beginning of his Introduction to Social Psychology. Macdougall considered that a study of these tendencies was an indispensable preliminary to the elaboration of any satisfactory treatment of the psychological aspects of society. It is true that their significance is not seen solely in their social functions: "Directly or indirectly the instincts are the prime movers of all human activity." But it is at the same time claimed that they have particularly important social expressions. And Macdougall has repeated his belief in the necessity and also in the substantial adequacy of his list of instincts, in that more extended treatment of social psychology which has appeared under the title of The Group Mind 2.

1 London,1908.

2 "I wish to make it clear. that this volume is a sequel to my Introduction to Social Psychology, that it builds upon that book and assumes that the reader is acquainted with it." The Group Mind, Cambridge, 1920, p. viii.

It would be out of place, in this book, to attempt a criticism of the criteria used by Macdougall in arriving at the list of primary instincts which he proposes. The criteria may be doubtful, or even definitely erroneous, but nobody has ever denied, or is ever likely to deny, that the list itself is one of very great interest.

"She principal instincts, according to Macdougall, are: of flight, of repulsion, of curiosity, of pugnacity, of self-abasement, and self-assertion, of reproduction (i. e. the sexual instinct), of acquisition, of construction, of feeding, together with the parental, and the gregarious instincts 1. Of these the instincts of reproduction, of acquisition, of construction, and the gregarious instinct are apparently the least clearly marked, or, in Macdou-gall's phraseology, are less clearly accompanied by specific emotional excitement than the others. We have to add " a number of minor instincts, such as those that prompt to crawling and walking 2," and very closely related to the instincts, but having no specific emotions and impulses attached, are the "general innate tendencies" of sympathetic induction of the emotions, of suggestibility, of imitation, of play, and of habit-formation with its necessary consequence of preferring the familiar to the unfamiliar 3. All of these form elements in the native equipment of man, and it is maintained that they are of particular interest in the psychological study of social life.

Now there are two things that must immediately strike everybody who looks thoughtfully at this list. The first is that although all these instincts and tendencies are dealt with side by side and as it were as 1 Introduction to Social Psycfiology, ch. in.

Op. cit. 13th ed. 1918, p. 82. 3 Op. tit. ch. iv.

equals in a book leading directly to the study of social psychology, they are by no means all of them equally immediately related to social facts. It is evident that what is called the "gregarious instinct," is a tendency which requires a social setting for its expression. If, that is, there is a specific response which we can call the response of being gregarious, it is not found a, all out of relation to some form of social grouping. But this is not true of flight, of repulsion, of curiosity, or probably of acquisition. Reproduction, again, or the sexual instinct is in one sense, though in rather a narrow one, a social response, and the parental instinct falls clearly into the same class. But the position of pugnacity, of self-abasement and self-assertion, and of con-structiveness, in this respect, is less clear. Constructive-ness, as I shall try to show later, seems to have a characteristic and exceedingly important social form. Self-assertion and self-abasement are, according to Macdougall, specifically social, though not everybody would be inclined to agree with him. As for pugnacity, that has sometimes been treated as an essentially antagonistic response towards others of like kind, but again, disagreement might well be expressed with this view.

The "minor instincts" appear to have no specifically restricted social expression; and when we turn to the general innate tendencies, we find nothing remarkably or exclusively social about habit-formation, and preferring the familiar to the unfamiliar, while sympathetic induction of the emotions, suggestibility 1, imitation, 1 It may, however, be noted that Prideaux and for that matter many others speak of auto-suggestion where no social relationship seems to be involved. (Brit. Jour, of Psychol x, 1920, p. 229.) For my part I think auto-suggestion to be probably a secondary and derivative process.

and probably play are all directly social forms of response. Macdougall's list, that is to say, furnishes us with some responses which are, and with others which are not, distinctively and immediately social.

The second consideration is that the various members of the list are treated too much as if each were a separate response, capable of being regarded as complete in itself. It is highly probable that no single one of the responses on Macdougall's list can be regarded as thoroughly analysed. There may well be several distinguishable kinds of fear 1, each with its specific avoidance reaction, no one of which can with confidence be said to be prior to the others. And the same may be true of the other instincts as they here appear. Moreover it is perfectly certain that in actual life no instinct ever does occur in what we are often pleased to call its "primitive simplicity," and it may well be the case that this "primitive simplicity" is merely a fiction of our sophisticated method of thinking.

But what is more important is that when we look into Macdougall's list we see that the instincts as he treats them show different degrees of independence in their relation one to another. Flight clearly in no way grows out of, or depends upon, pugnacity, or pugnacity upon acquisitiveness, or acquisitiveness upon self-submission. But in their social forms, with which we are particularly concerned, each of these may depend upon how the 1 It seems possible that these differences in kind of fear may be more apparent in primitive than in modern society. "An old resident of these islands," writes the Rev. W. Deane, "showed me a list of the different kinds of fear which was prepared for him by an intelligent native. There were no fewer than eleven kinds in all." Fijian Society, London, 1921, p. 24. Unfortunately the list is not reproduced so that we have no means of saying on what the classification is based.

instinct of gregariousness finds expression. While supposing we compare gregariousness itself with the "general innate tendency" of "sympathetic induction of the emotions," it at once becomes clear that between these two there is the closest relation. This Macdougall points out himself.

It would (he says) seem to be a general rule, the explanation of which is to be found in the principle of sympathetic emotion, that the more numerous the herd or crowd or society in which the individual finds himself the more complete is the satisfaction of the gregarious impulse 1.

His statement seems quite clearly to mean that the gregarious instinct, in its development, depends directly upon the general tendency of sympathetic emotion.

But we seem bound to go farther than this. Macdougall, in search of primitive simplicity, describes the gregarious instinct as: "a mere uneasiness in isolation, and satisfaction in being one of a herd 1." There are, that is, two outstanding features of the gregarious instinct, the one negative "a mere uneasiness in isolation" the other positive "satisfaction in being one of a herd." The distinction between these two features is, I think, more important than has generally been recognised. The first, the uneasiness, comes into play only when the animal or human being is separated, or is in danger of being separated, from his group. Then, with unceasing search, he tries to find his comrades again, or to guard against the impending separation. The group recovered, or the danger over, the uneasiness disappears. While the uneasiness is undoubtedly socially determined, it is 1 Op. tit. p. 84.

expressed only in the absence, or impending absence, of comrades; the satisfaction demands the actual presence of the group.

The moment we seriously consider this satisfaction, we can see that it stands in need of further and more definite characterisation. Satisfaction is a general term, ana may name an experience which arises in a non-social situation. There may be satisfaction in a good meal, or a new discovery, in fact in the unimpeded expression of any tendency whatsoever, fundamental or derived.

Macdougall obviously cannot mean that sort of satisfaction. He is speaking of "satisfaction in being one of a herd" a specifically social response. He must mean some peculiar social satisfaction, and this seems to be based upon a high degree of readiness to be influenced by other members of the herd or group. If we try to characterise this "readiness to be influenced" more definitely, we seem driven exactly to that "sympathetic induction of the emotions" which Macdougall calls a general innate tendency. In fact, if gregariousness is to be treated as an instinct in Macdougall's sense, there is some ground for confining it to "uneasiness in isolation." Its more positive character of social satisfaction belongs rather to the general innate tendencies. At the same time there is no good reason for confining this " readiness to be influenced " to emotions. Similarly bodily actions, and the materials of cognitive processes, may be sympathetically induced. With gregariousness, in the narrow sense of uneasiness in isolation, we shall have no great concern, for our main interest is in tendencies to response which occur actually within the groups whose culture we shall study.

Turning, then, to that side of gregariousness which indicates a readiness to be influenced by other members of the herd or group, we are at once reminded of two of the instincts which Macdougall calls primary. These are the two instincts which, most emphatically of all, he considers to be social: they are the tendencies to self-assertion and to self-submission. Macdoug ll's names are, I believe, bad ones, because they use the very confusing term "self" where it would be better omitted. Consequently I propose to speak of assertive-ness and submissiveness, or of dominance and acceptance. The mere change of terminology is, however, of little importance.

Submissiveness, and, in a way, assertiveness also, most clearly involve a readiness to be influenced by others. Their most striking illustration is to be found in the case of hypnotic suggestion, where one person is wholly ready to do, think, or feel as another commands him.

At first sight we may be tempted to say that whenever human beings in a group respond readily one to another, there is assertiveness on the one hand and submissiveness on the other. This is the view which Macdougall inclines to adopt. It would follow that, on its positive side, gregariousness is little more than a general name for that degree of responsiveness without which there can be no true group life, such responsiveness having the two specific forms of dominance and acceptance.

But readiness to respond to social influences does not always involve the relationships of assertiveness and submissiveness. Equally important, and equally fundamental, is the response one to another of equals. This I propose to call the tendency towards " primitive comradeship." The tendency towards primitive com- radeship has as much right to be called instinctive as have assertiveness and submissivencss, and is equally essential for the development of group life.

Gregariousness, then, may be treated, either as an instinct in the narrower sense and as naming a specific response, or it may be treated as a general name for a nuthber of responses. If the first alternative is accepted, gregariousness indicates a tendency to seek the company of one's kind, irrespective of the particular nature of the social relationship involved. If the second alternative is adopted, gregariousness includes not only the tendency to seek company, but also certain specific tendencies to be influenced by one's fellows which arise when certain social relationships are secured. The three fundamental relationships are: primitive comradeship, assertiveness, and submissiveness.

For my part, I prefer to use gregariousness strictly of the mere tendency to seek company, and to distinguish this from the root, instinctive social relationship tendencies of "primitive comradeship," "assertive-ness" and "submissiveness." These latter are not merely formal names for the relationships which may hold between members of a social group, but they indicate tendencies which actually operate, just as all other instinctive tendencies do 1, in determining the behaviour of one member of a group to others, or of a member of one group to members of a different group.

In actual life, the connexion between these three social relationship forms is exceedingly close, and, as we shall see in the next chapter, it is often remarkably easy to pass rapidly from one to another. No doubt primitive comradeship comes most frequently into play 1 See chapter x.

in shaping the ordinary working reactions of companion members of the same group, or of groups belonging to the same community. It is not, however, restricted to this narrow field. It influences the results of the contact of members of different groups, or of groups belonging to different communities. In somewhat the same fashion, assertiveness and submissiveness are ijpt to find their most frequent illustration when members of different social groups, or groups belonging to different communities, meet together. But they, also, have reference beyond this field, and may often be seen at work within a single group or a single community.

All three of these tendencies characterise a state of readiness to be influenced by others. If a group is prone to take over the opinions, modes of behaviour, or emotions of one of its members, we tend to assume at once that the latter must be in a position of superiority. Except as considered from the outside, he need not be. He may be leader and companion at once. In the primitive group there is reason to think that he frequently is 1. Precisely the same may be true of the relationship between one group and another. Moreover, there is a kind of leadership which mainly depends upon the swift responsiveness of the leader to desires, emotions, tendencies to action, and opinions of the general members of the group. Such leadership, whether it is exercised by an individual, or by a group, is of the primitive comradeship type 2, as contrasted with that which, based upon assertiveness, enforces commands upon followers by sheer weight of dominance. The three tendencies are all alike, in that they promote that interchange of emotions, opinions, and behaviour without 1 Cf. p. 79. 2 Cf. pp. 182, 184.

which no genuine social life in the group is possible. They differ, in that while assertiveness and submissiveness both involve a social relationship of superiors to inferiors, primitive comradeship characterises a relationship from which all such suggestion of inequality is absent.

By far the most important point, however, in regard to these social relationship tendencies, is the way in which they may direct the expression of any other tendency which is simultaneously excited. Suppose, for example, that fear is called into play in a social setting, the prevailing responsiveness being that of primitive comradeship, it is apt to assume the characteristic form of panic, and the group or groups affected may disintegrate, or stampede. But if the prevailing social response is one of assertiveness a far more complicated series of results follows. The social aspect of the constructive instinct is likely to be immediately aroused, and thereafter definite social mechanisms of persecution and cruelty, swiftly hardening into institutions will appear. Again, if the underlying social response is chiefly one of submissiveness, the effects once more follow a different line, and a slave class with its own typical modes of organisation will arise. It is the same with the other instincts. Pugnacity with primitive comradeship develops organisations in which rivalry has friendly expression, and many forms of group play here find their place; with assertiveness it produces social despotisms, and with submission, it may give rise to groups or bands of aggressive outlaws. We thus accomplish little when we merely make out a list of underlying modes of human response. For the important thing is not merely that there are these responses, but that they vary in most important ways according to the manner in which they are related one to another. All equally basic in the sense that we cannot get to the origin of any, they may yet exhibit a relation of dependence among themselves, and in particular may vary immensely in their social significance according to which of them are contemporaneously stimulated, and which among these arc dominant. Further, from our point, of view, that of the study of primitive culture, the most immediately important are those of primitive comradeship, assertion and submission. For according as one or other of these is the prevailing fundamental form of social response whether within or beyond the limits of a single group so the other specific instinct responses assume varied social expressions.

It should be evident that I am suggesting far more than a mere change of terminology. It is a definition of the whole point of view from which the fundamental human responses should be studied by the student of culture, whether his concern is with primitive or with modern society. It is the assertion of the prime importance of a consideration of the organic relations which subsist between the various fundamental human impulses or tendencies. As such it is wholly in line with the position adopted in the previous chapter, where it was urged that our task throughout is to analyse the nature of the inter-relationships of the chief tendencies which issue in human behaviour, and to elucidate the results which follow when one group of tendencies comes immediately into touch with another group.

Our position is in some respects similar to that taken up by Dr W. H. R. Rivers. He considers that: " Instincts may be classified as of three main kinds those of self-preservation; those which subserve the continuance of the race; and those which maintain the cohesion of the group 1." Of the third variety of instinctive response he says: "Its main constituent is the gregarious instinct with its different aspects of suggestion, sympathy, imitation and intuition 2." Here gregariousness is, according to the second of the alternatives indicated above, treated as a group of instinct-responses of which four are specified and discussed 3. It docs not affect Rivers's position to urge that these four in no way exhaust the numerous responses which, if this view is accepted, may be considered to fall under the gregarious group. But I have tried to go farther, and to throw light upon the important question, hitherto very little discussed, of an underlying essential structure or arrangement of certain fundamental human responses. And I have been induced to do so in consideration of another of the principles enunciated in the preceding chapter, namely, that we have to study, not merely this or that social reaction, but definitely this or that social individual.

So far, then, three primary and directly social responses have been distinguished: primitive comradeship, asser-tiveness and submissiveness. These are all largely of an affective character. They always involve, and perhaps may even be considered to grow out of, emotional, or affective, relationships. Can this enumeration be regarded as adequate? Let us turn again to Macdougalps list of general innate tendencies. In this list is an extremely interesting "tendency of preferring the familiar to the unfamiliar." At first sight this may appear 1 Instinct and the Unconscious, Cambridge, 1920,1st ed. p. 52.

2 Op. cit. p. 53.

3 Dr Myers points out to me that Rivers eventually treated suggestibility as the most fundamental social instinct possessing the three forms of sympathy, imitation and intuition.

to have no specific social reference whatsoever. Undoubtedly outside of the social group such preference may be found easily enough. But within the group this tendency has a specific character and outstanding results of the highest degree of importance. It marks that tendency which practically all students of primitive culture, whether they have attempted a general survey, or have restricted their attention to particular communities, have emphasised, the tendency towards conservation. The interesting thing about this tendency is that while undoubtedly possessing an affective character, it is largely cognitive in its nature. We can see this if we describe it as a tendency to prefer the familiar to the unfamiliar. The actual preferring is no doubt commonly accompanied by no small amount of feeling; but what is preferred is first, at least dimly, cognised, and is known in fact as familiar. The conserving tendency provides a basis for the continuance of institutions, just as the fundamental social form of constructiveness gives us a basis for the formation of institutions.

The next point has an importance which it is almost impossible to exaggerate. It is that this tendency towards conservation is selective in its operation. The facts show that no social group preserves equally all its institutions. Take, for example, the case of a number of marriage regulations and restrictions and the correlated set of relationship terms. Both may be preserved, but as a rule the latter will long outlast the former. Numerous illustrations are to be found. Among the North American Indians, for instance, are many tribes, who possessed formerly a clan system of social organisation, with exogamic grouping, and the consequent classificatory system of relationship. Owing to the operation of varied causes the clan system, in a number of cases, partially or wholly broke down, but the system of naming still persists [1].

The selective operation of the principle of conservation provides, in fact, some extraordinarily interesting problems for the psychological student of primitive culture, with some of which I shall deal in detail later. At present I merely wish to draw attention to this selective and discriminatory character, since it seems further to justify us in ranking this important tendency as one which has largely a social cognitive nature, in distinction to the mainly affective character of those tendencies which have hitherto been discussed.

The tendency towards conservation is seen mainly in the social attitude adopted towards more or less established traditions and institutions. But the actual establishment of such traditions and institutions seems to bring us face to face with another underlying human response, which we may call the social form of the instinct of construction. This it is which definitely promotes social organisation. In the mere form of a "simple desire to make something [2]" the instinct of construction clearly cannot be said to have any marked social reference. But Rivers has pointed out that "its most complete and striking developments are connected with the parental occupation of nest-building, and with [1] There is, it should be admitted, still much controversy with regard to the correct interpretation of the facts. The view indicated in the text seems, however, to be gaining ground among authorities. Dr Radin, who has made a particularly careful study of the social organisation of the Winnebago Indians, assures me that in this and like cases, it is practically certain that a process of degeneration has occurred in which the names have outlived the institutions.

[2] Macdougall, Introduction to Social Psychology, p. 88.

the social ends of the honey-bee 1." They are then the outcome of a social setting. On its strictly social side, in fact, the instinct of construction has a characteristic expression, and is at the basis of all social organisation.

This tendency towards organisation, in the course of which the varied social elements of a group are built together and come to have more or less well-determined functions, is found to be already operative in any group whatever that is open to our observation. We have then every right to treat it as instinctive from our point of view. But what are of particular interest are the various forms which it takes in its relation to the other underlying social tendencies. To refer to illustrations already given, supposing the specific fear instinct is aroused within a group in which the dominant social relationship is one of primitive comradeship, panic may occur and in that case the tendency towards organisation seems to be practically absent. But fear with assertiveness leads speedily to organised cruelty and persecution, and with submissiveness may lead to slave organisation.

The social tendency towards organisation will come up again for discussion when we attempt to determine the principles governing both the conflict, and the mutual re-inforcement of the root social impulses 2. Meanwhile we appear to be justified in maintaining that while the organising tendency is in definite operation in the primitive group, it is in a way dependent, both for its occurrence and for its form, upon the other tendencies which are simultaneously operative. Moreover it may turn out to be broadly true that when the underlying social relationship is one of primitive 1 Instinct and the Unconscious, p. 53.

2 See chapter iv.

comradeship, the organising tendency, if it is aroused at all, operates unwittingly; whereas, when the underlying social relationship is one of dominance or acceptance the organising tendency is of necessity stimulated, and in general its operations are definitely witting 1, though in no case are the whole of its results foreseen. Supposing that this view can be substantiated, we see once again the importance of a study of the mode of arrangement of the primitive social responses.

Now when we turn to a study of the institutions and modes of response of any primitive group whatsoever, the list of social tendencies which we have so far considered must appear woefully inadequate. Even when we add the fact that each of the underlying social relationships of comradeship, dominance and acceptance may vary in its expression according to its relation to any of the specific individual instincts which psychologists usually recognise, we have a scheme far short of the complexity of life in any known social group. For as a result, largely, of the operation of the tendencies toward construction and conservation, characteristic institutions arise within a group and are perpetuated. Such institutions vary in their nature from group to group in accordance with the inter-play of the social relationships involved, the specific interests that are aroused, and the nature of the group's external environment. But once an institution is formed and persists, around it cluster special tendencies having a social reference and all the appearance of original simplicity.

This point has important consequences and deserves to be illustrated in detail. I shall take my first illustration from an interesting study in the psychology of 1 For a concrete discussion of this point, see chapter vi.

Ritualism 1. At the outset the author of the monograph in question states his position with the utmost clearness though with less reserve than might perhaps be desired: "The thesis which we shall defend is that the type of reaction designated as ritualism is always social 2." And again: "The ceremony is always a social reaction. There is always implicit or explicit reference to other selves, be they real or imagined 3." And yet again: "The position which I shall defend in the present undertaking is that every ceremony, every rite, is social 4." Shall we then speak of a social tendency towards ritual, or ceremonialism, and treat it as on all fours with the other tendencies so far discussed? If we do this there appears to be no good reason why we should not go a good deal farther. Henke points out that in primitive society the established ritual may refer to "every act of life."

In 1887 and 1888 (he reminds us) about six hundred sacred formulas were obtained on the Cherokee reservation in North Carolina. They cover "every subject pertaining to the daily life and thought of the Indian, including medicine, love, hunting, fishing, war, self-protection, destruction of enemies, witchcraft, the crops, the council, the ball play, etc., and in fact embodying almost the whole of the ancient religion of the Chero-kees 5."

Very similar remarks might be made concerning the ritual of many other primitive people.

At the same time the ceremonial may have a specific 1 A Study in the Psychology of Ritualism, by Frederick Goodrich Henke, University of Chicago Press, 1910.

2 Op. cit. p. 3. 3 Op. cit. p. 8. 4 Op. cit. p. 9.

5 Op. cit. p. 10; the last part is a quotation from J. Mooney, Seventh Ann. Rep. Am. Bur. of Ethnology, Washington, 1891, p. 307.

character according to the subject with which it deals. Ritual practices attached to medicine, for example, may differ from those attached to war, within the same tribe; while again rites attached to the same activity may vary very greatly in different communities. Once a form of ceremonial has arisen and become fairly stereotyped within a social group, it may, from the point of view of the community, appear as simple, as inexplicable and as inevitable a mode of social response as any of the fundamental tendencies with which we have hitherto been concerned. We should thus have, not merely a tendency towards ritual, but several tendencies each directed towards a particular form of ritual. Moreover practically every community would yield illustrations of many such special tendencies.

At this point misgiving may well arise. Must these specialised tendencies, which differentiate one group from another, be considered definitely as group responses? They direct the activities of the particular social organisation concerned,, and for the most part, to the individuals belonging to that society, they appear to stand in no need of explanation, or at any rate of that kind of explanation which points to pre-existing conditions. But in the first chapter our main concern was said to be with the socially determined individual response. From the point of view of the community we may assert that a specialised tendency towards, say, a particular form of ceremonialism is displayed. Yet when we turn to the individuals concerned we find wide differences of attitude adopted towards, and even during, the practice of the ceremonial, and this in spite of the fact that the group as it engages in the ritual shows all the marks of common action, Shall we say then that these

"group difference tendencies" 1 are essentially of the nature of group responses, or group possessions, and as such have no place in a properly psychological treatment?

Here I would first call attention to the fact that in dealing with the relation of psychology to sociology, in the preceding chapter, I urged that while the latter eculd confine itself to social facts, the former is not able wholly to restrict its attention to facts of the individual life. For many individual responses are directly socially determined, and these social determinants have to be taken into account, if the individual responses are to be explained. The group difference tendencies of which I am now speaking may, in this way, be justly brought within the scope of our disciission.

To make this more clear, let us consider another illustration, taking this time a form of social life belonging to the modern world. When an individual joins a college he finds that masses of conventions, and numerous institutions have become stereotyped before his entrance. In this case the underlying social relationship involved is as a rule one either of acceptance 2, or of comradeship. This, operating together with the tendency towards conservation, predisposes the individual to accept some of these conventions and institutions without question, and to take part in the activities with which they are connected. Whatever may be the subtleties of his individual attitude towards them, from the point of view of social response he is 1 For this descriptive term I am indebted to Dr C. S. Myers.

2 I would like to point out here that Macdougalps term "self-abasement" seems to indicate a fur more marked degree of inferiority than the facts in general warrant.

simply one of his group. And the whole group appears to function together in the expression of a number of formed and relatively settled tendencies. Obviously the tendencies thus finding expression vary greatly among themselves. Some organisations within the group express work tendencies, others play tendencies, and others, such for example, as a debating club, express alternatively responses now belonging to the one class, and now to the other. Moreover every such tendency has a history within the group. It has arrived gradually, through many changes, at its stereotyped form. But the individual now takes part in the expression of the tendency without any consideration as to the vicissitudes through which it may have passed. To him the tendency is there, mature, to be accepted and to find expression in his behaviour.

Clearly the social tendencies which are expressed in group conventions and institutions operate directly as social determinants of individual response. They are group difference tendencies in that each tradition or institution possesses its own field of reference, and its own restricted range of application.

Now there are two ways in which we may treat these tendencies. Suppose that at that stage in the organisation of a group at which certain of the tendencies have already reached a stereotyped form, we take the group in question for the subject of our study. In the first place we may consider complex, formed and specialised tendencies, attempting to trace their development through the inter-play of the broader, less differentiated and more individual tendencies to which they owe their origin. The group difference tendencies in this case constitute our problem. But we may reverse this procedure, and, without enquiring into the history of the stereotyped social responses, we may accept them as our starting-point and attempt to work out the further changes that are introduced as they come into effective relationship one with another, and as, in new combinations, they act as social determinants of individual behaviour. The group difference responses now fqrm, not our problems, but our data.

The first mode of approach will give us an analysis to all appearance very far short of the complexity of any actual state of affairs. We may be criticised for replacing the subtlety and movement of real life by incredibly lifeless and shadowy conceptions. The criticism may mean one of two things. It may indicate that our enumeration of tendencies is strikingly incomplete. Incomplete it certainly is. But the criticism ignores the fact that the whole aim of this type of argument is to show the simpler conditions of that complexity which characterises a particular stage of social development, and not to exhibit all the tendencies that operate at any stage whatever of social life and growth. Or on the other hand the criticism may mean that the individual attitudes towards the tendencies dealt with vary far more than do the tendencies themselves. This cannot be doubted, but once again the aim of the analysis is misunderstood. For our attempt is not to work out the varieties of individual attitude towards, say, a ceremonial convention, in all their delicacy, but rather to discover the determining factors which lead all the individuals in a given group to respond in certain directions in a unitary manner. The point is that, once they are established, all conventions and institutions gain a direct, controlling function of their own over the individual. Thus we may speak of them as specialised tendencies exerting an immediate influence upon the social responses of the different members of a group. In this way they come within the scope of our study.

In another, and a more intimate way these specialised tendencies are perhaps of interest to us. As we have alremdy pointed out every person, at the outset of his life, is endowed with certain predispositions, both of the instinctive and of the individual kind. But there can be little doubt that in the course of his life he develops new tendencies, or that a very leading part in this process of acquisition is played by the influence of the community in which he lives. Now it may possibly be the case that many of those social modes of response which are expressed in conventions and institutions do, in a way, become possessions of the individual. The situation seems to be somewhat as follows. When an individual enters into a community, the underlying tendencies towards acceptance and conservation produce an exceedingly ready assimilation of the established customs and conventions. It may be that after these conventions have been observed a number of times the individual does actually acquire a tendency to behave in a particular manner, and further that this tendency gains a more or less independent status, and comes to operate by itself as a driving force in the person's life 1. This suggestion, however, is put forward only in the most tentative manner. The point that I wish to make is that the group difference tendencies certainly come within our purview as determinants of individual response, even if they are not themselves to be considered as individual in their character. 1 Cf. pp. 272-3.

We may now at once apply our " principle of discrimination" in regard to problems of origin. For, however primitive the organisation with which we are concerned, such group difference tendencies, clustering about social and religious institutions, and expressing themselves in characteristic social responses, may always be found.

Of every one of the broad and generalised responses discussed in the earlier parts of this chapter we may say that to put forward a problem as to its origin is illegitimate. The case is otherwise with these group difference tendencies. They all form problematic material. But they do not present problems which we are in all cases bound to pursue. I shall later attempt to show that the psychological study of primitive culture can develop satisfactorily only on a basis of the detailed investigation of specific communities. To attempt to settle great questions of psychological interest affecting the life of nations when as yet we know practically nothing about the laws affecting the inter-play of social tendencies within m specific group, simply leads to endless theorising. Now if we do take the specific community as our object of study, and concentrate our attention upon the results of the inter-play of tendencies within that group, we shall in all instances be justified in accepting as starting-points for our investigations various specialised social responses. This is only to urge, in yet another form, that the important thing is not any mere list of tendencies that may be obtained, but the elucidation of the functional arrangement and relations of those tendencies, together with the results consequent upon that arrangement.

Thus our analysis of those social responses with which we have to begin our researches into the psychology of primitive culture is admittedly and necessarily incomplete. To the broad and fundamental tendencies which we have distinguished we shall find ourselves compelled to add, upon occasion, more specialised responses differentiating one group from another. Precisely what those responses are we can tell only when we know with what particular community we are to be concerned, and at what stage of its history we are to begin its study. This is the answer, both to those who urge that lists of original tendencies are generally incomplete, and also to those who, adopting a precisely opposite point of view, say that such lists commonly contain members which are themselves in need of explanation by derivation from more simple forms of response.

One other point should be made clear. I have spoken of the fundamental forms of social relationship response; of the social influence of conservation and of that social construct! veness which produces new forms of organisation; and of the group difference tendencies. But the recognition of these need not lead us to ignore the more specifically individual instinct reactions, such as the various forms of avoidance, of curiosity, of acquisitiveness and the like, or the more narrowly social forms, such as the sexual and parental responses. These are not in any way unimportant from our present standpoint, but they vary in their social effects and significance, according to their relationship to the fundamental social responses with which in this chapter we have been mainly concerned.

Further, our concrete studies will furnish us with many illustrations of the importance of individual tendencies which distinguish one person from another.

All of these, however, are best discussed as they may be found to occur in particular instances of life in the primitive community.

This completes the general consideration of the foundations upon which our course of study is to be built. The argument may at times have appeared somewhat abstract, but it seemed desirable to attempt to provide a general basis for our future more concrete studies.

In the next chapter I propose to show how the general principles already outlined may be shown to have concrete application to the study of a specific form of social expression. This could be done in connexion with an analysis of primitive ceremonial, or by a study of primitive group games, or, in fact, by investigation into any kind of early social behaviour. But I propose to take, as my leading illustration, the folk story, treating it definitely as a social product. We shall be able to see in actual operation in this field the modes of response which so far have been named rather than given definite application. The purpose of this discussion, and of the succeeding chapters, will be to show that the scheme adumbrated will actually work.

Next we must proceed to determine in greater detail, and again by a study of actually observed material, certain important results of the inter-play of tendencies. Here I propose to deal more particularly with the psychological effects upon primitive culture of the conflict and mutual re-inforcement of tendencies.

This discussion will continually force upon our notice some of the extraordinarily important questions which psychology must endeavour to face with regard to the effects of "contact of peoples." We shall have to try to say what, with our present range of knowledge, can be said, from a psychological point of view, in respect to the dissemination, the elaboration, and the no less important disintegration of culture.

This line of study will serve to display again and again what are the primary requirements for the development of St truly psychological treatment of primitive culture. In the conclusion I shall try to state as definitely as possible what I conceive to be the essential needs for further development within this field. It will then, I believe, become clear that social psychology must follow lines of growth essentially analogous to the development of more general psychological study.

Finally I shall return to the principles already considered, shall re-interpret them in the light of the discussions entered into in the course of the general argument, and shall attempt a more complete and definite exposition of the peculiar point of view from which the psychologist should approach the analysis of social phenomena. I shall endeavour to show precisely how this point of view, in relation to its field of study, is connected with the problems of psychology in general, as these problems appear to the student of contemporary social affairs.

I may now summarise the present chapter: 1. A consideration of the native equipment of man, as dealt with by Macdougall in his Introduction to Social Psychology, showed that some of the principal instincts and innate tendencies distinguished by Macdougall are immediately and specifically social, while others are not. To the first class belong: of the principal instincts: gregariousness, self-assertion, and self-abasement, in a narrow sense the sexual and parental instincts, and, with some doubt, pugnacity, ancj a s9cialform of the con- structive instinct; of the innate tendencies: sympathetic induction of the emotions, suggestibility, imitation, and probably play.

2. The instincts and tendencies distinguished by Macdougall show, as regards their social forms, different relations of independence one to another, specific instincts leading to a different social response according to that type of fundamental social relationship which is simultaneously in operation.

3. Three forms of fundamental social relationship are to be discriminated: the tendency to primitive comradeship a relationship of equals and the tendencies of

assertiveness and submissiveness, or of dominance and acceptance a relationship of superiors and inferiors.

4. These three are mainly affective in character. As largely cognitive we have the social tendency to conservation, the selective nature of which must not be forgotten. We must also add a social constructive tendency which is at the basis of all social organisation.

5. The study of any definite social group reveals further the operation of numerous specific tendencies clustering in the main about various forms of institution. While in most, if not in all cases, it would be possible to consider profitably the origin of these group difference tendencies, we are, as a rule, justified in taking them, already formed, as starting-points for the discussion of our problems. In any case the important thing is not merely to obtain a list of the tendencies but to study the relationships which in given cases they bear one to another, and to elucidate the effects of these relationships.

6. We shall from this point be concerned to develop in a more concrete fashion the method of approach to the study of primitive culture which it has been our business in the first two chapters to describe in general terms.

CHAPTER III

PSYCHOLOGY AND THE FOLK STORY

The Argument: The folk story, the myth and the legend are ll to be studied as social products. They frequently grow out of established institutions and customs, and so express group difference tendencies. They illustrate the ways in which the fundamental social relationship forms affect the primitive community. Particularly as regards their dramatic character, their drojl, and their fantastic features they are directly influenced by facts arising from their social functions within the group to which, or within which, they are told. They help to show how the more individual instinctive tendencies come into play in the early group, and how these may produce very different results according as they enter into different combinations one with another and with the social relationship forms. Finally they give some evidence of the influence of the individual characteristics of the story tellers, as factors determining the form and matter of the stories. It is the aim of this chapter to show how all these conditions may come together and aid in the shaping of the stories, and thus to provide a concrete illustration of the application of the general scheme, the main outlines of which have already been set forth.

In a sense the whole of the rest of the book will be an illustration and development of the point of view already expressed. In the present discussion, however, I shall, in particular, show how the tendencies whose nature and relations were discussed in the preceding chapter may be seen actually at work in the folk story.

On the whole, psychologists have given less consideration to the popular tale, than the interest of the subject warrants. And when they have discussed it they have usually adopted an unnecessarily narrow point of view. They have tended to ignore the social character of the folk story, and to regard it simply as an imaginative expression of more or less uniform individual tendencies. They have said that all individuals, confronted by the striking phenomena of nature, the rising and setting of the sun, the passage of the stars in their courses, the succession of the seasons, tend to fasten upon the same objects of interest, and to think of these in the same ways. This is done, it is argued, by the very laws of the constitution of the mental life, and not in any sense by social compulsion. Or it may be that, leaving the contemplation of natural phenomena aside, the psychologist has urged that the folk tale, like the dream, springs almost wholly from one or two deep-seated individual needs, or desires, or wishes. These needs are implanted in every man, no matter in what social group he is to be found, and it is by them that the popular story is mainly produced. Or yet again, some less recondite explanation may be attempted. The folk tale, it may be said, is a kind of primitive recreation. The early storyteller rests, as he speaks, from the fatigues of the day. But he is tired, and his weariness heightens and renders fantastic his imagination. Once again the appeal is made to laws of psychological reaction which affect the individual as such, and operate alike within or without the social group, and if within, then in very much the same way whatever the group may be.

Now all of these theories, whatever else may be said about them, tend to become views concerning the absolute origin of the folk story. Each in its own way seeks some simple and comprehensive hypothesis, by which the whole of the vast structure of mythology, legend, and folk tale may be explained. Moreover the hypothesis always concerns a reaction which is distinctively individual. It is the individual who contemplates natural phenomena; it is the individual who seeks an imaginative fulfilment of his wishes; it is th? individual who feels fatigue and yields himself to phantasy; and, to revert to one of the earliest of all the forms of theory, it is the individual within whom is the stirring of "elementary thoughts," which come from nowhere, but are from the beginning, as it were, fully formed in the mental life.

All of these theories must inevitably fail to give satisfaction. In the first place, there is no way of discovering the absolute origin of the folk story, and it is best to be honest, and to say so. This is only one special case, though, so far as the history of the subject goes, it is an outstanding case, of the futility of the investigation of absolute origins. But as the general question has already been considered, I do not propose to say anything more about it here.

In the second place, these theories are all extraordinary examples of illicit simplification. There is no reason for doubting that the folk tale, precisely as in the case of many other products that are studied by psychology, comes from a variety of sources. All through this chapter we shall have continually to be reminding ourselves of this fact. A folk tale, or a part of one, quoted to illustrate one tendency, principle, or characteristic, will be found to illustrate half-a-dozen others equally well. Into popular tales, as we have to deal with them, come influences varied in their nature and source, and not less varied in their effects. They mingle, play one upon another in complex and often in subtle ways, and in the production of the result the tale with which we have to deal they all co-operate. If, at the very time at which we are considering the character and formation of the stories, we merge all these influences into one, we adopt a hopelessly unpsychological procedure.

In the third place the folk story cannot be treated solely as an individual response. Many of the complex influences that take a part in shaping it, come directly from the social group. It has been said already that to recognise these does not involve the rejection of the psychological method of approach. Throughout this chapter I shall again and again insist, that in certain perfectly definite respects the myth, the legend and the popular story, are immediately affected by influences arising from the social setting in which they take form and grow. This will be shown to be true both as regards the material with which they deal, and as regards the form which they assume. In them will be found the expression of those deep-seated instinctive tendencies which actually require a social setting for their stimulation. Playing upon them will be found the influence of diverse group difference tendencies which not only require a social setting, but which presuppose a social group having a particular history, and particular forms of institution. Moulding their form will be found tendencies which arise directly from the fact that the tales are told to listeners, individual tendencies, that is to say, which are socially determined. While running through them all, as themes which recur over and over again, are the instinctive responses which are truly individual in their character, though their expression is here mainly determined by the prevailing social relationships.

It will, I think, help to bring out the coherence and essential unity of this lengthy chapter, if, before proceeding to concrete illustration of the various points to be discussed, I first develop rapidly the plan of treatment that will be adopted.

First, then, I shall try to say exactly what I mean wb en I call the folk story a social product.

Next I propose to show how the group difference tendencies find expression in the popular tale. I shall attack this question thus early, not because these group difference tendencies are to be regarded as themselves the most fundamental, but because I wish in every possible way, to differentiate the method of approach which I am adopting from that which strives after absolute origins. Supposing it to be true that the folk story often simply takes up and expresses tendencies which are already stabilised in the form of institutions, it is clear that its study may legitimately presuppose a long order of development. For not only psychological probability, but also all available evidence, suggests that in these cases, it is not the institution that is derived from the story, but the story from the institution.

I shall pass next to a study of how the general underlying and instinctive forms of social relationship: primitive comradeship, assertiveness and submissive-ness: come into the tales, and of how their exceedingly intimate inter-relations are illustrated.

This will lead us to a consideration of the precise ways in which the form of the stories is conditioned by influences arising at once from the social group.

Last of all I shall endeavour to illustrate how the individual instinct responses come into play, and to show how in the folk story we may find concrete illustration of the importance of that structural arrangement of instincts which was a main point of emphasis in the last chapter.

We may begin our discussion of what is meant by calling the folk story a social product, by reminding ourselves that all such stories are essentially for listeners. Called into being by the inter-play of characteristic needs, emotions and interests within a group, they are transformed and developed by the influence of the same factors. This may be illustrated by examples taken from the folk tales of the Ila-speaking peoples of Northern Rhodesia. These peopled inhabit the country to the north of the Batoka plateau, above the middle Zambesi, in the fertile plains some two hundred miles north of the Victoria Falls. A remarkably vivid and instructive account of their manners, customs, and institutions has been written by the Rev. E. W. Smith and Captain A. M. Dale 1. At the conclusion of their work the authors have collected a number of the folk tales current among the Ba-ila.

One listens (they write) to a clever story-teller such as our old friend. from whom we derived many of these tales. Speak of eloquence! Here was no lip mumbling, but every muscle of face and body spoke, a swift gesture often supplying the place of a whole sentence. He would have made a fortune as a raconteur upon the English stage. The animals spoke, each in his own tone: the deep rumbling voice of Momba, the ground hornbill, for example, contrasting vividly with the piping accents of Sulwe, the hare. It was all good to listen to impossible to put on paper. Ask him now to repeat the story slowly so that you may write it. You will, with patience, get the gist of it, but the unnaturalness of the circumstance disconcerts him, your repeated request for the repetition

The lla-Speaking Peoples of Northern Rhodesia, London, 1920.

of a phrase, the absence of the encouragement of his friends, and above all, the hampering slowness of your pen, all combine to kill the spirit of story telling 1.

The whole force of the description brings vividly before us a social setting. It will be noticed that all the comparisons used refer to a group, and that the writers poi t to the story-teller as being a centre of attention within such a group. They think of him as on the "English stage." They talk of his "eloquence." They are sure that he is adversely affected when he lacks social encouragement. It is obvious that the mere fact that the tales are told in a social milieu, and must appeal to a sympathetic group of auditors, is of immense importance. And this description of the story-teller among the Ila-speaking peoples, is wholly confirmed by the accounts of writers who have discussed the telling of popular tales among other peoples. To consider the story-teller outside of his group is as futile as to discuss the orator without his audience.

That the folk story is a social product, implies, among other things, that in its matter the popular tale must make a common appeal, and in its form it must be so shaped as to call forth a widely and readily shared response. For both of these characters spring at once from the fact that the folk story is largely a mode of social intercourse.

One interesting conclusion may perhaps be drawn at once from these considerations. It will be generally admitted that the folk story affords, on the whole, a very fine illustration of the working of that social instinct of conservation of which we spoke in the last chapter. Doubtless stories change from time to time. 1 Op. tit. ii. p. 386.

They suffer transformation as they pass from people to people. Yet it remains true that within a given group they are often remarkably persistent. Not only does their theme remain unaltered, but the very terms in which the story is told suffer but slight change.

If these stories could be treated independently of influences arising from the group this would be ifluch more extraordinary than it is. The fact is that the auditors of a folk story commonly form a group which displays to a remarkable degree the character of harmonious thinking, acting and feeling. They are people among whom that instinctive response which I have called "primitive comradeship," is exhibited to a high degree. A tendency to any kind of reaction arising in one part of the group is reflected with remarkable rapidity in every other part.

In the islands of Barra (says J. F. Campbell).,. during the recitation of these tales, the emotions of the reciter are occasionally very strongly excited, and so are those of the listeners who maybe found almost shedding tears at one time, and giving way to loud laughter at another 1.

Now it may be the case that any group, whether large or small, within which the fundamental relation of "primitive comradeship" holds sway, is particularly prone to preserve the material with which it deals and to adhere to the behaviour which it adopts, with little or no change. At first sight, it is possible that this may seem somewhat unlikely. The comradeship response involves a ready reflexion of all feelings, behaviour, or thoughts which find expression in any member of the group concerned. It may thus appear to be precisely 1 Popular Tales of the West Highlands, London, 1890, vol. i, pp. 4r-5.

that relationship which provides a social milieu in which change will be welcomed. And indeed in its developed form comradeship does seem to have this result. Of William James, for example, it has been said:

Men and women of all sorts felt at ease with him. He was distinctly not a man who required a submissive audience to put him in the vein. A kind of admiring attention that made him self-conscious was as certain to reduce him to silence as a manly give and take was sure to bring him out. It never seemed to occur to him to debate or talk for victory 1.

There seems little doubt that it was largely from this developed form of comradeship that the high degree of responsiveness to new ideas which characterised James's mental adventures sprang.

It is, however, a psychological principle of interest and importance that tendencies which persist at all levels of human development may have apparently opposed results at different stages. Especially in its early forms of expression, there is an exceedingly close relation between the conserving tendency and the comradeship response. Each helps and intensifies the other. The comradeship tendency is most likely to be prevalent and effective in a group in reference to modes of thought, feeling and action which have already acquired familiarity through repetition. At the same time, any group which expresses the comradeship response is, by that very fact, all the more likely to repeat its various social activities without change. Between comradeship and social conservation there holds good that circular relationship which is frequently illustrated among human impulses. They may both originally come into play under the same 1 The Letters of William James, London, 1920, p. 26. B. 5 general conditions, and in reference to the same general type of material. The expression of either tends to intensify the expression of the other. In certain of its later developments the conserving tendency may become more consciously selective, and the comradeship response may acquire a more independent status. But at first the two are closely connected, and by their joint action the folk story is rendered doubly likely to persist with but little change. Its preservation is thus due largely to its social character.

Whatever explanation may be put forward there is no doubt that popular tales do persist with remarkable sameness from period to period. Take the report on the Ba-ila again:

Many of the tales (we are told) are known far and wide, others in lesser areas. But, however often the people hear them, they never seem weary of the repetition. They never say: u Oh, that's an old tale! 55 or make sarcastic references to chestnuts, but enter into the spirit of the thing all the more for knowing all that is to come. They heard the tales first as children from their mothers or grandmothers, but nevertheless they will, with no trace of boredom, come in with their ejaculations, just at the right points, take, it may be, a sentence out of the narrator's mouth, or even keep up a running echo of his words 1.

In fact, if we confine our attention to stories which have grown up within the community we are investigating, or which, introduced from another group, have been assimilated to popular tales already existing within 1 Op. cit. p. 336. One is here reminded forcibly of Perrault's description of children as they listen to fairy stories: "On les voit dans la tristesse et dans 1abattement tout que le h6ros ou F heroine du conte sont dans le malheur, et s' crier de joie quand le temps de leur bonheur arrive."

the community, we find that they are almost always remarkably persistent. It appears fair to say that their conservation is partially consequent upon the fact that the folk tale group is one which normally displays to a high degree the character of "primitive comradeship."

There is, however, another reason why the conservation tendency is very strong in reference to folk stories. And with the consideration of this we shall pass to our second point, and see how in the popular tale may be found evidence of the effect of various group difference tendencies. To a very large extent indeed, myth, legend and folk tale grow out of established social institutions and customs. As this fact will exercise an important influence upon our attitude in dealing with the tales, it must be given careful consideration.

In Fiji there is a legend which tells how great competitions are held between the natives of some specified place and a number of visitors, the lives of the defeated being at the mercy of the will of the victors 1. The competitions always include an eating contest, each side being bound to eat all that the other side provides, and to leave nothing over under forfeit of life. Now within the communities which possess this story there are inter-marrying tribes or clans known as veitambani, a word which signifies "related as one half to the other." These groups are looked upon by the natives as belonging together: it is a disgrace for them (they say) that the report should go that they have been overwhelmed or weak in war, or in exchanges, or in eating, or in drinking. It is better that they should die in battle than run away; it is better 1 "The Common Sense of Myth," by A, M. Hocart, Amer. Anthropol. N. S. 1916, pp. 307-18, that they should be poor rather than that their contribution of stuff to the exchange should be small; it is better that their bellies should burst, and their stomachs be rent than that food and water should be left, it must all be eaten up.

There is, that is to say, a definite custom embodying the eating competition. o

When we turn to the Fijian popular stories we find one which tells how ten brothers go to Tonga to marry ten sisters. The usual contests follow, and there is the eating competition. Now, says A. M. Hocart, from whom I have taken this illustration, the brothers and the Tongans stand in the relation of veitambani. The story is the direct reflexion of an already established social custom. There seems to be no reason for doubting that he is right. Here, then, is a custom already grown up, complete and often in operation within a given community; and here is a story centred about this custom, and told to various auditors within the community. The atmosphere in which the story is told is one of excitement, emotional sympathy, and "primitive comradeship." The tale requires no explanation. It is immediately received. The tendencies which cluster about the institution of veitambani are stirred again as the tale is told. No doubt the custom itself may have had its history. But the important point for us is that now it is there. And it is partly owing to this fact that the story which is based thereon is precisely of the kind that can be most immediately received, and is most perfectly preserved within this community. The legend is the direct expression of various group difference tendencies.

Hocart's example is no isolated case. He gives a number of others himself, and his conclusion is most emphatic.

So long (says he) as the mythologist is content with taking myths in isolation, and constructing a rationalised version out of his own head, he can never get any further. There are so many possible ways of rationalising a myth according to the temperament, bias, nationality and age of the mythologist, but each remains a bare possibility with no power to convince any one. The truta may be very different from what we all expected, and that is only to be attained from a systematic study of the whole culture to which the myth belongs, together with neighbouring cultures. Then the facts will force the conclusion on us, and not we on the facts.

For my part I should agree with this absolutely, with the sole addition that what we need is not merely a knowledge of specific customs and beliefs, but of how those customs and beliefs act upon the story-telling group as we find it in whatever people we may be studying.

This conclusion is assuredly borne out in what is probably one of the most complete of recent researches into comparative folk lore, the Comparative Study of Tsimshian Mythology, by Dr Franz Boas 1. The Tsim-shians are one of a group of tribes inhabiting the northernmost portion of the North Pacific coast. They display perhaps the most strongly of all the tribes in that region the "characteristic traits of North Pacific coast culture." They are an energetic people, dwelling in the "valleys of the Nass and Skeena rivers and the channels and islands southward as far as Milbank Sound," fishing, and hunting, and having a fairly well developed material culture. They possess a wealth of myths, legends and tales.

Boas takes a wide and exhaustive survey of the stories 1 Thirty-first Ann. Rep. of the Bur. of Am. Ethnology, 1909-10.

which are current among the Tsimshians and neighbouring tribes of the Northern Pacific coast. And as a result he concludes that most of the tales are built upon some simple event or other which is characteristic of the social life of the communities in which they are told.

The material presented in the present work (he says, after a most detailed analysis) if examined in its relation to the folk tales of neighbouring tribes, and in its probable historical development, shows nothing that would necessitate the assumption that it originated from the contemplation of natural phenomena. It rather emphasises the fact that its origin must be looked for in the imaginative tales dealing with the social life of the people 1.

Boas, indeed, here speaks of origin, and talks as if he means literal beginning. He may be, and probably he is, correct. Yet to this view a certain speculative element must necessarily attach. My own position is clearer and simpler. However a story may actually have originated, it cannot for one moment be doubted that the study of these popular tales does show that in many instances they refer directly to social institutions already established in the community within which they are told. The tendencies clustering about the institutions are reflected again in the stories, and from the point of view of the study of the formative influences of the tales, and of their effect upon listeners, may legitimately be taken as starting-points for analysis.

The most impressive proof of this contention is to be found in the Description of the Tsimshlan based upon their mythology, which Boas presents to his readers 2. Here is 1 Op. cit. p. 881. 2 Op. cit. pp. 393-477.

an account occupying almost one hundred large pages, and comprising nearly every department of social life and interest, giving for every custom referred to its illustrative equivalent from the popular stories. The list of activities thus represented in the tales is a formidable one. We find customs and institutions illustrated connected with: Towns, houses, household goods, and manufactures; dress and ornament; fishing, hunting and food-gathering; travel; playing and gambling; quarrels and war; social organisation; family life; chiefs, attendants, slaves and council; visitors and festivals; marriage and death; ethical ideas and emotional responses; religious and magical practices; current beliefs; and shamanism. When we turn to the actual details the facts are equally striking. Take, for example, the case of family life. The tales show clearly that the family in the strict sense remains an effective unit of social organisation in spite of the four-fold exogamic clan division which the Tsimshians possess. The kinds of duties to be shared by wife and husband are often related, and how in cases of danger women and children may be " placed in canoes and sent to places of safety." The relations between brothers and sisters, parents and children, are described in great detail: how and when they live together, what, in certain cases, each owes the other in the way of gifts, and there are innumerable narratives concerning their common emotional relations. No one who reads Boas's description, and who follows it up by a careful study of the stories themselves, can fail to see how through the whole of the tales runs the influence of a many-sided social life, and of the various specialised tendencies which this life involves. "All of these stories," says Boas, in conclusion, "show a unity of the underlying idea. They are built up on some simple event that is characteristic of the social life of the people, and that stirs the emotions of the hearers 1." He claims that the stories: have "the merit of bringing out those points in their ethnology which are of interest to the people themselves. They present in a way an autobiography of the tribe 2."

In almost the same words the authors who write of the Ba-ila state their views. As is commonly the case, many of the stories of the Ba-ila are told about animals. These, on the face of it, may seem to have little to do with social custom. But: in sketching these animals (say Smith and Dale). the Ba-ila are sketching themselves. The virtues they esteem, the vices they condemn, the follies they ridicule all are here in the animals. It is a picture of the Ba-ila, drawn by the Ba-ila, albeit unconsciously, and valuable accordingly 3.

We see then, that the folk stories of a particular people commonly centre about social customs and values which either are or have been practised or accepted within the community. In the last chapter it was urged that group difference tendencies cluster about specific social institutions, and that these may act directly as determinants of individual response. Here we get our first definite illustration of these facts. The primitive story-teller, and each of his listeners, is directly affected by tendencies arising from the relatively settled modes of behaviour of their group. When we are analysing the formative influences giving rise to popular tales, we need not attempt to trace these tendencies to their own 1 Boas, op. cit p. 875. 2 Boas, op. cit. p. 398.

8 Smith and Dale, op. cit. n, p. 841.

origin. We are justified in taking them as starting-points for the purposes of our treatment. Their number and their character, but not their function or their mode of operation, may vary greatly from group to group. On the one hand they serve to heighten the harmony of the group, while on the other hand the fact that the very constitution of the group favours harmony itself makes it easier for them to do their work.

Thus, together with the fact that the story-telling group is on the whole one in which " primitive comradeship" is uppermost, the group difference tendencies help to secure the conservation of the tales.

As for the mechanism of the operation of these tendencies, however diverse they may be, they always produce, as Boas points out, a stirring of emotion in the hearers. Sir James Frazer has said that:

A study of the emotional basis of folk lore has hardly yet been attempted; inquirers have confined their attention exclusively to its logical and rational, or, as some might put it, its illogical and irrational elements 1.

In the attempt to fill up this gap in the study of folk tales, a recognition of the readiness with which the group difference tendencies arouse emotions must have an important place.

We must next pass to a study of how those instinctive forms of social relation which, as we saw in the last chapter, underly all the more narrowly defined tendencies, and are at the basis of all social activities, find illustration in the folk tale. Of these the most commonly recognised are assertiveness and submissiveness, but I have urged that equally fundamental is the response which I have called " primitive comradeship." 1 Folk Lore of the Old Testament, m, 454.

In studying the expression in popular story of these tendencies, we have continually to remember in what subtle and intimate ways all the various influences which, for the purposes of our treatment, we have to deal with separately, may come simultaneously into operation. It is a point that has often been insisted upon, in reference to many different problems of primitive culture.

One half of a custom (says Hocart) will lie within religion, the other within social organisation; a myth will have some of its roots in technology, others in religion, others in something which we do not know how to classify 1.

In the discussion which follows I shall attempt to quote from actual stories, il-lustrations of the relationships of "primitive comradeship," of assertiveness, and of sub-missiveness. But the illustrations will never be of one tendency alone. They will show how fluid are all possible boundaries in this field; how one primitive form may, with extraordinary ease, slide into another, and how the ways in which the various tendencies come together may make an important difference to the character of their influence.

We will begin with the instinctive response of "primitive comradeship." This, in its earliest forms, gives us simply a ready and harmonious response to the thoughts, feelings and actions of certain members of the community, with no trace of an attitude of superiority on the part of the persons who are the source of the change, or of inferiority on the part of those who respond. We sometimes speak of how " waves of feeling " may sweep through a whole community. There may similarly be " waves " of action, or of ways of regarding a situation. In all these 1 Op. cit. p. 310.

cases the different members of a group tend to feel, act, and think more or less alike. But it is no less important to remember that concerted responses, where the different actors play diverse parts, may just as well spring from "primitive comradeship" as may response in unison, where all the actors do the same things. Thus Rivers tefls how among the Solomon Islanders he frequently noticed that different members of a boat's crew would work together in complete harmony upon different tasks, though he could discover no trace "of an understanding by which the members of the crew arranged who should undertake the different kinds of work 1."

The story-telling group certainly appears to exhibit the relationship of primitive comradeship to a high degree. Yet this response has not set its mark upon the folk story as deeply as have the responses of dominance and acceptance. At first this circumstance seems curious and unexpected, but brief reflexion will show that it is perfectly natural. There is no obvious reason why the atmosphere in which the story is told should determine the subject-matter of the tale. Indeed, it is a fact of common observation that auditors often best enjoy stories about characteristics which they do not themselves possess, or about types of conduct which they seldom or never practise. Most important of all, however, is the consideration that primitive comradeship lacks dramatic quality. It affects individuals, but by itself it does not clearly stand out as mark of individual character. It is, in fact, the ordinary, everyday, working, social attitude of companion members of a community who do not stand out prominently from their fellows. As we shall see in detail shortly, however, folk stories 1 Instinct and the Unconscious, pp. 94-6.

must be considered as forms to be told to listeners. The story-teller is always subject to influences arising from his own position in the group. He therefore not only deals with material which, because it at once fits in with already formed social tendencies, evokes a teady emotional response, but he must deal with this material in such a way as to hold attention, and if possible to Increase his own prestige as a centre of interest in the group. It is at least partly in consequence of this that the tales gain their marked dramatic form. The value of such a form reacts upon the material of the stories, and influences the types of social relationship that are displayed most prominently. Yet it is still true that any collection of tales will yield evidence of the less striking, and "coloured" response which I have called "primitive comradeship."

Let me introduce my illustrations by a suggestion which is certainly somewhat speculative. Popular stories everywhere often attribute to the mere spoken word a remarkable influence. To speak and to do are regarded as almost the same thing. Yet the speaker may neither be given nor need he assume a position of superiority, and those who are affected by his speech are not thereby rendered inferior. Turn again to the description of the tales of Ba-ila.

It seems (we read) that in ancient time, when things were still fluid, before animals and men had assumed their final forms, it was possible for one creature to affect another, favourably or adversely, by merely pronouncing its destiny. Thus Mintengwe, the blackbird, dooms the rest of the feathered tribe to persecution and death; and tortoise confers on hare the dignity of preeminent wisdom. Here we have the world-wide belief in the efficacy of the spoken word, whether for curse or for blessing 1.

How "magic" words and formulae may open caves, recover treasure, and vastly influence the destiny of living people, is familiar to all students of folk lore.

Now I think it just possible, though naturally I do noft wish to insist upon the view, that here we have an illustration of the remarkably rapid way in which a pronouncement may spread throughout a community the various members of which stand one to another in the relationship of primitive comradeship. Not only does the pronouncement spread and become known far and wide, but it is met everywhere with an acquiescence which is far from being an admission of inferiority. The word is law not because of the dominant, or domineering position of the speaker, but because of the "comradeship" of the hearers.

Apart from this conjecture, however, we often find a direct picture of the response of "primitive comradeship." I will take a story from the collection of Tsim-shian mythology, entitled The Meeting of the Wild Animals. The animals, finding themselves hunted all the year round, are in dire distress. So they have a meeting, and all the large animals are invited by the Grizzly Bear 2. But the Wolf says: I have something to say. Let us invite all the small animals, even such as Porcupine, Beaver, Raccoon, Marten, Mink, down to such small animals as the Mouse and the Insects that move on the earth, for they might come forth and protest against us and all our advice might come to nought!

So the invitation is extended and all the animals come 1 Smith and Dale, op. cit. u, pp. 337-8. a Boas, op. cit. pp. 106-8.

together, both small and great. The small animals all sit together on the one side, and the large animals on the other. Then the Grizzly Bear suggests that they should ask "Him Who Made Us" for very cold winters as a protection against the hunters. The Panther speaks up and says: "I fully agree to this wise counsel" and all the large animals agreed.

So far the situation is one of perfect concord, with no animal really in the ascendant and with none oppressed. But the Porcupine, being invited to speak, points out that the Grizzly Bear's suggestion is well suited to the needs of the large animals: "for you have plenty of warm fur even for the most severe cold"; but for the small and unprotected animals, severe weather will be a great hardship. The prevailing unity seems likely to be disturbed, although still no section of the meeting assumes any notable position of assertiveness. The large animals merely remark mildly that they have already made up their minds and cannot change. Thereupon the Porcupine tries again, and this time points out that extreme cold will make it very hard for the large animals to get adequate supplies of food. At this:

All the large animals were speechless because they wondered at the wisdom of Porcupine. Finally Grizzly Bear arose and said: "It is true what you have said." Thus spoke Grizzly Bear to Porcupine, and all the large animals chose Porcupine to be their wise man, and to be the first among all the small animals; and they agreed that the cold in winter should be much as it is now. They made six months for the winter and six months for summer.

Then Porcupine spoke again out of his wisdom, and said: "In winter we shall have ice and snow. In spring we shall have showers of rain, and the plants shall be green. In summer we shall have warmer weather, and all the fishes shall go up the rivers. In the fall, the leaves shall fall; it shall rain, and the rivers and brooks shall overflow their banks. Then all the animals, large and small, and those that creep upon the ground, shall go into their dens and hide themselves for six months!" Thus spoke the wise Porcupine to all the animals. Then they agreed to what Porcupine had proposed.

They all went joyfully to their own homes. Thus it happens that all the wild animals take to their dens in winter, and that all the large animals are in their dens in winter.

Here we have the story of a council in which there is a considerable amount of give and take without superiority or inferiority. The spokesmen, Grizzly Bear, Panther and Porcupine, occupy a most interesting position. They seem rather mouthpieces of a group than law-givers to a group. In one way, they stand out from the others, but there is hardly a trace of anything really meriting the title of assertiveness. There is differentiation of function without the dominance of high rank or the submission of low. The Porcupine, in particular, who is definitely chosen as "their wise man," really seems only to say what all the rest are thinking, or to formulate something that all the others have, so to speak, already accepted without formulation. Perhaps we can see here something of the relationship in which a chief may often stand to a primitive group. It is a relationship in which leadership does not depend mainly upon domination or assertion, but upon a ready susceptibility to the thoughts, feelings and actions of the members of the group. The chief, that is, expresses the group rather than impresses it. This is the kind of relationship, entirely different, it seems to me, from dominance and assertiveness, that runs all through the story I have quoted. And it is a matter of no difficulty to find the same kind of relationship depicted in many other tales belonging to an early level of culture. It may be not without significance that the story which has been quoted as illustrating the instinctive response of "primitive comradeship," contains also as good an example as could be wished o the "efficacy of the spoken word."

Attention has already been drawn to the way in which this working relationship of equals a relationship that is fundamental for the development of social life continually tends to swing over into the emphatic forms of dominance on the one hand, and of subservience on the other. Take the very story which I have just quoted. When the first opinion of the Porcupine meets with but little response, the Porcupine is, in the original version of the story, pictured as for the moment full of fury, and as if he were an inferior fighting for an equal status. Again, the tale arranges the big animals on one side of the council and the small animals on the other, as though to mark an entente that may easily pass into difference. Finally, immediately after the narrative tells us that all the animals go to their dens in the winter, "large animals as well as small ones," it goes on:

The large animals refused the advice that Porcupine gave; and Porcupine was full of rage, went to those animals that had slighted him, and struck them with the quills of his tail, and the large animals were killed by them. Therefore all the animals are afraid of Porcupine to this day.

So in the end comradeship breaks down, and we get dominance on the one side, while on the other there i fear, with presumably some degree of submissiveness.

There can indeed be no doubt that of the three fundamental instinctive forms of social relationship, dominance or assertion of some kind or another is the one that comes the most readily into the folk story. We shall now consider the reasons why this should be so.

Assertiveness, being a fundamental social instinct, is boitnd to find its way into so largely social a form of expression as the popular story. Moreover, in certain of its manifestations, dominance is precisely that relationship to hear of which produces lively feelings of pleasure and amusement in any ordinarily constituted group of listeners. We may go once more to the Ba-ila, and look through their varied accounts of the adventures of Sulwe, the hare.

He deserves (say Smith and Dale) a section to himself. He is the most popular of all the dramatis personae. In the minds of the Ba-ila he embodies all subtlety. He is skilful in practical jokes; he is cruel, he is cunning, he is false; a Machiavel, a Tartuffe, a downright rogue. He should be a despicable character, but the Ba-ila shake and roll about with laughter as they listen, for the hundredth time to his adventures. Nor can we resist joining in the laughter; he is such a droll creature that we forget his treacherous conduct.

Sulwe is only a small creature, but with one exception, all the animals are as clay in his hands 1.

Changing the names we could say very much the same about the Coyote tales of the south-western plains of North America 2, of many of the Raven tales of the North Western Pacific coast 3, and of innumerable other series of stories. In the Ba-ila series, by trickery Hare "makes Hippopotamus and Rhinoceros engage in a 1 Op. cit. ii, pp. 339-40.

8 See Boas, op. cit. and references.

Tug-of-War "; " deceives Lion and burns him to death "; " secures the spear of Hornbill"; " scares Hyena "; " gets him stung to death by bees"; "breaks all Lion's teeth and so kills him"; "eats Lion's children." But in the end he is himself overcome. He is first caught by fraud, and "then the big ones came, they seized Hare, and killed him." The whole chain of stories revolves around the struggle for position between the Hare and all the other animals, with the Hare almost always in a position of ultimate superiority until his death by fraud and by force at the end. In the Raven series the superiority is more frequently due directly to force, yet fraud still has a large part to play. How the two may be intermingled is well illustrated in the tale of how the Raven made war on the South Wind 1.

It had been a long period of bad weather, and all the people with whom Raven was at that time living were in trouble because they could not get food. "Raven's eyes were sore on account of the smoke which the south wind blew down through the smoke hole, and which filled his little hut." Raven called together all the Fish, and urged that something should be done. The Devil Fish and the Hallibut counselled war upon the South Wind, and they borrowed the canoe of Killer Whale. Then Devil Fish, Hallibut, Red Cod, Cockle, and the other fishes, led by Raven, set out upon their war journey. Cockle boasted that he would kick the South Wind down the beach, but when the time came he could do nothing, and Raven "took him up and broke him." It was Raven who laid the plan of campaign, though he stayed in the canoe himself. Red Cod went to the house of South Wind, and lit a fire there; and the smoke from 1 Boas, op. cit. pp. 79-81.

the fire drove South Wind outside. There, with his eyes all bleared and dim, he slipped on Hallibut, and rolled down the beach to the canoe where were Devil Fish and Raven. Then Devil Fish sucked him, and held him tight; and Raven's time was come. Trickery was discarded for brute force.

Kaven said to his peoples: "Kill him with stones, kill him right away!" Thus spoke Raven to his companions. Then he spoke again, and said: "Go on warriors! Club and kill him 1" Then the chief, the Master of the South Wind, spoke at once and said: " O chief Raven! Why do you intend to do this to me? " Raven said at once: " O chief, Master of the South Wind! I do this because we always have bad weather." Then the Master of the South Wind spoke again and said: "There shall be alternately one fine day and one bad day." Raven said at once, "Kill him, for what is the use of one day fine and another bad weather? What does that help us?" Then the chief, the Master of the South Wind, spoke again and said: "There shall be two good days in succession." Raven said: "I don't want that either. Goon! Kill him!" Thus spoke Raven to his warriors. Then the chief, the Master of the South Wind, said: "It shall always be summer in your world." Raven said: "That is too much. It is enough to have four days fine weather at a time!" Thus said Raven to the chief, the Master of the South Wind. Then Raven said again, "O chief, Master of the South Wind! Don't lie, else we shall come again upon you, and make war on you."

And in that way the matter was settled.

There is no doubt that a number of diverse influences come together in the formation and preservation of a story such as that which I have just quoted. But when we take it in conjunction with many of the other tales in the Raven series, we can see that a central point is the triumph of Raven over the chief of the South Wind. The triumph is, moreover, essentially one by dominance and not by comradeship. And it involves eventual abject submissiveness on the part of the conquered enemy.

Although assertiveness involves a correlated submissiveness, the two are by no means always equally emphasised. This raises some interesting considerations with regard to the ways in which the three primary social responses are related to one another. Already we have seen how the comradeship relation often seems, as it were, to tremble in a balance, and to be ready to topple over towards dominance on the one side or acceptance on the other. Even in the Raven story just quoted Raven's relationships to Hallibut, Devil Fish, and Red Cod, though he is regarded as their leader, seem to be largely those of comradeship, while his attitude to Cockle is at first that of a comrade, but soon after changes into one of very emphatic dominance. In the same way assertion may rapidly give way to submission. In the Sulwe chain, for example, after being in a position of superiority throughout the whole series, the Hare is finally overcome and has an ignominious end. In another Raven tale, Raven makes a slave, who then tricks him, only to be destroyed in his turn 1. This swift transition from one fundamental form to another is exceedingly common. But in so far as assertiveness is concerned, it seems on the whole more likely to occur where the dominance is secured by fraud than where it is expressed by brute force.

We here come back to a fresh realisation of the complexity of the inter-play of tendencies in the primitive 1 Boas, op: cit. pp. 689-91.

group. How these primitive instinctive social relationships find expression in the folk tale, is determined not merely by the fact that they are operative within the group, but by the contemporaneous action of other tendencies also. A fighting people, developing popular tales at a period of their vigour, are likely to express in these stories a forceful and triumphant superiority. But once conquest gives place to a more many-sided set of relations between a given group and others, superiority by force begins to be displaced from its position in the stories by superiority by fraud. While, again, when we have an oppressed, or submissive, or maybe a slave type of people developing popular stories, we shall often find series in which enemies are shown to win temporary supremacy by trickery, but in the end suffer forceful overthrow.

It goes without saying that this simple scheme will not actually meet the complexity of the facts. Stories of all types find their way into the popular collections of all peoples. Yet when we compare, say, the Norseland sagas with many negro series, or the latter with the tales current among American Indians or African tribes who have many points of contact one with another, and are neither vigorously dominant nor persistently submissive, we may suspect something of the kind I have suggested. At any rate the matter is worthy of careful investigation, and whatever else such investigation may reveal, it will furnish yet another line of evidence to prove the social determination of the popular story. This fact leads naturally to the third step of our chain of illustration, and helps to show how the form of the stories is directly affected by influences arising from a group of listeners.

Let a man write down in his study a story which he has heard. Then let him tell it to a group of auditors; and compare the two versions. The chances are that with the second form of the narration all the dramatic qualities of the story will leap into greater prominence. The contrasts will be heightened, and a tendency to exaggerate any remarkable events will be apparent?! It is especially interesting that laughable or astonishing incidents will tend to become more central in the tale as told to listeners, and the apparent coherence of the story may also suffer. I am not merely speculating about these differences. What I have suggested may be observed by any person who takes the trouble to carry out a few experiments.

The essential thing to remember is that the narrator, in the second of the above cases, is being subjected directly to influences which come from the social group of which he is one member. Two tendencies in particular gain an immediate access of strength: that to create astonishment, and that to produce laughter. Other influences also find new or increased play, but it is certain that these two together produce a marked effect upon the form of the folk tale, and operate quite as much upon the primitive story-teller as upon his modern counterpart. I will make one further broad generalisation before proceeding to illustration of these points. I think it probable that on the whole, the stories which grow up and become popular in a group that is assertive in respect to other groups, very readily give place to details meant to produce astonishment; while the stories which become current in a group that is chiefly of the submissive or comradeship type in reference to other groups somewhat more readily introduce details of a laughable

The influences arising from the relationship of the story-teller to the group affect the form of the stories in the most direct manner possible. Cumulative stories, for example, are common, and are appreciated in the primitive group the world over 1. Cumulation undoubtedly creates astonishment. It may also with great facflity produce laughter, particularly when, as is very often the case, the cumulation is effected by a repetition of the same type of incident, or of the same formulae. Sharp contrasts great power with little size; huge bulk with little wit; vast efforts and little done are also extremely common and all minister, both to surprise and to amusement. The effect of such contrasts may often be heightened by an elliptical and a metaphorical mode of expression. The former aids in producing the very incoherent and inconsecutive appearance of the narrative form as it is commonly found in the primitive group. As for the place of the metaphor in the popular tale, this opens up a great field of study hardly as yet explored, but offering immense possibilities for interesting research 2. Set formulae again, conventionalised beginnings and endings 3, undoubtedly are connected with the fact that the tales are told to listeners, though here other tendencies are involved besides those which produce laughter and astonishment. Taken together, these points show how influences arising from his audience affect the story-teller as soon as he begins his narration, and are reflected in the form which his tale assumes.

1 See e. g., W. L. Clouston, Popular Tales and Traditions, Edinburgh, 1887, vol. i, pp. 289-313. Cumulative stories are those of "The House that Jack Built" or of "The Old Woman who went to Market" type.

2 See e. g. Rev. de Trad. Pop. 1902, pp. 259-70, also Die Urspriinge der Metaphor, by H. Werner, Leipzic, 1919.

3 Rev. de Trad. Pop. 1902, pp. 233, 347, 462, 536.

In this realm, however, as in every other, form and material go together, and influences that affect the one affect also the other. Laughter and astonishment are only partially a question of the arrangement of material, and are as much, if not more, dependent on the selection of material to be arranged. The incoherent appearance, again, which almost inevitably marks the spoken nalra-tive, produces its effect not merely by virtue of incon-secutiveness, but by reason of the particular nature of the links that are dropped.

Once more, therefore, our attention is drawn to the relatively prominent place occupied in the folk tale generally by the type of relationship involving either definite superiority or marked submissiveness. For the more sharply-cut the relationship the better adapted it is to arouse an admiring, amused, or surprised response on the part of the auditors. This is a part of the reason why the hero tale possessing some well-marked central character, is exceedingly common; while the fact that hero stories almost always run in cycles, or series, thus piling superiority upon superiority, is a question primarily of form.

Not only do the tendencies which arise from the relation of the story-teller to the group, thus affect the type of relationship depicted, and the general theme of a particular story, but in even more marked ways, they determine the details of the material dealt with. Take, for example, a common comic form, the Story of the Bungling Host 1. Here an animal, or a man, stupidly allows himself to be tricked into taking a part of his own body, which he cuts off or pulls out, and presenting it as food to his more clever guest. There are a large 1 See Boas, op. cit. pp. 694-702.

number of variants of this tale among the American Indians. From version to version the animals involved change considerably. Sometimes we find the Seal, often the Bear, or it may be a species of Deer; in one place it is a Fat Man, in another a Badger and in another a Bee; Birds may be involved, or Squirrels, or Beavers, or Mountain Sheep. The fact is that as the story is told from group to group, while its theme remains constant its characters change, and they must do so, if the tale is to meet with the approbation of listeners, since as it travels from place to place it passes through varied natural environments. The animal chosen is one with whose habits the listeners have some familiarity.

These influences which the group brings directly to play upon the narrator may be one of the many reasons contributing to the well-marked tendency for proper names to change rapidly from one version to another of a story. It has often been pointed out that immense importance is attached to names at the primitive levels of culture. This is partly because they are frequently of a descriptive character. And as we pass from group to group, even while we remain within the sphere of influence of the same general culture, we find that the names of the chief character of a tale arc apt to be varied. In the Raven series, for example, the name of the hero changes from tribe to tribe. No less than ten variants are to be found, all of them current among tribal divisions having much the same culture 1.

There is, we may be sure, no perfectly simple psychological explanation for this position of the proper name. It is transformed, or it persists, for a number of reasons, and not all of these are directly psychological. But 1 Boas, op. cit. p. 584.

certainly the attitude of the auditors to the story-teller plays its part. The narrator finds a change of name necessary if the tale is to produce any notable effect upon the hearers, though this, in its turn 4 may be due to the fact that certain names are a kind of property within the tribe an ethnological rather than a psychological consideration. u In another way it seems possible to me that the swift change of names may have something to do with the influence of the individual group upon the particular story-teller. There is a curious connexion between certain names, whether given to people or to animals, and a marked effect of comicality. It is, for example, extremely easy to set children laughing over mere names. Although I confess that I can give no evidence worth noting, I suspect that something of the same thing may occur with the primitive group. But what sort, or what sound, of a name seems amusing changes remarkably rapidly from one group to another. The matter depends very largely upon small local differences of dialect, or perhaps on local catchwords, or upon names and associations of the locality. If names, owing to the way in which they are regarded at the primitive level, stand out from a narrative, and if, as seems likely, they can easily excite the risible tendencies of a group of listeners, we may have one of the reasons for the rapid transformation of names as tales pass from group to group; and to some extent the same fact may explain the tendency, which is occasionally marked, for names to persist unaltered 1 where the auditors belong almost always to the same group.

Not only does the relation of the story-teller to his 1 Cf. Mallery, "Picture Writing of the American Indians," Rep. Ann. Bur. Eth. 1888-9, p. 443.

group affect the form of the folk tale; riot only does it frequently determine directly particular details of the material dealt with; not only does it influence the general type of social relationship that will be most often depicted among a given people; but it may, together with the group difference tendencies, and the individual instincts, settle the dominant themes of the tales, and how those themes are developed. The wide distribution of droll stories over all the world has already been remarked. We can say, both that the comic tale will appeal to a group of auditors most readily, and that, when the group is a primitive one, there are fair chances that the humour will lie in the situation, and the situation will present a practical joke. Of the Ba-ila we read: "The rough, practical jokes of Sulwe, with his absurd dressing up, his slashing and chopping, his breaking of teeth, and all the rest of it are distinctly humourous to them 1." It is the same with other people: the story of the Bungling Host, which has already been referred to, is a case in point. Some animal, or man, often one who in everyday life plays a part of some importance, is in the story made to look extremely foolish. If the practical joker can be depicted as insignificant in bulk, or in position, in relation to his victim so much the better. For here the tendency to create astonishment and to produce amusement both are served: "The mildness of the Hare and the ferocity of the Lion in actual life make it all the more amusing when Sulwe ties the Lion up and deceives him in other ways 2."

Enough has been said to illustrate how the relation of the story-teller to the group may affect both the form and the matter of the folk tale, through the operation 1 Smith and Dale, op. cit. n, p. 844. 2 Ibid. p. 344.

upon him of tendencies that arise from the presence of auditors. If a complete analysis of all the influences upon the folk tale that are of interest in psychology were being attempted, much more would have to be considered at this point. But such complete analysis is not my present aim: and I may therefore now pass on to give a few examples of how the individual instincts find a place in the popular story.

It may be asserted with confidence that there is no primitive appetite, and no instinctive response, which has not definitely set its mark upon the folk story. So far I have considered only the basic social instinctive responses. But there are others, important as regards their social expression, yet wholly or largely individual as regards their character. Curiosity, acquisition, many of the forms of constructiveness, danger responses, the search for food and its enjoyment while they all find frequent expression within the social group, nevertheless do not appear to be wholly dependent upon the social group for their occurrence. The case is not clear as regards pugnacity, while sexual instinct, though it certainly involves some social relation for its expression, hardly presupposes what may be fairly called a "group." Boasting, or vaingloriousness again, which seems probably to have an instinctive character at the human level hardly arises except in a social setting, and yet within such setting appears distinctively as an individual response.

The study of these individual instinct responses is of particular interest in relation to the folk tale, because we often find special groups tending to prefer certain instinctive themes to others. Thus an analysis of popular tales may, in the case of the primitive group, possess an interest analogous to that of a consideration of early autobiographies in the case of the individual. By learning the kind of events that are regarded as worth recording we may discover at least some of the types of response occupying a prominent position. For example, if we take an autobiography prepared by an Indian called Running Antelope, in 1873 and presented in eleven drawings, we find that seven of the eleven pictures have to do with the killing of enemies 1. Again, the deeply interesting Autobiography of a Winnebago Indian, secured and edited by Dr Paul Radin, displays the constantly recurrent themes of fighting, sex, and ceremonial 2. Similarly in the tales that are current throughout a particular community, some special type of instinctive response is often found to be given the most prominent place. Thus we may examine the culture-hero tales of the North-west region of North America, and compare those of the northernmost part of the coast area with those of Vancouver Island, and the delta of the Fraser, and again with those of the south-western interior of British Columbia. Roughly speaking the first series tend to centre about Raven as hero, the second about Mink and the third about Coyote. The dominant topic of the first is greed, or voraciousness; of the second is sex as expressed in marked amorous propensities; and of the third is vaingloriousness or boasting.

Raven's voraciousness (says Boas) that induces him to cheat people and to steal their provisions, is an ever recurring theme, the point of which is regularly to induce the people to run away and leave their property.

1 Mallery, op. cit. pp. 571-5.
2 University of California Publication in American Archaeology md Ethnology, vol. xvi, No. 7, pp. 381-473.

Mink's amorousness has led to the development of a long series of tales referring to his marriages, all of which are of the same type 1.

Now it seems to me that this frequent appearance of a certain characteristic having a direct instinctive basis in the popular tales of a given set of people may be a matter of the greatest interest. In the first place what we may call the "preferred response" may clearly vary from group to group. Thus any conclusion that we may be tempted ttf draw concerning the foundation of all folk stories upon some particular instinct is extremely likely to be erroneous, unless we definitely limit it to a given social setting. For example anyone who should confine his attention mainly to the Mink series could get some remarkably cogent illustrations of the sexual character of the motives behind popular stories. His illustrations would require considerably less distortion than has often been found necessary when this view has been developed 2. But the student of the Raven series could equally plausibly urge that a grasping greed is the basic motive of the tales; while the champion of the Coyote would similarly urge the claim of self-display or vaingloriousness.

In the next place, we are clearly dealing here with a condition which operates directly in determining the matter of the stories. The more individual instincts, in fact, come near to the group difference tendencies in their intimate relation to the details of the popular narrative. While the group difference tendencies, however, have to do with the direction in which the theme 1 Boas, op. cit. pp. 876-7.

2 As, for example, in Ricklin's Wish Fulfilment and Symbolism in Fairy Tales, Eng. trans. New York, 1915, or in Rank's The Myth of the Birth of the Hero, Eng. trans. New York, 1914.

is developed and with the details to which it is applied, the individual instincts mainly settle the themes themselves. The instincts are less varied and less numerous than the group difference tendencies, and in fact the themes are far less varied than the details into which they are worked. We may say then that the expression of tle fundamental responses of comradeship, dominance and subservience affects the type of relationship depicted; the influences arising directly from the presence of the listeners affect the form of the tales directly and their matter indirectly; but both the group difference tendencies, and the particular individual instincts, determine in the most immediate way the themes of the tales. Supposing the dominant individual instinctive tendency is voraciousness, then assertiveness, for example, is expressed mainly in the fight for food, and submissiveness largely in getting the worst of this fight. But when the chief instinctive tendency is one of sex, assertiveness and submissiveness, though no less prominent in the tales, are connected with an entirely different set of details. It is the same when pugnacity is uppermost, though here quarrel and fighting may occur in reference to the blocking of any one of the instinctive tendencies.

A study of the influence of the various individual instincts upon the popular tale, thus points to the importance of admitting an order of effectiveness among these tendencies. Where the story is one of a series with a central character this order of effectiveness is apt to remain fairly constant. But in the case of stories of a more isolated character it must be admitted that it is often hard to find any constant order of relationship among the instincts as they find expression in a primitive community. Where any central instinctive impulse is to be found, however, its function is always the same. Such impulse provides the type of material upon which all the other tendencies dealt with in this chapter work, or within which they are illustrated.

Now there can be no doubt whatever that certain of the individual instinct tendencies are much more prominent in the primitive folk tale than the rest. These are: all the group of activities connected with securing and enjoying food; all those connected with sex; those which express a more or less violent pugnacity; and, probably, also those in which the hero indulges in outrageous boasting.

Although nobody can doubt that danger responses are primitive and instinctive, yet on the whole they seem to take a relatively inconspicuous position in the earliest folk tales. That is to say, danger is either sought or shunned, and on the whole is far more often sought than shunned, under the influence of one of the other instinctive tendencies. In particular, fear is not very often definitely pictured, and even when it is present, it seems rarely to occupy the foreground of the story. Moreover it occurs most frequently in connexion with the supernatural. This does not in the least mean that the various forms of fear reactions are less outstanding at the primitive level, but rather that the folk tale is hardly a suitable medium for their expression. Not only the influence of the auditors, but also that of the storyteller himself, has the effect of driving fear out of the popular tale. At no level is the description of fear pleasing either to a speaker or to listeners, least of all when danger is imminent, as it often is to the primitive group. Danger and death are very common in the tales, but fear and flight are far less often depicted. When we turn, however, to another department of primitive culture, and pass from the folk tale to the ceremonial, we find that the production of fear at once assumes a most important role.

Our consideration of the expression of the individual instincts in the folk story points to an important conclusion. These instincts never act without check. Sometimes one type of instinctive response tends to take the lead and sometimes another. It is therefore necessary to consider how the order of importance amongst instincts is determined.

In the first place much undoubtedly depends upon the nature of the external environment, in its connexion with the social organisation of the time. The very great dominance in some cases of the group of food impulses rests mainly upon this factor. There can be no doubt that when large quantities of food are necessary, but the environment is such as to make abundance of food difficult to obtain, voraciousness immediately tends to spring into prominence. Where the environment is kinder, and the social organisation is of a relatively settled type, the food-seeking impulse grows less marked and may yield its first position to one of the others.

In the second place much depends upon the sphere of primitive culture with which we are concerned. If, for example, we were to confine our attention to the folk story, we should often be tempted to say that the influence of fear, fright, or awe upon primitive life and interests was relatively slight. But it is not so. That very instinct response which is in the background in one group of social activities may be in the foreground in another. The folk tale serves, on the whole, a recreative function. It involves, as a rule, a comradeship group. To make fear, fright, extreme alarm, or trembling awe very prominent tends to destroy the relationship and to break up the recreative aspect of the story. But with the ceremonial group both bond and function are different, and fear may hold sway. Thus as we pass from one activity to another, and from one external environment to another, we find that the inter-relations of the instincts may vary. And the variation depends largely upon the material with which the tendencies have to deal.

In the third place we have to admit the possible direct influence of the individual characteristics of the taleteller. All of the illustrations with which we have so far dealt in this chapter have concerned tendencies definitely demanding a social grouping; or influences brought to bear upon the individual by the fact of his working in a group; or individual instinctive responses expressing themselves in social relations. But these are not all of the influences that are at work. The individual taleteller may also set his mark upon the tale. I propose to lead up to a discussion of this point by first considering an admittedly instinctive response which so far has not been mentioned I mean the response of curiosity.

Many folk tales picture an adventurer. And of course all adventure involves curiosity. Bird, beast, fish, or man goes in search of fire, weapons, food, companions, and so on. But in none of these stories, until we reach a fairly developed level, does it seem to be the curiosity as such that holds the interest. It is the search as directed and controlled by some other instinct or interest that takes the prominent place. In curiosity, in fact, we have an instinctive response which rather produces the folk story ab extra than plays a prominent part within it. By common consent we must accept many myths, legends and stories as having an explanatory value within the community in which they are current. Whether or not they are to be regarded as having developed out of an imaginative treatment of certain facts of social life, they are accepted as accounting for puzzling facts of observation. That is to say behind them, and moulding them, making for their development, persistence and often for their transmission to a new group of people, is the instinct of curiosity. And this instinct, in working out the connexions of things, uses all the other instincts in its search for explanations. It is instructive to look through the origin stories of the Tsimshian people. There was a time when: the whole world was still covered with darkness. When the sky was clear, the people would have a little light from the stars; and when clouds were in the sky, it was very dark all over the land. The people were distressed by this. Then Giant thought it would be hard for him to obtain his food if it were always dark 1.

And that was the beginning of numerous adventures and a long search, as a result of which daylight was found and brought to earth. When people began to multiply, great distress arose "because they had no fire to cook their food and to warm themselves in winter 2." From this began the search which ended in the capture of fire for the world. About the same time "the tide was always high, and did not turn for several days, until the new moon came, and all the people were anxious for clams and sea-food 3." It was to get food that the "Giant" was stimulated to discover the secret of the 1 Boas, op. cit. p. 60. a Op. cit. p. 63. 3 Op. cit. p. 64.

tides, and to obtain a tide twice daily. The search and the adventures, in all of these stories, undoubtedly give us instances of the expression of curiosity. But the curiosity is, in every case, set going and carried through owing to its connexion with the dominant instinctive demand for food.

Further, whatever may be the particular details described in stories of this type, they certainly make their appeal through the curiosity instinct. Rarely, unless some late version is being considered, do they appear from their mere form to be explanatory in function. But as a matter of fact that is what they are. Without making any definite pretence, they satisfy questions.

It is usual (say Smith and Dale) to regard savages as uneducated people, and, as far as books are concerned, they certainly are, but in the book of Nature they are well read. From an early age they learn to recognise the animals, to distinguish their footprints and cries, to know their names, their habitats and customs. And not only are they keen observers, they reflect on the facts, and comparing the facts one with another, they want to know the reasons of things 1.

The want is not often clearly formulated, and so curiosity as such rarely is itself a centre of interest in the folk talc. But the fact remains that many of the tales are popular because they satisfy an impulse to know which is never itself formulated and consciously acknowledged.

This brings us to the question of the influence of the individual upon the stories. It is extraordinarily interesting to follow the development of the curiosity tendency. At first it merely satisfies an unformulated desire, but later on problems are definitely set and their 1 Op. cit. ii, p. 337.

solution sought. Thus it may be that curiosity is awakened when old stories are brought into a new and strange setting: It seems likely (remarks Boas) that there is a distinction between the way in which the stories were told to the older generation, that followed the old way of living, ar? d the manner in which they are related to white people or to the younger generation that has forgotten many of the old ways. It is not unlikely that some explanatory matter has been included in the tales that in olden times would not have been present. On the whole, however, my impression is that only a slight amount of descriptive material has been introduced in this way 1.

Apart altogether from this result of the migration of stories, it is a question of great interest whether the occurrence of explicit explanatory forms the use of terms such as "thus," "therefore," "because," "for this reason," and the like marks a response to a tendency as social in its determination and expression as, say, that of comradeship, or whether it should rather be set down to the influence of individual character upon the tales. There seems strikingly little data for an answer to this question. It may be that only through the development of a certain sort of social milieu does that questioning attitude which the instinct of curiosity always produces come to consciousness. For example, a careful survey of a large number of the different versions of stories collected by Boas and others rather suggests that the Tlingit tales consistently tend to show a greater amount of what may be called "explicit satisfying of curiosity" than do any of the other versions. If it is so, we should still have to ask whether this 1 Op. cit. p. 893.

is due to the particular social arrangements of the Tlingit, or whether it may not be an individual characteristic, due to the narrator who furnished the versions, or even to the investigator who collected them.

That characteristic individual additions are often made to the popular tale when we reach a high level of culture, is perfectly certain. For example, Andrew Lang tells how a certain French authoress produced embroidered versions of a number of popular stories: she wonders that the Contes should have been handed down to us from age to age without anyone taking the trouble to write them out. Then she herself takes the trouble to write the story of Diamonds and Toads. and hopelessly spoils it by her broiderie, and by the introduction of a lay figure called Eloquentia Nativa 1,

The illustration is particularly interesting as showing the influence both of social and individual factors. For the lay figure is a convention of the time simply taken over from social usage; while some of the other additions mark the individual character of the author.

Beyond doubt this also occurs at a much more primitive level. Very often indeed the story-teller is widely known throughout a community. It is his business to tell tales. In a way the stories become almost his property. He thus acquires a reputation with his groups of listeners, and to keep up his reputation he does not scruple to invent, or to transform. Dr Radin has told how in collecting versions of tales, he has noticed that some of the most marked variations from a socially accredited pattern are introduced in this manner.

Thus to all that play of varying influences already 1 Introduction to Perrault's Popular Tales, Oxford, 1888, pp. xxv-xxvi.

referred to, must be added those which spring from the individual character of the story-teller. Not only does the group compel him to tell them the tale in certain ways, but he for his part forces them to listen to certain variations which are his own. However, since the influence of the individual is a point that we shall have to tiiscuss again in connexion with the psychological study of the contact of peoples, and the borrowing of culture, I need not develop it further now.

It remains to summarise the main points of this chapter.

1. The folk story is always to be regarded as primarily a social product, developed for and told to auditors, and consequently both as regards its form and its matter making, within its own community, a common emotional appeal.

2. Its remarkable persistence within its own group is in part to be traced to the comradeship response which holds this group together, and in part to the expression in the popular tale of group difference tendencies clustering about the life and institutions of the people concerned.

3. In the popular tale may be found frequent illustrations of the expression of each one of the primitive instinctive social relationship tendencies: comradeship, assertiveness, and submissiveness. Of these three, however, the second and third tend to be the most strongly marked.

4. Directly affecting the form, and indirectly affecting the matter, of the popular story are tendencies which are brought to bear upon the narrator of the tale by the group of auditors; prominent among these are the tendencies to provoke astonishment and laughter.

5. Just as the group difference tendencies which are connected with pre-existing institutions directly settle many of the details of the stories, so the specific indi-104 PSYCHOLOGY AND THE FOLK STORY vidual instincts settle their general themes. Particularly when the narratives fall into series it is often possible to show how one of the instinct responses is dominant, and how the rest fall into order about this one. In determining which of such instincts takes the first place external environment plays a large part; the particular sphere of culture involved may be important; while the individual characteristics of the narrator also exercise a strong influence.

6. Certain tendencies e. g. curiosity which rarely appear within the cultural product in an undisguised form, may yet have much to do in shaping and maintaining the product.

7. All of the tendencies and factors which have been discussed co-operate in the production of popular stories. A similar combination of conditions may be observed in other departments of activity within the primitive group.

To some of the results of this intricate inter-play of factors we must now turn our attention.

CHAPTER IV

THE CONFLICT OF TENDENCIES AND THEIR MUTUAL REINFORCEMENT

The Argument: None of the tendencies which have been considered operates entirely by itself in determining the behaviour of man in society. We must therefore discuss what happens when, in reference to the same situation, more than one tendency is called into activity, and must deal in particular with the conflict of tendencies, and their mutual reinforcement.

The first mode which society has of dealing with conflict is that each of the conflicting agencies is assigned its own characteristic sphere of activity, or its own recognised time of expression. Thereupon, in each sphere, and in reference to the satisfaction of the tendency which is dominant within that sphere, a special social group is apt to be formed.

No instinctive tendency, however, is readily controlled in its expression. The segregated impulse may burst into activity beyond its due limits. Moreover, any social group is almost sure, sooner or later, to try to increase its dominance in the community. This it does by carrying its peculiar practices into realms beyond those which were originally its special concern.

Whenever tendencies, the operation of which has been restricted in some manner, are brought into play regardless of the restrictions, they are likely to attract social disapproval. The practices associated with them may be driven into secret. In secret they persist, however, and they may, under conditions which we must be prepared to state, bring about crises which have all the appearance of reversions to a more primitive level of behaviour.

How socially-disowned tendencies may persist for long periods is a matter which we must particularly consider. In part the persistence is due to the continuous life of the special group, and in part to some not very clearly defined influence connected with primitive comradeship.

Where tendencies which do not radically conflict are simultaneously operative, new modes of social response are commonly produced. As to what modes do actually arise in this manner, the two most important determining conditions are: the form of underlying social relationship which obtains, and the sphere of culture which is affected.

In other cases tendencies merely supplement one another, and produce, not a new mode of behaviour, but a more vigorous expression of some already existing mode of response. In this mutual reinforcement of tendencies, probably the influences arising immediately from a man's place in his group all that is included under the term "social approval" play the chief parts.

The last chapter has revealed something of the complexity of the influences that, in the primitive group, are brought to bear upon the formation and development of the popular story. These influences differ, not only in their source, but in their character and functions also. While some of them work harmoniously together, each reinforcing the others, some are antagonistic. For example, we saw how the tendency to create astonishment, and the deep-seated social instinct of dominance, may both work in harmony to give to assertiveness a prominent place in the folk tale. But dominance tends to destroy comradeship, and so, on the whole, do the specific danger responses which are connected with fright.

THEIR MUTUAL REINFORCEMENT 107

What is in this respect true of the folk story, is equally true of every other department of primitive culture. Wherever we turn we find a great variety of influences at work, some of them helping and some of them hindering one another. A sound psychological treatment must not only recognise and disentangle this multiplicity of influences, but it must at least attempt to find out in what ways they combine, and with what results they conflict. Our first step is to admit that many tendencies are at work, and that it is impossible to reduce these to some one fundamental form: we have taken this step in the preceding chapters. Next we must discover the main modes of the inter-play of these tendencies, and illustrate its effects upon primitive culture: we shall attempt to do this in the present chapter.

Let us begin with an interesting fact which has already been noticed. Although fear, alarm, and flight are fairly often depicted in the folk story, they seldom form leading motives, at any rate at a really primitive level. This is because they express tendencies which may conflict with the most important formative influences of the popular tale. Fear, alarm and flight, on the whole, tend to destroy comradeship; and are pleasing neither to the story-teller nor to his auditors; this leads to their suppression, and, except in an incidental way, to their disappearance from the stories. When they are described, however, they are connected not infrequently with the supernatural. And the moment we turn to those other departments of primitive culture which are wholly concerned with the attempt to enter into relations with supernatural powers, we find the fear tendency springing into an important place.

The ideas which are current in any community with regard to supernatural powers are apt to be exceedingly vague. This is a favourite subject of comment by authors who write about primitive people 1. But as a matter of actual fact, if only we cared to make unbiassed observation, we should find that the modern community shows little difference in this respect. The important point at present, however, is that whether or not these powers are sufficiently defined to be regarded as malevolent or beneficent, to have intercourse with them is usually believed to be dangerous. For the Ila-speaking peoples, to take a good illustration, there are vaguely defined forces pervading all things, neutral in themselves, but available for those who have the "secret of manipulation." These forces however: are dangerous things to interfere with. They are therefore tonda (taboo). For an ordinary person, under ordinary circumstances, and without an antidote, to interfere with them is forbidden; it is dangerous to himself and the community. By saying certain things, doing certain actions, eating certain foods, he may liberate these energies with fatal consequences to himself and his neighbours. Persons in certain conditions, and things put to certain uses, come into intimate contact with these forces and are therefore tonda. It is as if at certain times the separating medium becomes attenuate, the insulating rubber, so tojspeak, gets worn off the live wire, and people come into close contact with the forces 2.

1 Cf. J. H. Hutton, The Angami Nagas, London, 1921: "In approaching a subject such as the religious beliefs of the Angami, one is met at the outset by an obstacle

of very great difficulty. In common with other savage races the Angami regards the supernatural in general from a point of view that is sublimely vague."

2 Smith and Dale, op. cit. IT, p. 83.

THEIR MUTUAL REINFORCEMENT 109

Again the account of the ceremonial practices of the Angami Nagas, reveals a very similar situation. These people are a tribe inhabiting a section of the northern portion of a strip of irregular hill country dividing Assam and Bengal from Burmah. As usual their religious ideas appear to the observer to be vagueness itself, but their religious practices are perfectly definite. "Acts of worship," are spoken of, in Button's account of the people 1, as "gennas,",.

because there is no suitable English word which describes them, and the word genna, though by derivation from the Angami kenna signifying forbidden merely, has become regularly used in the Naga Hills for the various incidents of a magico-religious rite,

Genna has three sides or constituents. " First of all we have kenna (or Kenyti), that is to say prohibition." Kenna has an extremely wide application, but it has always to do with something that is forbidden to the individual or the household. In the second place there is Penna.

While kenna is the prohibition laid on a unit of the community, penna is the prohibition laid on the whole community. Penna really is kenna applied to the community instead of to the individual.

The third character of ceremonial observance is called Nanu, and includes the positive and active side of a rite, as well as the negative, prohibitory sides which are indicated by kenna and penna. The point here is that much of the ceremonial of worship thus deals with things which must not be done. And the avoidances have two main functions. They increase the awe and fear of the practices on the part of those who may suffer from them; and as in the case of the Ila-speaking people, they safeguard those who engage in the rites against harm.

As an example of the first of their effects we may cite the case of two women from one community who went to catch snails in the terraces of the men of another village group at the time when the paddy was ripening. Some of the men of the second group annoyed at the possibility of damage to their crop, threw mud at the women. They were not even struck by the mud, but when some of the men's fellow-villagers threatened to do a genna consisting in this case of a day's penna."for the loss of two heads," the two women, fearing that they would die as the result of such a genna, hurried into Kohima to get orders against its observance 1.

What makes this particular instance especially interesting is its clear illustration of the social, communal nature which certain prohibitory ceremonial may possess.

A writer upon the psychology of Fijian society, again, shows how the whole of the Fijian religion centres around fear. He quotes with the utmost approval the statement that "A principle of fear seems to be the only motive to religious observances." Repeatedly he reverts to the same characteristic. The very fact that the supernatural powers are undefined, renders them the more fear-inspiring 2.

Yet when we turn to the popular stories of any of these three peoples, descriptions of fear seem to occupy no very important position. Precisely analogous facts may be observed in many other communities. The conclusion seems irresistible. Taking the underlying forms 1 Hutton, op. cit. p. 193.

2 Deane, W., Fijian Society, or the Sociology and Psychology of the Fijians, London, 1921, ch. m.

THEIR MUTUAL REINFORCEMENT 111 of human response which go to the shaping of primitive culture, we find some whose simultaneous action within the same sphere is antagonistic. What then happens is not that one of the underlying forms of response is altogether inhibited, though, as will be shown presently, this may occur given appropriate conditions. Instead of this, each type of response gradually becomes restricted to a more or less well defined sphere of activity, within which it is dominant. The process is not, it need hardly be said, a conscious process, but its outcome is that each type of response gains full scope for expression within its own field, and so the violently disintegrating effects of conflict are avoided.

Since this delimitation of opposed responses to different fields of behaviour depends upon an inherent antagonism between certain primitive reactions, it is clearly a matter of direct psychological interest. To some extent, as every psychologist knows, processes of exactly the same character take place within the limits of the individual mental life. Different interests, which collide one with another, or different instinctive reactions which will not harmonise, may be preserved through the attainment by each of a characteristic sphere of expression. But within the primitive community the consequences of this determination of boundaries are perhaps of even greater significance. For it follows, not merely that particular types of institutions or spheres of custom are dominated by some outstanding tendency towards response, but that round about such institutions and customs persons are collected who have special social functions. I do not think that the influence of antagonistic impulses in leading to specialised social functions, and the development of cults, has ever been thoroughly investigated. But beyond doubt that influence is both far-reaching and persistent.

Take the case of ceremonial, for example. It is generally agreed that the development of religious ritual is very closely connected with fear, though to urge that ritualistic practices spring from this root alone would be absurd, and in violent opposition to our leading contention that numerous factors determine all branches of culture. Moreover fear does not gain its special sphere of expression in religious and magical ceremonies simply because it is allowed a small place in the folk story. Not only in story-telling, but in many other primitive activities, the expression of fear is disturbing and unwelcome. But by whatever reason fear gains its own territory in the sphere of religion, there thus arises a social group whose members have the reputation of being in close contact with the dangerous supernatural powers. This is a part of the social psychology which gives us the wizard and the priest, and also a part of what gives to these their very great power in the primitive community.

The first point, then, is that sets of impulses which are relatively incompatible may be preserved within a community, by acquiring different spheres of influence. In this way each set may continue without constantly warring upon the other, and so producing social disorder and disease.

Now the indirect determination of differences of social grouping through the limitation of the main spheres of influence of antagonistic impulses, may clearly have a long and complicated series of consequences. Let us briefly trace a few of these in reference to the group of ceremonial leaders. Once give to any social group a THEIR MUTUAL REINFORCEMENT 113 reputation within the community, and immediately the influences brought to bear upon any member of that group, by other members of the community tend to take specialised directions. What does obtaining a reputation mean from the point of view of social psychology? It means that within a group certain persons are generally looked upon as possessing to a high degree certain qualities or abilities. These are the qualities and abilities that immediately spring to the mind whenever such persons are seen. These are the abilities and qualities which all the other members of the group expect to see illustrated in the activities of the persons with the reputation. A reputation, that is to say, is always more or less a matter of over-weighting in certain directions. It is important to remember that receiving a reputation and keeping up that reputation are in the majority of instances and particularly within the primitive group inseparable social responses. The chain of occurrences is something like this: Partly through the antagonism of primitive impulses, certain tendencies acquire special spheres of expression. Within these spheres characteristic institutions arise, shaped so as to express and maintain these tendencies. About the institutions cluster special social groups who develop determinate functions. This endows any member of the group with a reputation. Thereupon he may become a marked man in the community. Other people look to see him show and sustain certain qualities, and this usually has the effect of making him all the more likely to display and even to exaggerate these qualities. Very rapidly the qualities in question become conventionalised attributes of a group. Leading individual members of the group then tend to develop character- istics having a strong family likeness, and in line with these conventions. Ordinary members of the group share in its general reputation, and so often come to be considered by the rest of the community as displaying qualities and abilities which in point of fact they by no means possess. Into the production of all these results factors arising within the special social group, and factors brought into operation by the ways in which the rest of the community regard the special group, mingle in intricate fashion.

Among the Ba-ila are "prophets" who are in the closest touch with the vague but dangerous unseen powers 1.

These prophets play a very important part in the life of the Ba-ila. As the mouth-pieces of the divinities they are the legislators of the community and, generally speaking, they receive a great deal of credit. Sometimes the message they deliver is harmless enough, sometimes it is distinctly good, but sometimes it is noxious. The word of the prophet is sufficient to condemn to death for witchcraft a perfectly inno-cent man or woman. And such is the extraordinary credulity of the people, that often they will destroy their grain or cattle at the bidding of a prophet 2.

The character and career of several of the prophets of the Ba-ila have been described with some detail. There is a strong likeness in them all, both as to what they actually do, or pretend, and also as to what the community expect them to do. The same is true of the succession of "Messiahs" who led the various forms of the Ghost Dance religion, among different tribes of North American Indians. No doubt in this case we have 1 Smith and Dale, op. tit. n, 141 et seq. a Op. tit. n, 141.

THEIR MUTUAL REINFORCEMENT 115 to do with a complex ceremonial to the formation and development of which a large number of different impulses contributed. But many of them were impulses which, largely owing to the position of the Indian tribes in relation to a conquering people, could not well be expressed in everyday practical activity. They were, that is, driven into a less open sphere of their own. And there they produced leaders in whom many of the same characteristics appeared again and again 1.

This driving apart of antagonistic tendencies into fields of expression of their own, often has further social consequences which are of the very greatest importance. Its immediate effect is to preserve within the community both of two conflicting forces. But it may also have the further result in certain cases, of producing social disapprobation of one of the conflicting tendencies. We are familiar with this process in the individual mental life. Certain deeply implanted tendencies turn out, in the course of development, to be incompatible. They can neither be rooted out, nor can the antagonism give place to fusion. Each tendency thereupon gains its own sphere of expression, but there is war between the different spheres, and from the conflict results arise which possess great psychological interest. The whole process is closely paralleled within the primitive social group.

Many of the most striking illustrations are, in the field of primitive culture, connected with that very fear tendency the dominant expression of which, in the primitive group, seems often to be found, as we have 1 Mooney, J., "The Ghost Dance Religion and the Sioux Outbreak of 1890," I4th Ann. Rep. of the Bur. of Amer. Eth. t Washington, 1896, Part u.

seen, in the realm of religious ceremonial. Fear is associated with danger. Now danger cannot be escaped. It is a present and pressing possibility, particularly within the primitive group. But its harmful results may be counteracted; the dangerous situation may have two issues. Out of risk may come individual and general good, or individual and general disaster. As we tiave seen, the actual powers of the unseen are rarely defined at any level, so that from the same source may proceed both good and ill. But they are apt to be secured in different ways and to appear through different instruments. Thus the Ba-ila have not only their prophets, but their witches, wizards and sorcerers. The diliberate invocation by any person of the aid of the hidden powers "for the purpose of harming and killing his fellows is the most monstrous of all crimes in their eyes 1." Persons who do this are Balozhi, witches, warlocks and sorcerers. The prophets are revered, the witches hated. But as in the case of the prophets, so in the case of the wizard and sorcerer the same characteristics recur over and over again. Indeed, in this case the repeated appearance of the same qualities is more striking than ever. For the exploitation of fear produces, alongside of the recognised institutions and social groups others that are outside the general life of the community and are consequently looked upon with suspicion, so that eventually they may get driven underground. All pathological social developments appear to have a history of this sort. Based, in the beginning, upon tendencies which are inherently antagonistic to others that work within the same community, the initial step is the separation of the warring elements and the delimitation of the spheres of their 1 Smith and Dale, n, 90-9.

THEIR MUTUAL REINFORCEMENT 117 social expression. Then certain of the elements attract strong and general dislike. Finally they are driven into concealment. Their expression is forcibly opposed. Often the special social group who have them in charge are persecuted. Social disintegration, confusion, and ill-harmony may speedily follow.

So far all the illustrations that I have given have to do with the specialisation of the expression of fear. But there are, on the same instinctive level, other instances also. Take, for example, the instinctive tendency towards conservation and the instinctive tendency of curiosity. These two are clearly in a broad sense opposed. Curiosity prompts exploration of the novel; the basis of conservatism rests in blind acceptance of the old. This provides a situation favourable to a delimitation of the field of expression of the two tendencies. A primitive group, curious and enterprising in its exploration of many of the natural processes by which they are surrounded, will at once relapse into pure conservatism if really novel situations are presented. Often, indeed, this conserving tendency is not unconnected with fear: It is to be noticed that it is especially strange, unusual things, uncommon sights, newfangled habits, strange foods and ways of doing things, that are regarded as manifestations of the hidden powers. It is here that we find the root of the conservatism of the Ba-ila, and their hatred of new ways. When, e. g. bananas were first introduced by us at Kasenga, we offered some of the fruit to Mungalo. He turned from it with expressions of great horror. "No! No! I have never seen that before! It is tonda 1."

The history of every primitive group, in fact, reveals certain spheres of activity within which curiosity is not readily to be allowed full sway. The limitation does not necessarily produce social disorder. Curiosity is assigned its own realm. And within this realm its reign is recognised, as for example, in most initiation ceremonies; it may also possess its own special social groups, to keep it within due bounds.

But this method of dealing with the opposition is f apt, sooner or later, to cause trouble. The instinctive curiosity breaks out, not only in its own proper place, but in the realm where conservation holds sway too. Then there is conflict, and all the searchers for the novel who defy tradition are contemned by the majority. This is how primitive science got driven into its underground beginnings.

In the same way the primitive sexual response may in certain of its expressions very easily run counter to any of the other forms of instinctive social reaction; or dominance may break up comradeship, and then dominance and pugnacity together may wage war upon submission and vindictiveness.

Such examples as these serve to show, not only that incompatible responses at the instinctive level do often result in pathological states within the primitive group, but they indicate also the most important general condition why this should occur. Simply because the responses are on the instinctive level, they are never easily contained each within a specially delimited sphere. Fear is right and proper when dangerous powers are, with adequate precautions, being propitiated, or being used to serve practical ends which appeal to the various members of a community. But when it pushes its way into all the spheres of daily life, when it is made to serve the ends of a few persons only, when it is invoked with-

THEIR MUTUAL REINFORCEMENT 119 out any of the safe-guards that are the concern of the special ceremonial social group, it must be stamped out. Swift social crises, sudden religious revivals, sexual orgies carrying away a whole group, outbursts of persecution all are evidence of the thrusting into forbidden spheres of deep-lying tendencies which have their own reatm of expression. With them is connected the further fact, which also follows from our preliminary analysis, that once any social group is formed, and its reputation set, the great social instinct towards dominance will often carry the group beyond that sphere within which it was originally formed, and make it bid for authority in new directions.

At this point another consideration forces itself upon our notice. Suppose antagonistic tendencies are at work in a community, with a consequent delimitation of spheres of activity. Then suppose one of the tendencies, either because it persists in seeking expression beyond its limits, or for some other reason, falls into disrepute among the members of the community, and so gets eventually driven into secret expression. It will still tend to have its own social group formed about it. Now the very constitution of a group tends to give both to the tendencies and to the allied practices enormous powers of persistence. For normally a group never disappears all at once. It has a continuous life running, in almost all cases, far beyond the bounds of individual existence. This is one reason why practices that are socially condemned may, long after they seem to have disappeared from a community, apparently leap into sudden activity. They have not disappeared. They have only been driven underground. All the time they have been seeking expression in realms denied to them. The group for whom they are a cult, like any other group, has its share of the tendency to secure dominance. Let its aggressiveness be increased, possibly by the appearance of a new and unusually dominant leader; or let the powers of resistance of the community as a whole be lessened, and the old practices suddenly spring into new fields of activity, usually attaching themselves to tendencies which are generally acknowledged and approved. This is a part of the mechanism of social reversions, upon which much has been written. What is particularly interesting is that the most striking illustrations of reversion appear to have occurred within those very realms that have provided most of our illustrations in this chapter and to have been concerned with the exercise of religious observances, sexual excesses, and over-bearing pugnacity.

Such sudden outbursts of tendencies whose operation has been driven into secret may occur at any level of cultural development. But they are especially interesting to us for two main reasons. The first is that on the whole the more primitive the community the more subject it is to these reversion phenomena; and the second is that whenever they do occur they seem to provide striking illustrations of a state of affairs which may characterise a very lowly level of society. They show how antagonistic impulses may be operative together, without any clear limitation of their fields of activity.

Let me state definitely that I do not for a moment suppose that all the reversions which are illustrated in the study of social crises are produced solely by the mechanism which I have just described. They all, I believe, do lead us back to a state which, in general, is characteristic of very early developments in primitive

THEIR MUTUAL REINFORCEMENT 121 culture 1, in which opposed tendencies are but imperfectly confined to their own spheres, and so may come into operation together. But there is no need to postulate the survival, in every case, of a social group having a continuous history and regularly practising in secret the rites or behaviour that the majority repudiate. We may have not only the sphere, but the time for the operation of certain tendencies defined. This is very often indeed the case within the primitive group, with regard to violent and explosive sexual expressions. It is so, for example, with funeral practices among the Ba-ila. After quoting certain songs of a directly sexual character which are sung by women at Ba-ila funerals, Smith and Dale go on 2:

When we have expressed our astonishment at women singing such songs for it is the women that sing them the elders have quoted the proverb."A mourner is not to be passed before the face," i. e. has licence to do whatever he or she pleases. Under ordinary circumstances it would be reckoned taboo for women to utter such things in the presence of men; but at funerals all restraints are removed. People do as they like. Grass may be plucked out of the thatched roofs; the fields may be robbed of the growing corn; all passions are let loose.

Clearly enough outbreaks of this sort do not involve specialised social groups continuously practising in secret. We have here another way of dealing with root tendencies which conflict, the establishing for certain of them of distinct times and seasons. And once more the nature of a community, with its large amount of 1 I do not, however, for one moment maintain that the reversion does actually present us with a truly primitive state, in all respects the same as that attained in the early history of society.

overlapping of the length of life of individuals, and with its continuous traditions, makes the very long persistence of relatively rarely expressed tendencies perfectly possible. But when every allowance has been made for the continuous practice of certain tendencies by special social groups, and for the more sporadic occurrence of such tendencies in the group as a whole by the establishment of times and seasons, it is certain that there are facts of reversion, as they are illustrated in social life, that yet await explanation. Tendencies which seem to have disappeared wholly out of social life may yet apparently, under certain conditions, be revived with great vigour. Many of the practices which mark states of great religious excitement at a relatively advanced stage of social development seem to illustrate this fact. Maybe the resurgence of the old impulses are deferred consequences of ways in which antagonistic impulses have been dealt with at a primitive stage, rather than phenomena which have themselves been present at a remote period. Davenport's description of the negro preacher gives us an illustration.

The negro preacher is a figure of singular interest. The descendant of the medicine-man of the African clan he early appeared on the plantation. The southern minister. has been always the emotional orator swaying his audience at will, expounding the doctrines of depravity and damnation, and too often illustrating them in his daily practice, appealing to the instinctive emotions of fear and hate as well as love, the mourner, the shouter, the visioner, rioting in word pictures, his preaching an incoherent, irrational, rhythmic ecstasy. Here is a primitive man with primitive traits in a modern environment 1.

1 Davenport, E. M., Primitive Traits in Religious Revivals, New York, 1905, pp. 49-50.

THEIR MUTUAL REINFORCEMENT 123

The persistence of these tendencies, long disowned by society, seems rarely to be manifested in the individual as such. It is in the man as he is related to his group that they are to be seen. And it is when the group is collected together that the expression of the tendencies becomes most unmistakeable and most violent.

At many of the " big quarterlies " and the " protracted meetin's" which are held in the South of the United States, there are scenes of frenzy, of human passion, of collapse, of catalepsy, of foaming at the mouth, of convulsion, of total loss of inhibition. To be "mad with supernatural joy" is with the negro the great test of supernatural presence. The influence of the. worship of his ancestors in the African forest is still interwoven with the mental prepossessions and the nervous organisation of the race 1.

There seems in fact to be no escaping from the conclusion, that, even more certainly as regards individuals in social relationships than as regards individuals considered by themselves, tendencies which, because of their antagonism to other tendencies, have been first assigned a separate sphere, or distinct times, for their expression, and then driven underground, persist. Such persistence is not limited to the root instinctive tendencies. Specialised tendencies growing up and clustering about particular institutions may exhibit the same characteristics, and thus these sporadic reversions take different forms in different groups. Any tendencies, in fact, which have, for considerable periods, obtained social sanction and expression, though they may be displaced by others, are yet liable to return. It may indeed be doubted whether they ever lapse into complete impotence. They may appear to do so, but perhaps 1 Davenport, loc. cit.

all kinds of stimuli, which do not rouse the displaced impulses to overt expression, yet keep them ready for use. Perhaps an important part of the social significance of symbols is that they help to keep overlaid, or disowned tendencies from complete disappearance. I do not know by what precise mechanism the persistence of primitive traits and tendencies is thus maintained. For my part, however, I think it not improbable that that deep-seated, and but little investigated response which I have called "primitive social comradeship" has something to do with the matter.

In a descriptive account of the Ibos of Nigeria 1, we are reminded that a fact which must always be borne in mind by the foreign inquirer into primitive customs is that the ideas of the native are indefinite. He has no fixed thoughts. He is under the influence of an atmosphere which emanates from the whole tribe. This subliminal consciousness by which all his movements are controlled, becomes practically a "sixth sense." It is inexpressible in words, but nevertheless extremely powerful in action.

Primitive comradeship ought not to be called a " sixth sense." It is nothing of the kind. But it is a real response. It renders companion members of a community very sensitive to influences passing from one to the others. The nature, and even the fact of these influences, need not be known, either by those who transmit or by those who receive them. About every social custom, and particularly about every social symbol, there tend, for example, to cluster a group of meanings, only a few of which are ever in the full consciousness of those who practise the custom or use 1 Basden, G. T., Among the Ibos of Nigeria, London, 1921, pp. 0-10.

THEIR MUTUAL REINFORCEMENT 125 the symbol. The meanings, or associations, which are, at any particular time, in the background may have an influence no less great because it is unacknowledged. Such an influence is, however, effective, only when certain social conditions are realised. The most important of these is that the members of a group, apart from any assumption of superiority, or position of submissiveness, should be extremely readily susceptible to thoughts, feelings, and tendencies to action which are finding slight, unacknowledged, but nevertheless real expression in the daily behaviour of their companions.

Suppose, for example, some custom has come to be regarded as socially objectionable. Its open practice disappears. But if it has been pursued in a group continuously, for any length of time, the tendencies and meanings which cluster about it disappear less readily than the mere practices themselves. Maybe the old custom is replaced by something new, and less socially objectionable. Then the tendencies and meanings which belonged to the old are transferred to the new, though they are unacknowledged, and though the persons who practise the new custom may be wholly unaware that the old tendencies and meanings are in any way whatever affecting their behaviour. Possibly no new custom is adopted. Nevertheless the old tendencies and meanings still find subtle ways of obtaining satisfaction. They are, though once again in a manner which never receives social acknowledgment, attached to other customs of the group or community.

Once get a social atmosphere in which unacknowledged tendencies call forth a ready response, and an enormously increased power of persistence is given to factors which, to ordinary observation, do not seem to have any place whatever in social behaviour. Such is the atmosphere produced by primitive comradeship. Thus the subtle and ready comradeship response, operating within the community, helps to give a strong power of persistence to tendencies which have been expressed within the group, but have long been disowned by it. So when the social crisis comes, any community may find itself back in a more primitive stage, and antagonistic tendencies may either wage war openly one upon another, or, operating together, may fling the whole group into confusion. The antagonism of tendencies does not concern the deep-lying instinctive tendencies only. With the group difference tendencies, in fact, the field of possible opposition is enormously widened. Part of our future discussion of the social psychology of contact of peoples will be concerned with the effects of the clash of the group difference tendencies. But there is one point that must be noticed here. Antagonism among the instinctive responses may lead to social limitations of their expression, to social disapprobation when certain of them are expressed, and so to the driving of many social practices into secret operation. But there is no evidence that any of these tendencies are stamped out completely. It may be otherwise with the group difference tendencies. These are to the group as "interests " are to the individual. They differentiate one group from another. They may even differentiate a group at one period from what we call "the same" group at a different period. They change from group to group, and from time to time. To all appearance they may, through antagonism, disappear completely.

Here, for example, we get the interesting social facts connected with "The disappearance of useful Arts."

THEIR MUTUAL REINFORCEMENT 127

The clearest illustrations have been brought forward by Dr Rivers 1. He has shown how the canoe, the making of pottery, and the use of the bow and arrow have all disappeared from certain parts of Oceania. The explanation which he advances turns definitely on the limitation of production of the articles concerned to special groups and to particular places. Limitation of this sort is precisely the most characteristic first step resulting from the opposition of tendencies. When we remember that the canoe almost certainly, and the bow and arrow probably, were very closely associated with a specific religious ceremonial, the case for segregation as the result of opposition is strengthened. The social process which produces a group having charge of religious ceremonial, also commits to that group the secrets of certain material arts. Whether the disappearance of the particular craft involved was thereafter due to the dying out of the special social group; to the destruction of the place of manufacture; to the weakening of certain features of religious authority; to the incoming of an alien people; or in large measure to mere changes of fashion, is not clear. Perhaps more than one of these influences combined. They all, except the first two, involve opposition affecting specialised tendencies, and the art which was the expression of the tendency apparently disappeared completely.

We must, however, pass on now to a very brief consideration of the integration and mutual reinforcement of tendencies as they are expressed in the social group. It need hardly be remarked that no tendency ever really operates in isolation. All that we can assert is that in 1 The Disappearance of Useful Arts, Festscrift Tillagnad Edward Westermarck, Helsingfors, 1912, pp. 109-30.

reference to certain types of activity certain tendencies are most prominent. But as they are expressed in social life, about these tendencies cluster many others, and, by the mingling of them all, new impulses are developed, or the old impulses are given increased impetus. Take, for example, the case of primitive ceremonial. In the development of many of the early forms of religious ritual fear takes a central place. All the situations originally involved are danger situations, to be approached with care, and by the help, as a general rule, of a special group, or a special person. But this is not all. There is practically no instinctive or acquired tendency the purposes of which may not be served by ceremonial. Sex, curiosity, the search for food, dominance, submissiveness, pugnacity all may find ceremonial expression in characteristic forms. If it is agreed that, at an early stage, ceremonial frequently has reference to a situation which is regarded as dangerous, and hence as one to be approached with fear, it will be seen that ceremonial practices are particularly likely to yield instances of the social relationships of dominance on the one hand and submission on the other. In general the situation is a dangerous one. The powers invoked are very strong. They must be approached with care. But if due caution is taken, the person, or group, approaching these powers may itself gain strength. Supposing the approach is combined with anger against an enemy. Charms and incantations are developed. Nothing can avail against these. The enemy is to be conquered, the worshipper made triumphant.

Turn now to play, as it occurs in the primitive group. In a very large number of cases the participants are divided into parties. One party is arrayed against the

THEIR MUTUAL REINFORCEMENT 129 others. But the underlying relationship here is one of comradeship. The division into contending parties, instead of producing charms to carry death and destruction to one side, produces a new tendency of friendly rivalry or of competition. Boys, among the Ba-ila, have fierce mimic battles, using long shafts of grass as spears. They charge and retreat and charge again and shout with glee when they succeed in transfixing the enemy. Generally speaking such games are carried out with good temper, but sometimes a sham fight develops into a real one, when sticks are grasped instead of grass and broker heads result. We remember one instance when a little boy often gravely brought a charge against another of the same age for hurting him in one of these sham fights, and claimed an ox as compensation 1.

Now here is the same root tendency towards pugnacity. United with fear in a social relationship of dominance it produces the making of charms and incantations to do their fell work in secret; united with a simple, straight effort to secure superiority it produces a downright fight; united with a relationship of primitive comradeship it produces social competition and friendly rivalry.

Take dancing again. This is a form of expression very common indeed in almost all primitive groups. But it may take widely different forms, and give rise to widely different impulses according to the other tendencies with which it is connected. There is the dance of the wizard or the warlock, and like the charm it is intended to bring death to an enemy. There is the dance of the initiation ceremony, which may often be mimetic, and intended to promote certain knowledge, and to excite 1 Smith and Dale, op. til. n, p. 243.

certain specific passions. There is the dance of pure gaiety, which promotes good fellowship and co-operation. The underlying impulse towards rhythmic bodily expression in circumstances of emotional excitement is the same. But the form and purpose of the expression, and the tendencies which are excited or produced, vary with the other impulses that are brought into play at the same time.

So we might go on and so, in fact, a complete psychological study of primitive culture would have to go on to consider the effects of the integration of tendencies. All through, the most important facts to consider are: first, whether the underlying social relationship involved is one of dominance, submissiveness or comradeship, and, secondly, in what special realm of activity the various combinations of impulses are expressed, and with what particular group difference tendencies they are connected. It is probable that the department of primitive culture which, beyond any other, displays the most striking illustrations of the effects of the integration of tendencies, is to be found in the realm of play.

Mutual reinforcement may be distinguished from integration, in that while the latter is concerned in the production of new forms of expression or of new tendencies, the former gives us the case of supplementary tendencies coming in to aid some leading motive without thereby turning it in a new direction. I cannot enter upon this study now, interesting as it is, further than to make one suggestion. We have seen already how the socially initiated tendency to create astonishment may very directly supplement an already existing instinct towards dominance, by enhancing the position of a

THEIR MUTUAL REINFORCEMENT 131 story-teller in relation to his audience. In general, I believe, it will be found that the most interesting and outstanding cases of mutual reinforcement arise from some form or other of social approval which is brought to bear upon an individual by virtue of his position within a community.

Much still remains to be discussed with regard to the inter-play of tendencies. But I hope that enough has been said both to indicate the nature of the problems that arise, and to suggest their very great importance. In passing on to a more detailed study of the psychological processes which are illustrated in the primitive group as a result of " contact of cultures," the same type of problem will continue to occupy attention. For it is evident that, when an alien culture comes into relation with one which is already established, what immediately ensues is a very complicated process of the inter-play of tendencies.

The results of our discussion in the present chapter may now be summarised: 1. Every department of primitive culture shows a number of tendencies simultaneously in operation. We must attempt to say how these tendencies react one upon another.

2. When two tendencies, or groups of tendencies, are antagonistic they tend to get separated, and each acquires its characteristic field of expression.

3. As a consequence of this social groups develop having specialised functions.

4. But, particularly in the case of instinctive tendencies, there will always be an effort on the part of the more or less segregated impulse to seek expression beyond its lawful limits. The dominance instinct as expressed in specialised social groups works in the same direction.

5. For these, or other reasons, social disapprobation of certain of the antagonistic tendencies may arise, as a result of which these tendencies, and their related practices, are driven into secret.

6. But in secret they persist, and may precipitate social crises, which consequently have all the appearance of reversions to a more primitive level of culture.

7. Persistence of displaced tendencies may be secured by the continuous life of the group, or of the community, or in some other manner connected closely with primitive social comradeship.

8. Tendencies which do not radically conflict may combine or be integrated, and new modes of social response may thus develop. In the determination of these it is probable that the most important factors are the primitive forms of instinctive social relationship.

9. Moreover, tendencies may simply supplement one another in the growth of primitive culture; not producing new lines of advance, but leading to the more vigorous prosecution of old developments. Here probably the socially initiated tendencies due to a man's place in the group, or to what we broadly call social approbation, play the most important parts.

CHAPTER V

THE PSYCHOLOGICAL STUDY OF THE CONTACT OF PEOPLES

The Argument: We may distinguish between the transmission of culture by means of the contact of peoples, and by means of borrowing. In the former case, migrating groups travel long distances, taking their cultural possessions with them. These groups, settling eventually in a new environment, stamp the impress of their culture upon an indigenous population. In the case of " borrowing," the new cultural elements are introduced, not through the movements of groups as a whole, but through the influence of individuals who, having travelled from their home, return again bringing the new elements with them. Transmission by contact appears the more important the more primitive the social organisation with which we are concerned.

The psychological determination of the results of contact depends in the first place upon the instinctive social relationship form which holds good within and between the groups involved.

In general, it can be shown that if, between the groups which meet, there is a relationship of primitive comradeship, the most probable result is a true blending of cultures. If one of the groups is very forceful and dominant, the others being submissive, within certain limits, it is likely that the culture of the submissive peoples will be overthrown and replaced by that of the dominant group. That form of dominance of one group over others which is secured by quality of culture, favours the replacement of certain details of the cultural possessions of the relatively submissive peoples, the development of

"compromise formations," and the growth of a more complex culture.

In the second place, the results of contact depend upon those social instinctive tendencies of which conservation and constructiveness are the most important examples. By virtue of the former, when two or more groups come into contact, if their cultures possess points of likeness, details will almost inevitably be exchanged. For conservation is always selective, and thus only parts of a complex culture are maintained without change. This, in itself, renders possible the acceptance of new features, in place of those features of the old which are not conserved. Particularly when the emotions and emotional attitudes which were attached to materials belonging to the old culture can be transferred to new details, the new is apt to be fitted into the background of the old.

The old and the new are not, however, left side by side. They are worked up into distinctive " cultural patterns." This is one of the tasks of the tendency towards social constructiveness.

In the third place, the group difference tendencies come into play. They function chiefly in determining the further modifications which elements undergo, after their transference to the culture of a new group.

The fourth set of factors to be dealt with are the individual instincts those which do not demand a group for their occurrence, though they may have important social expressions. These exercise their influence in a variety of ways. Their chief function, in regard to the contact of peoples, is to help to determine what particular sphere of culture, or what special social activities, are affected.

Finally, we must always be prepared to admit that the influence of the personality of outstanding individuals may be important. Such influence, however, seems in all probability to be less effective at the primitive than at more highly developed levels of social life.

There is little significance in saying that certain beliefs, myths, objects, etc., are borrowed, when they are found in two areas between which diffusion is possible. What we want to know is what lies at the bottom of the facts that just these have been borrowed, and how they were borrowed. How did the recipient culture and the person or persons who were the actual trafhsmitters of the new features limit the elements borrowed? Was there an inert substitution of a new for an old feature; was there a re-interpretation of the old in terms of the new; or, lastly, a re-interpretation of the old in terms of its own culture, but due to stimulation from without? 1 It is in these words that Dr Paul Radin points the moral of his investigation of the growth and dissemination of the Peyote Cult of the Winnebago Indians. The questions which he asks are of the very greatest importance to the psychological study of primitive culture. We are often told that some element, or elements, of culture are borrowed, or have been adopted through the contact of peoples. But, at least from the psychological point of view, this statement ought never to be accepted as the end of research. Rather it should be treated as the beginning of further study. All contact, all borrowing, involves a great amount of that inter-play of social and individual tendencies, the complexity of which in certain directions was the subject of our study in the last chapter. Underlying all spreading of elements from one culture to another are the social relationships of the people involved; the group difference tendencies that have already been developed on both sides; the nature of the material about which those tendencies cluster; the specific individual instincts; and in many cases the 1 " A Sketch of the Peyote Cult of the Winnebago: A Study in Borrowing," Jour, of Religious Psychology, Jan. 1914, vn, 1-22.

temperament, interests and aptitudes of outstanding individuals. Here again, that is to say, we find in operation all those factors which have been discussed in the preceding chapter. I will now try to show them at work in the determination of the processes by which elements pass from one culture to another.

In this chapter I propose to confine my attentiorf to the main conditions governing transmission by contact, and to show how these conditions operate. In the next two chapters I shall deal with the conditions of the borrowing of cultural elements, and with what happens to the borrowed material in the course of its assimilation.

I wish at the outset to make a distinction between transmission by contact arid transmission by borrowing. In the first case we have a body of people migrating, coming into a new home, and carrying with them a culture which consists of a number of different elements. In the second case we have elements introduced into a new home by individuals, who by travel, or for some other reason, have become acquainted with these elements in an alien environment. Intermediate between the two cases, but perhaps somewhat nearer to constant proper than to borrowing, is the transmission by contact intercommunication which profoundly affects the cultural possessions of neighbouring peoples, especially when these are in friendly relation one with another. No doubt many common conditions are at work in these cases, but the differences between contact and borrowing are sufficiently important to justify their separate discussion. Strictly speaking, the contact of cultures generally, if not always, involves a blending of peoples. But introduction of alien elements through the medium of influential individuals does not do so. On the whole there seems justification for asserting that the former exerts relatively greater influence at the more primitive levels; while the latter becomes increasingly important with the development of more complex social systems. This position is in agreement with that adopted by Dr Rivers, who says: in rude society external influence is the chief, if not the only, condition which can set up a process of social transference similar to that which among ourselves falls to the lot of a great social or religious reformer 1. And though no doubt it is true that the more remote the society the more difficult it is to get any real appreciation of the influence of the individual, there seems to be no good reason for disputing Rivers's statement. Accordingly I propose to devote this chapter to a study of the conditions, so far as they are of psychological interest, of the modification of culture through contact of peoples.

In his History of Melanesian Society, and elsewhere 3, Dr Rivers has attacked very much the same problem, though his standpoint has generally been less definitely that of the psychologist 4. He points out that an attempt ought to be made "to formulate some of the conditions which determine the nature of the compound which results from the settlement of a migrant people among an indigenous population."

Since, so far as I know, nobody else has attempted a systematic search for these conditions, it will be best to begin from the suggestions made by Rivers himself.

1 Folk Lore, vol. xxxu, 1921, p. 26: "Presidential Address on Conservatism and Plasticity."

2 Cambridge, 1914, vol. n, ch. xxvu.

8 See especially Essays and Studies Presented to William Ridgeway, Cambridge, 1913, p. 474.

4 This does not apply to the Folk Lore paper.

The conditions influencing the mode of interaction between a migrant and a settled people which arise out of the nature of the peoples themselves and of their respective cultures are (he says) of four chief kinds: those arising out of the disposition of the people, especially whether they are inclined to peace or war; those arising out of their numerical proportions; those due to their differences in physical and cultural endowment; and those due to the proportion of the sexes, this condition being especially important in the case of the incoming people 1.

He points out that the most important of these conditions is the inclination of the peoples concerned to " peaceful or warlike behaviour," but that this again is dependent for its specific effects upon the relation between the peoples in numbers and in cultural endowment. "Another general feature of the character of a people," he goes on, "which is of obvious importance, is adaptability as opposed to conservatism 2."

Concerning this proposed basis for our general problem two remarks must be made. In the first place while everybody must at once admit the importance of the conditions enumerated, it is equally clear that no attempt has been made here to describe them in a specially psychological manner. And in the second place, if we try to look at the conditions in the light of the scheme of psychological responses which we have proposed to make the basis of our studies, we shall see that according to this scheme, they are not all upon the same level. Take, for example, "the inclination of the peoples towards peaceful or warlike behaviour" and compare it with "adaptability as opposed to conservatism." The first is in part a matter of the underlying 1 History of Melanesian Society, n, 293. 2 Loc. cit.

THE CONTACT OF PEOPLES 139 instinctive social relationship within a community: whether it is one of primitive comradeship, or of asser-tiveness, or of submissiveness. Partly, also, it is a matter of the degree of importance in a social group of the individual instinctive tendency towards pugnacity. The second is an immediately social instinct of a special character whose operation and sphere of influence seem often to depend upon the nature of the underlying social relationship. This comes out clearly from Rivers's own discussion in the paper on " Conservatism and Plasticity," to which reference has already been made.

Innate disposition (he there says) almost certainly contributes to determine whether a person readily follows the accepted custom of his group or rebels against it, but his attitude, and certainly the details of his attitude and the nature of the affects accompanying it, are largely determined by the relation of the child to those who exert authority over it in its early years. And owing to the nature of the institution of the family, the father occupies a most important position among those persons 1.

When he turns to find a possible social parallel for this fact of individual psychology, he is reminded of the position of the elders in a primitive group:

There is reason to believe that, in many parts of Melanesia at least, the place of the father is taken by the old men of the community in general. The old men occupy a commanding position of authority, and are so intimately related to the whole of the small community they dominate that they count as much as, if not more than, the father, or the mother's brother as the wielders of authority and influence 2.

To this dominant position of the elders, then, much of the strength of conservatism in the small Melanesian 1 "Conservatism and Plasticity," Folk Lore, xxxn, pp. 15-16.

communities is traced. That is to say, conservatism and indirectly adaptability also, are tendencies upon a somewhat different level from the primitive social relationships of comradeship, dominance and subservience. For they appear at once less generalised in their character, and in a way actually dependent upon the latter for their expression.

Again, if we turn to differences which arise from the physical and cultural endowments of the people concerned, we shall immediately find ourselves face to face with inter-play among the group difference tendencies. For it is largely upon differences in physical and cultural endowment that a group's distinctive institutions are based. And if we examine the effects of the factors which arise from the proportion of the sexes we shall soon see that some, at least, of these spring immediately from social expressions of the individual instincts.

For the purpose of disentangling the various conditions of interaction between peoples, therefore, we shall do well to study first the influence of the fundamental instinctive social relationship forms; to pass thence to the social instincts which are somewhat more specialised than the relationship tendencies, and which may depend upon the latter for their spheres of operation; next to discuss the importance of the group difference tendencies; then to illustrate the social influence of the individual instincts; and finally to lead up to our study of borrowing through a discussion of the possible influence of the peculiar characteristics of important individuals.

Supposing two groups come into contact one with the other, and friendly relationships ensue, neither side
THE CONTACT OF PEOPLES 141 being markedly superior. This is the case in which true blending of cultures is most likely of all to follow. As our illustration will show, elements of either culture will be assimilated by the other, though, as in all instances, both the amount and the nature of the as milation possible will be determined by the already existing group difference tendencies, and by the particular instincts and aptitudes that are called into play. Take, for example, the ceremonial known as The Hako, a series of social and religious ritual observances prevalent among the Pawnee Indians. According to Miss Alice Fletcher 1 this ceremony has a two-fold purpose: to secure the perpetuation of a family, or other social group, by children, long life, and plenty of food; and to promote social harmony among different groups. The ceremony is a very old one and has probably spread from the region of the Mexican plateau and the South Western plains, suffering modifications in the course of its diffusion, in accordance with the character of the different environments through which it has passed. The nature of some of the ritual and regalia suggests that the primary instigation of the ceremony was desire for offspring, so that a clan or kinship group might increase its strength and be perpetuated through the birth of children. The secondary purpose, the promotion of social harmony, was an outgrowth of the first, and seems to have facilitated the diffusion of the ceremony. Some of the groups concerned were originally antagonistic, but as a more settled mode of life was adopted, and more friendly relations were established, the antagonists of old days accepted common ceremonial customs. Thereupon the ritual materials became more
1 See 22nd Ann. Rep. Bur. Am. Ethn.
complicated, elements being interchanged from different cultural settings.
Not only did the ceremonial practices then spread more rapidly, but as the regalia used were taken from one group to another, manufactures peculiar to one tribe were widely dispersed, and the handicraft of, f ne region became known to other sections. When the underlying relationship is one mainly of comradeship, knowledge of any of the cultural possessions of one group is apt to lead at once to the adoption of similar practices in another group. It is not the knowledge alone that leads to the practice, but the knowledge reinforced by the affective relationship of comradeship and by all that this involves. Thus it is that friendly intercourse and entertainment become most powerful agents in the diffusion of ceremonial. And if we are right in urging that the relationship of comradeship has a primitive and instinctive basis, there can be no doubt that, even at the most primitive levels, it has played a very great part in the blending of cultures. It is worth while noticing that this is a condition which may operate in entire independence of the relative numbers of persons concerned on the two sides.
Comradeship may involve all degrees of intimacy of personal relations; and the completeness with which cultural possessions are affected is correspondingly great. At every stage the comradeship response promotes blending, but we ought to distinguish between merely giving or receiving an element of culture, and taking over also its original significance, or purpose. As Lowie points out 1, a tribe which does not possess certain 1 See "Ceremonialism in North America," Amer. Anthropol N. S. 16, 1919, p. 602.

THE CONTACT OF PEOPLES 148 cultural characters might, merely as spectators of the performances of other groups, become acquainted with those characters, and adopt them. In Australia: U A tribe will learn and sing by rote whole corrobborces in a language absolutely remote from its own, and not or word of which the audience, or performer, can understand the meaning of 1." What undoubtedly happens in this case is that the foreign element is accepted into an existing culture, and given a significance within that culture, which may be peculiar to the people who have received it. When this occurs subsequent modification is on the whole far more likely than if the transmission involves a greater degree of personal intimacy.

While comradeship favours blending in the true sense, dominance on the whole favours displacement. But here we must be cautious. There are different types of dominance. Dominance by mere force of numbers may mean simply the extermination of one side, and the most extreme form of displacement. This is not, however, a common, and cannot be called a distinctively psychological, process. The superiority that is psychologically important is not of numbers or of brute force, but of quality of culture. Thus Rivers finds it possible to use as a guide to the past the principle that the extent of the effect of a migrating people upon those among whom they settle is proportional to the degree of superiority of the immigrant culture, and from this it will follow that the greater be the superiority of an introduced culture, the smaller need be the number of its introducers 2.

In all cases the superiority of which we here speak is 1 Quoted by Lowie from Roth. 2 Contact of Peoples, p. 477.

"thefact that an introduced culture seems to those who adopt it to be higher than their own," though in practice it is not necessary that there should be explicit, conscious admission of superiority. And if we ask how an introduced culture can seem to be "higher" there are two answers. First, the culture must have some fa ly obvious point of contact with that to which it is introduced, and secondly, it must have some practical value that appeals to the primitive instincts or to the social tendencies marking a particular group, and that makes it seem unusually well adapted to meet the ends of these tendencies. As Rivers remarks, the second point is the more important the ruder the social organisation with which we have to do.

It is the knife and the match, the steamship, the house and its furniture, but above and beyond all, the firearms of the European which impress the man of rude culture and lead him to regard their possessors as beings of a higher order than himself 1.

To this I should like to add, in view of the first of our two general conditions of superiority that the possession of certain ceremonial features is often just as important as the possession of material objects in producing a relatively submissive attitude towards an incoming culture.

It is, I think, evident, from what has been said that the particular effect achieved by dominance in any given case is dependent upon the attitude by which the dominant people are received. If dominance on the one side is answered by extreme submissiveness on the other, the most marked cases of replacement of one culture by others are produced. This is a common result when 1 Contact of Peoples, p. 478.

THE CONTACT OF PEOPLES 145 a forceful and pugnacious group, possessing, at the same time, a higher order of social development, comes into contact with a group much lower in the line of social growth. But even under these circumstances the replacement is not solely the outcome of dominance on the one side faced by submissiveness on the other. The institutions, customs, ceremonial and habits of the forceful people are seldom found to contain more than a few general characters in common with those of the submissive people. If the latter can be forced to accept them, therefore, they cannot be fitted into the already existing cultural patterns, but must replace, or be added to, the old forms of response. There is less blending, and more mixing of relatively incongruous elements; or more driving underground of the old, and superposition upon the apparently dead past of the new material. This is the social state which, probably beyond any other, leads to those pathological developments of social life discussed in the last chapter. It produces inevitable burdens burdens such as all vigorous and developed communities have had to bear who have attempted to colonise or govern more primitive peoples.

Most interesting of all are the cases in which a dominant but not overwhelmingly warlike migrant people come into touch with a settled people who are not, for their part, excessively submissive. Such a situation allows of fairly free intercourse between the peoples concerned, as a result of which many of the details of the incoming culture may replace details belonging to the old. But the replacement is generally partial; and since the relation involved is one of dominance based not upon mere pugnacity but upon inherent superiority, the new and the old have comparatively little in common. For a long time they may exist side by side, each chiefly affecting certain groups, or each having its assigned sphere of expression. They do not so readily fuse as do elements accepted through comradeship. And the result is a perplexing, but at the same time a vitalising, complexity of culture.

Undoubtedly, leaving aside the cases of conquest by brute force and superiority of numbers, this is the commonest of all the relations between a migrant and a settled people. Comradeship is a relation which very often holds good within a community, but it is less frequently found to overspread the boundaries of groups and to unite different communities. It may hold between different peoples who occupy neighbouring territories, and have achieved a settled life. But when a migratory people travel long distances they usually carry with them a culture which is in many respects markedly different from that already existing in their new home. If, then, this contact is to produce definite and longstanding results, it seems bound to be based upon dominance by superiority.

Of all the illustrations that are available of this process those which have been developed in reference to Australian and Melanesian culture by Dr Rivers are certainly the most complete and striking. He points out that a fictitious simplicity has frequently been attributed to Australian culture.

What. we find is that nearly every one of the chief known methods of disposal of the dead is practised in Australia. We find inhumation in the extended and the contracted positions; we find preservation on platforms, in trees and in caverns. There is embalming, though of a simple kind, and lastly there is cremation 1. 1 Contact of Peoples 9 p. 481.

How are we to suppose that this complexity of funeral custom has come about? "People do not," says Rivers, "adopt new funeral rites merely because they see or hear of them elsewhere 1." They certainly are most unlikely to do so, unless between the different groups wi h the diverse ceremonies there subsists the relationship of comradeship. But that, as we have seen, is apt to demand settled conditions, particularly if groups having a widely different social character are in question. It cannot possibly be the explanation in the instances under consideration. We seem bound to agree that these are examples of the influence of small but dominant migrant groups, who, by virtue of their social relationship to the indigenous people, are able to introduce new features into the old culture. Coming from afar, winning an immediate superiority, not by armed force, or by excessive submissiveness, but by their material arts if we may admit that they were people who held the secret of metal working 2 they settled in their new environment, and, because of their friendly dominance, exercised a far-reaching influence. The practice of their material arts often died out, in the way which we saw to be perfectly possible in the last chapter, but certain of their rites remained, and produced a complex culture comprising many features which were not completely blended or reconciled. This complexity "has arisen through the preponderating influence which falls to the lot of small bodies of immigrants whose culture seems great and wonderful to those among whom they settle 3."

With regard to the influence of underlying social 1 Loc. cit.

2 Cf. W. J. Perry, The Megalithic Culture of Indonesia, Manchester, 1918.

8 Contact of Peoples, p. 484.

10-2 instinctive relationships we may now sum up the results of our discussion.

Where the relationship of primitive comradeship holds, a true blending or fusion of cultures is likely to occur. But this relationship, in general, either holds good only between groups within a primitive community, or else, if different communities are involved, it demands contiguity of position, and a settled mode of life.

Where a migrant people come into contact with an indigenous group, and achieve dominance by sheer force, either through their own pugnacity or because of the great submissiveness of the indigenous group, the incoming culture tends rather to replace than to blend with the old. Under these conditions, however, the old may often persist in subterranean ways, and is liable to break out in the form of violent social reversions.

When a small immigrant body are received in friendly fashion, and win a dominance based upon the superiority of their culture, while much of the old culture persists openly, new elements are introduced, or replace some of the old details. There results a complexity of cultures presenting features which are not perfectly reconciled. This type of superiority is often gained through skill in material arts; nevertheless that very attainment which secures the welcome in the new home may disappear in course of time, though other elements which did not so directly contribute to the original dominance remain.

We must now pass on to consider the parts played by instinctive responses having a characteristic social expression, but somewhat more specifically directed to certain ends. Of these the most important seem to be conservation and that social form of the constructive instinct, of which, so far practically nothing has been said. But each of these is so bound up in its functions with the group difference tendencies, as well as with the instinctive social relationship forms of which we have ategady spoken, that they cannot be considered wholly by themselves.

The most Interesting thing about the tendency towards conservation is, as I suggested earlier, its selective character. Yet the apparent selection of this rather than that element of culture for survival, is not wholly a question of the operation of a conserving instinct. It is largely due to clash or to reinforcement among other tendencies. The fact is that the study of these instincts of conservation and constructiveness forces us to recognise an order of arrangement among primitive tendencies. Very broadly speaking, that is preserved which brings into play a number of reinforcing tendencies, and that is lost or distorted which stimulates conflicting impulses. At the same time it seems possible that what may be called the conserving instinct itself, does exercise a selective function. This is partly in consequence of its cognitive character. For example, every group tends to form what have been called "cultural patterns." When any new cultural element comes along, or new body of culture is introduced, it is either accepted, when it may be preserved unchanged, or may survive in a distorted form, or else it is rejected, according as it fits into an already existing pattern. To say that the instinct of conservation is brought into play whenever any new culture or element of culture is presented which is capable of fitting into an already existing cultural pattern is to make the conserving instinct selective. The selecting mechanism in such cases appears to be some kind of practical appreciation of whether or not the new culture "fits" the old conditions, and perhaps it is not too much to say that this appreciation gives to the whole process a cognitive character. However, nothing is served tf by arguing as if the instinct of conservation, in its social expressions, ever operated entirely by itself. Let us see one way in which it may bring a complicated mechanism into play.

Here, once more, we must turn to a paper by Dr Rivers, to which reference has already been made 1. The variety of funeral practices among the Melanesians must, he believes, be accounted for by the influence of small migrant groups in the way we have already discussed. Now these groups meet, in Australia and in Melanesia, communities in which the dominant social position which is again largely identified with the practice of magical and religious rites is held by the elders. The elders are venerated and obeyed. But, owing mainly to their superior material arts, the incoming visitors are also venerated and obeyed. They inspire, that is to say, much the same emotions and attitudes as the elders, and to that extent they fit into the already existing social arrangements of the indigenous people. But the visitors also have their ceremonial. And in proportion as they take the place of the group of elders, so those parts of their ceremonial which have to do with activities formerly controlled by the old men replace the earlier customs. At the same time fragments of the earlier customs persist, and acquire, perhaps, a symbolic significance. Acceptance of this view, demands first that the group 1 "Conservatism and Plasticity," Folk Lore, xxxn, pp. 10-27.

THE CONTACT OF PEOPLES 151 of indigenous people should experience very much the same emotions, and adopt very much the same attitudes, towards the new comers, as they have previously experienced and adopted towards a section of their own community. Seeing that there is every reason to believe tk t the relationship between the strangers and the natives was a friendly one, there is nothing unlikely in this. The superiority of the elders and of the immigrants was due to similar reasons and in neither case was it attributable to military dominance. Moreover the native groups were apparently of the comradeship type pre-eminently, and consequently, according to our general principles, particularly likely to display homogeneity of response among themselves.

In the second place the position demands a mechanism of the transference of customs in group life, through common emotions, similar to that of the transference of habits or of cognitive materials, for the same reasons, with which we are familiar in the individual life. Again, providing only that we assent to the view that here we have to do with groups the members of which in general act, feel, and think in very close harmony, there appears to be no objection to the mechanism proposed. Conservation, then, as it is expressed in social survivals may involve a complicated series of responses, in which the underlying social relationships, and the special individual emotions and instincts, together with that collection of group difference tendencies which produce cultural patterns, may all come into play.

Now if this view is correct, plasticity, which is almost as marked a feature of primitive social life as conservatism, may appear to be simply the opposite side of the conserving tendency. It is because the group is selectively conservative that it is also plastic. For the very changes which it accepts are, in a large measure, the indirect outcome of its constant attempt to secure the persistence of the old. The changed ceremonial, for example, and the new elements which are introduced, are due to a maintenance of the old attitude, and of ttj appeal to the old emotions and sentiments by new features of the environment.

Although this is a part of the truth, it would be perverse to insist that primitive constructiveness can be adequately characterised as mere negative conservatism. For not only are certain parts of the old perceived, but the coming of the new gives rise, as Rivers points out, to "compromise formations 1," in which the old and the new both persist, side by side, and are perhaps never entirely reconciled. And it must be remembered that, in all forms of social life, from the most primitive to the most advanced stages, the old and the new undergo continuous processes of elaboration and modification into forms which may become so characteristic for special communities that they are spoken of as "cultural patterns." Something more is implied than the persistence of parts only of the old culture, and something more than the consequent acceptance of new elements. The old that persists and the new that is accepted are gradually worked together into new forms. It is particularly this process of reconciliation that demands the recognition of a constructive tendency operative in the community and playing a most important part in the development of social institutions. Such a tendency, resulting in the elaboration of distinctive cultural patterns, must to 1 "Conservatism and Plasticity," Folk Lore, xxxn, pp. 18, 26.

THE CONTACT OF PEOPLES 153 some extent have helped to guide the results of all contact of peoples from the beginning 1.

By implication, at any rate, the importance of the group difference tendencies has already been shown. The subsequent changes of culture introduced to a given gypup depend, not merely upon the social relationships involved, and not merely upon the special social instincts brought into play, but also to a large degree upon the tendencies which centre about the already existing institutions and customs peculiar to the group concerned. Take for example statements such as those made of the Fijians:

The religious psychology of the Fijians after conversion to Christianity reveals the peculiar features to which we have constantly referred in the course of our study of their customs and character. All have volubility in preaching. As all can join in the building of a house, so each seems to think that he is able to preach. It is doubtful whether one male Christian could be found who could not fill in ten minutes or a quarter of an hour with a sermonette. There are certain ideas which seem to have become the property of the clan-mind, on which he can always fall back upon with the certainty of getting an attentive hearing. In view of these there is a remarkable sameness in the native preacher's public addresses.

Words and phrases fall into grooves, as is natural where there is a paucity of ideas and a multitude of words. In the training of preachers the greatest difficulty is found in bestirring them to think for themselves. As to style in public utterances, it may be said that the native is, almost without exception, an adept at drawing analogies and interpreting allegory 2.

1 For a fuller discussion of the significance of social construct! veness, see chapter vi.

2 Deane, op, cit. pp. 114-15. It must strike everyone that here again very much the same observations could be made about many sections of a highly civilised community-

The Fijian native is, in fact, bringing into play upon the new material and reactions, the old group difference tendencies which have grown up about the activities of his past life. As we have repeatedly seen, the group difference tendencies stand to the social group, very much as the individual interests and capacities star to the individual. They are, in each case, defining, differentiating characters. And in every instance new customs or materials, received into a group, for whatsoever reason they may be accepted, are immediately affected by their relationship to the old specialised tendencies. Thus while the fact of blending may be mainly a matter of the social relationship forms involved, the particular direction which the changes introduced take is mainly a question of the influence of the group difference tendencies.

All of the factors we have discussed are socially expressed, but they exert a direct influence upon the individual. For example they determine the attitude adopted towards new material. The Crow Indians, for instance, possess a number of societies forming a Tobacco Order. The members of this order have privileges with regard to the planting of sacred tobacco, but the order does not differ from others in its inner organisation except as regards its regalia, and the instructions which were conveyed in a vision to the founder. Such visions occur also among many other tribes of Indians. The Shoshoni have them, for instance, but apparently they possess no ceremonial pattern, no current set of ideas, by which the visions can be regularly integrated into a ceremonial order. Of this Lowie remarks:

A Crow who belonged to the Tobacco order, and stumbled across a nest of curiously shaped eggs, would

THE CONTACT OF PEOPLES 155 might experience precisely the same thrill under like conditions, but the same psychological experience could not possibly result in the same cultural epi-phenomenon 1,

As a matter of fact it is only in a very loose sense that the Crow and the Shoshoni Indian could be said to have 4 the same" psychological experience. The characteristic difference tendencies of each group find their expression in the members of the group, and although it may be true that the purely affective part of the experience would be the same, much besides this is involved. The two responses are, as Lowie indicates, from the point of view of the group, to be distinguished. They are different also from the point of view of the individual, and this is mainly because diverse group difference tendencies are operative in the two cases. Of course it might be said that the fact that different tendencies are operative need not affect the character of the experience. This raises a theoretical point of some importance, the discussion of which, however, may be postponed for the present. Whether they are facts of experience or not, the tendencies most certainly represent conditions belonging to psychology. They are mental conditions which affect the individual's response, and if they differ, then the total responses involved are psychologically different also.

To work out in full the effects of the group difference tendencies, we should have, by the very nature of the case, to consider the particular characteristics of large numbers of groups. But our point is simply that how, as well as what, material is received through contact depends to a considerable degree upon the operation of these differentiating tendencies of social groups.

1 "Ceremonialism in North America," Amer. Anthropol., N. S. 16, p. 620.

Here already, as our illustrations show, we are approaching the study of the part taken by individuals in the psychology of social contact. We move a step nearer when we consider the specific individual instincts. It is extremely difficult to trace these in operation in any detail so long as we confine our attention to contact of peoples proper, as distinguished from borrowing. In a short discussion little can be done beyond giving a bare indication of the principles which are involved.

The underlying instinctive social relationship forms all presuppose a group of some sort. The conserving and the constructive instincts have the very closest connexion with life in a community, and, as they are here considered, may equally be said to assume the group formation. The group difference tendencies, by their very definition, demand a group for their growth and development. All of these, that is to say, though they are expressed in individual relationships and by individual behaviour yet do, by their very nature, presuppose a social setting for the individual. Now it is not clearly so with the other special instinct tendencies. They have their social expressions, and it is certain of these with which we are here concerned. But they do not seem to be connected in quite the same way with the fact of the social grouping.

Pugnacity, for example, certainly has very characteristic social expressions, but it seems to be readily called into action by the thwarting of any other instinctive tendency, whether within or without a social group. We have been reminded already that pugnacity, as leading to a special form of dominance, may have an important effect upon the results of contact.

Again, differences in reference to the material with which a branch of culture deals may show the pre ponderating influence of certain individual instincts within a specific group. This, for example, does seem to be the case in regard to the earlier forms of the Hako Ceremony, and as we have seen it appears also to be true of very many folk-tale cycles. We get sexual instincts prominent in the first, and sex, food-seeking, greed and vaingloriousness, for example, prominent in the second. As Rivers says "The possession by visitors of useful arts or of attractive ideas may give them an influence far out of proportion to their numbers 1." If these special material and mental developments are due in any way to the predominant position gained in certain groups by specific individual instincts, the latter have an obvious bearing upon the effects of contact.

In another way, that cannot now be worked out, the individual instinct tendencies may be important. One of the general determining conditions which we accepted at the beginning of this chapter as influential in relation to contact of peoples was "the proportion of the sexes." Directly around relationships which arise from such sex distribution cluster, as will be generally agreed, many of the primitive instinct tendencies. "The proportion of the sexes " produces a part, though by no means all, of its effects by reason of its powerful appeal to the various specific instinct responses 2.

Moreover I would suggest that not a little of the influence upon contact exerted by the route followed by a migrant group, and the general and local environment of the people who receive the new culture, is produced 1 Rivers, History of Melanesian Society, n, 295.

2 Ibid. 295-6.

directly through the relation of these external factors to the specific instincts 1.

We come finally to the parts played by the characteristics of important individuals. Probably it is safe to conclude that at a primitive level the individual, so far as his personal distinguishing characteristics go, j relatively less effective than he appears to be at a higher stage. The Fijian, to refer again to Mr Deane's discussion, shows great interdependence.

Self reliance is a very evanescent quality amongst the native clansmen. A suggestion made quite casually by one of their number will sway the attitude of the whole company, while another inadvertent proposition will turn them like sheep in the opposite direction 2.

They are not the only lowly civilisation of which this is true. Yet even the most primitive community has its outstanding individuals 3, and the dominance illustrated in such a community is not invariably that of a group. Dominant individuals must have put their mark upon the effects of the contact of peoples. The mark may remain, but the stamp and the influence of the important person merge in the general effect. It is when we come to study the borrowing of specific cultural traits that we are better able to trace the social significance of the dominant individual. But this study we must postpone to our next chapter.

Our present discussion may now be summarised: 1. This chapter deals with the underlying conditions which are of direct psychological interest, in the determination of the effects of the contact of cultures.

2. These conditions fall into five groups: (a) the primitive instinctive relationship forms of comradeship, 1 Rivers, History of Melanesian Society, n, 296-303.

2 Ibid. 102. 3 Ibid. ch. vm.

THE CONTACT OF PEOPLES dominance and submissiveness; (6) the special so instinct tendencies of conservation and construct ness; (c) the group difference tendencies which differ entiate one group from another; (d) the individual instinct tendencies; (e) the influence of the individuality of important personages.

3. In a general sense primitive comradeship favours true blending; dominance with submissiveness favours extinction and replacement; dominance by quality of culture favours replacement of details and the growth of complex culture.

4. The conserving tendency facilitates the processes of replacement of detail by detail, working largely through the mechanism of transference by common emotions. Conservation, as it is found in society, is always selective. This in itself helps to render possible the incorporation of new elements of culture. Whatever is preserved is worked up into patterns which become distinctive of special groups. The production of cultural patterns bears witness to the influence of a tendency towards social constructiveness, and is found at all stages of the development of society.

5. The group difference tendencies have their main function in directing the processes of modification of new elements of culture subsequent to their reception.

6. The individual instincts may affect the results of contact by their connexion with the social relationship forms; or by giving to the cultural possessions of a particular group some outstanding characteristic; by way of the proportion of sexes in the migratory and settled people; or by their special stimulation through certain features belonging to the external environment.

7. The personality of outstanding individuals in shaping the results of contact is difficult to detect, but we cannot safely rule out the influences that may be traced to this source. When we turn to a study of the process of borrowing elements of culture, the part played by the individual can at once be seen to be of great importance.

CHAPTER VI

PSYCHOLOGICAL FACTORS IN THE TRANSMISSION OF CULTURE BY BORROWING

The Argument: By "borrowing" is meant the transmission of elements of culture through the personal influence of some important individual or individuals

Borrowing depends first upon the influence of specific individual instincts or interests, and no material is transmitted unless it arouses one or more of these. The very instinctive or interest factor which makes an individual notice and assimilate special features in an alien environment, also tends to bring such features into a working agreement with the already existing cultural possessions of his own group. For it is exactly along the line of his leading instincts or interests that the individual is most open to the influence of those group difference tendencies which define his native community. These, however, are the more important as the individual is of a comradeship type, and the less effective as he is of a dominant character.

As soon as the elements begin to find a footing in the community, the person who introduces them is subjected to strong influences arising both from the group accepting his innovations, and from the group rejecting them. These generally tend to excite in him an attitude of hostility towards the old culture, and the differences between the new and the old are thereupon defined and sharpened. Frequently the individual who has introduced the new elements now joins others who are prepared to accept yet more radical innovations.

The whole of this chain of processes marks the operation of social constructive tendencies. By the influence of these, the incoming new elements are inserted into the old cultural patterns, and the old is widened in fresh and often in striking ways.

In social constructiveness the influence of the individual instincts and interests frequently intermingles with that of the group difference tendencies, and from the resulting conflict the new developments arise. 1 ailarly the competition and co-operation of different individuals, each of whom contributes some new element to the old culture, stimulate the constructive tendency. The expansion of cultural patterns which results is rightly called constructive, but it has no necessary connexion with conscious purpose, and is, in fact, rarely or never foreseen by any individual.

Borrowed elements, if they are to maintain a position, must be disseminated throughout the group or groups to which they have come. The mode of dissemination depends partly upon the relationship of the innovator to the group concerned, partly upon the pre-existing social organisation of the group, and partly upon the sphere of culture which is affected. In general, with a comradeship type of innovator, dissemination is likely to follow existing lines of social organisation; the borrowing will be distinctly conservative in character, and the new will be the more readily assimilated to the old.

This is one of the reasons that make it extremely difficult to say, in any given case, how far an element of culture which has been transferred from one setting to another must originally have carried with it a mass of associated material, and how far it may have been transmitted by itself. But there is no doubt that, while the most typical cases of the transmission of culture by contact favour the movement of whole bodies of associated customs, ceremonies, beliefs and the like, borrowing is more likely to operate upon particular, or single, cultural traits, which are "lifted" from their setting.

Whenever, at any stage in the process of borrowing, or of dissemination, constructive processes come in, they do so as a result of the conflict of impulses, or of the competition of individuals and groups. The results achieved are never completely, and rarely to any large extent, the expression of an ideal consciously framed by any member of the groups involved.

The whole of this argument is worked out in relation to the story of the introduction of the peyote crl among the Winnebago Indians.

We have now to turn from the study of the contact of peoples to that of what I have called "borrowing," and to consider some of the psychological principles at work in the latter. Transmission by borrowing has already been defined as the process by which elements of culture are introduced into a new home through the influence of some individual who has himself acquired these cultural traits in the course of his travels or through some travelling group of individuals who eventually return to their old home. When we were dealing with the typical case of "contact of peoples," we pictured a migrating group, often small in numbers, travelling over considerable distances, and at length settling into a new home, among people very different from themselves. But this cannot be said to be the only means of transmission of culture, though, particularly at a lowly level, it may well be the most important means. A roving individual, or group of individuals, may go out from an original home, may wander among alien cultures, and, returning, may introduce new customs. These are the two typical processes, on the one hand of "contact," and on the other of "borrowing." There is a third process, already referred to in the preceding chapter 1, which seems to be intermediate between the two, in the sense that it possesses some of 1 p. 136.

the characteristics of both. This may be called transmission by constant inter-communication. It occurs when peoples who were originally distinct, though living in neighbouring districts, come frequently into touch with one another, through the movements back and r."rth of their individual members. In this case also Clements of culture will be interchanged, though the situation is not identical with that of the small group migrating over long distances, or with that of the individual, travelling from his own community to a foreign group, staying awhile, and then returning again to his people.

It has often been questioned how far, for the purposes of the study of transmission, a culture must be taken as itself a unit. Are there, that is to say, a whole group of customs, institutions, ceremonies, and perhaps beliefs, which must be regarded as moving together, so that if we find actual evidence of one we can assume that the others must at some time also have been present? This is clearly the case with the typical form of contact, where we have to picture the group moving as a group and carrying its complex culture with it into a new environment. But such a state of affairs does not always hold good. Both in "borrowing" proper, and in transmission by constant intercommunication, some element may actually be "lifted" out of its setting and put into a new frame. This possibility must be borne in mind throughout our discussion, and we will consider whether our illustrations give us instances in which this has occurred.

In one respect borrowing presents us perhaps with a somewhat easier problem than contact. The process of borrowing is going on under our immediate observation 11-2 almost every day. The same is also true of contact, particularly if we consider the relations of sub-ordinate groups within a large community. But here probably the processes are less easy to observe, and certainly they are less frequently noticed. While contact proper seems to be a mode of transmission whose importance at thx; truly primitive level is very considerable, borrowing, through individuals or by intercommunication, rapidly assumes the primary position as the course of civilisation advances. In spite of this, however, the conditions of borrowing are not by any means easy to demonstrate. The processes involved are complex, subtle, and intimately intertwined. And it is as true of borrowing as of contact that our present survey must be brief and incomplete.

To some extent precisely the same conditions come into play in borrowing, as in contact, and they work in the same way. Thus, in so far as the underlying primitive instinctive social relationships operate they produce the same effects; but they are more important in the case of contact, and in that of transmission by constant inter-communication than in borrowing proper. The conserving instinct, and, as I shall try to show, in a special manner the constructive instinct, come to the fore. Group difference tendencies serve much the same functions in both instances; but with borrowing the individual instinct tendencies and the influence of individual difference characters of the personality of the individual that is spring into greater prominence.

I propose to take the risk of offering a treatment which may appear somewhat narrow, and to make most of my remarks upon the process of borrowing centre about Dr Paul Radin's "Sketch of the Peyote Cult of the Winnebago 1," a case which is of special interest owing to the detailed record obtained. I believe that the conditions which will emerge as a result of a study of this illustration, will prove capable of application to numerous other instances.

"The peyote," we are told, "was introduced among the Winnebago by John Rave, a prominent member of the Bear clan 2." He had been a roving, unsettled sort of man, but knew all of the ceremonies of the Winnebago, except the Medicine Dance.

Up to 1901 he was a heavy drinker. In that year he went to Oklahoma and while there ate the peyote. He then returned to the Winnebago and tried to introduce it among them, but none with the exception of a few relatives would have anything to do with it. This did not in any way discourage him however, and he continued using the peyote, now and then getting a new convert 3.

Gradually the new cult made its way until a very large part of the tribe accepted its practices.

At the outset the use of the peyote appears to have had very little to do with religion, or at least it was in no sense the introduction of a new religion. After Rave had first eaten peyote he had depressing experiences, and bad visions. He then interpreted these phenomena, in a regular Winnebago fashion, as due to the peyote or medicine itself. " Help me medicine," he cried," I should have known that it was you from the very beginning. As long as the world exists I shall use you 4." He ate more peyote, had delightful visions, and became a convert. But it was not, at this time, a new religion to which he was converted. His attitude was "similar to 1 Amer. Jour, of Religious Psychol. vol. vu, 1914, pp. 1-22.

2 Op. cit. p. 8. 3 Op. cit. p. 7. 4 Op. cit. p. 8.

the average Winnebago attitude toward a medicinal herb obtained either as a gift or through purchase. There is only one new note stimulation by a narcotic 1."

He then believed himself cured of a disease by the peyote, and with some ritual performance he cured his wife of the same trouble. The ritual contained nothing new. "Rave's attitude throughout, both from his own testimony and that of others, seems to have been practically the old attitude of a Winnebago shaman."

We have, then, at the beginning, apparently only the introduction of one new element the peyote; with possibly a few Christian teachings derived by Rave from his experiences at Oklahoma. Everything else seems to be typically Winnebago, and in consonance with their shamanistic practices.

On the whole, the extension of the Winnebago cultural background seems to have been so instantaneous that as far as the specific cultural traits of the Winnebago are concerned, there was no introduction of a new element. This view does not, of course, interfere in the least with the fact that to the Winnebago themselves the presence of the peyote represented the introduction of a new element 2.

The next step is one of particular interest. At first the reformer's attitude to the old Winnebago life was "certainly passive and unantagonistic 3." Both his general behaviour and his adherence to the old ceremonial show that his attitude still remains that of a typical member of his specific group. The group difference tendencies which have collected about Winnebago religious or ceremonial practices are unquestioningly retained. The conserving instinct is uppermost. There is a minimum of innovation.

1 Op. eit. p. 92. a Op. cit. p. 9. 8 Op. dt. p. 9.

Then followed a change of attitude. For acquiescence came "violent hatred and antagonism 1." The older tribal practices were now heartily condemned. How the change came about is not clear.

It probably represented the interaction of many ele-vnents, the hostility of the tribe, the drawing of issues sharply around certain points, and the gradual assumption on the part of Rave of the role of a prophet who had solved the problem of the adjustment of the Winne-bago to the surrounding white civilisation 2.

As Radin points out, the questions that arise here rather concern the transformation of culture which may be produced as a result of changes within the community, "although the initial stimulus for the change came from without 3," We shall return to this later, but it is worth while pausing here to note one or two points.

In the first place, it appears fairly certain that Rave's change of attitude was due in part to susceptibility to those influences arising directly from a group, upon which comment has already been made. Rave was definitely the leader of the ceremonial practices at this time. Such delegation of leadership as occurred came later, when the cult had become more widely accepted, and even then was never complete. As the centre of attention in the ritual group, Rave was at once subject to influences which would lead him to emphasise his own peculiar position in the community. The assumption of the role of a prophet, with the function of reconciling the position of the tribe and the demands of a surrounding civilisation was Rave's answer to a socially initiated demand.

In the second place, the community on the whole 1 Op. cit. p. 9. a Op. cit. p. 10. 8 Op. cit. p. 10.

represents the old conserving tendencies. The social position of Rave, as leader of a new ceremonial group, tended to stimulate within him the constructive, radical tendencies. These came chiefly into operation, however, in making Rave sympathetic to a second set of changes introduced by another person.

It was, we are told, at a time when Rave's hostility to the old life was at its height that a new convert, Albert Hensley, revolutionised the entire cult by introducing the reading of the Bible and positing the dogma that the peyote opened the Bible to the understanding of the people; and by adding a number of Christian practices, such as, perhaps the interpretation of giving public testimony and Bible interpretation. He too had been in Oklahoma for a long time. He brought with him many peyote songs, generally in other languages, and dealing with Christian ideas, upon which subsequently Winnebago songs were modelled. He introduced likewise either baptism itself or an interpretation of baptism. 1.

There was no attempt to interpret the peyote itself in terms of the Bible. On the contrary the peyote remained central, as at the beginning, and it was through the peyote that the Bible was interpreted. All of the elements of old Winnebago culture that were now reinterpreted, had even in the former days been subject to "great variability in interpretation."

"Rave's attitude towards the innovation of Hensley seems to have been that of benevolent acquiescence 2." This, as I have already pointed out, is precisely what would have been expected to follow from Rave's new ceremonial position. But what is particularly interesting is that the Bible, once accepted, was immediately 1 Op. cit. p. 10. Op. cit. p. 11.

treated, like the drum or the rattle, as a part of the ceremonial regalia. The new object served its purpose by acting as a differentiating feature which distinguished the peyote cult from other ceremonial practices. Beyond that it was itself interpreted, by the help of the peyote, it is true, but in terms wholly in consonance with the old Winnebago culture.

There was subsequently a split between the two innovators, mainly produced by the headstrong nature of Hensley, the younger man. But the later borrowings had set a definite stamp upon the cult. The Bible continued a part of the ceremonial regalia, and there remained "the Christian conception of the giving of testimony, or confessions, and possibly the Christian conception of baptism 1." Moreover, when the ceremony was performed in the open air, a fireplace shaped like a horse-shoe was made. It had a small mound of earth at one end, and this was called Mount Sinai. In front of the mound was a cross, and on the mound, among other regalia was placed a small staff called a "shepherd's crook." New songs, peyote songs, were introduced, and a new kind of symbolic drawings was developed. The drawings were generally placed upon rattles, a type of regalia peculiar to the peyote cult, and represented visions or scenes taken from the Bible.

What is specially interesting about all this is that many of the elements of the new cult may be precisely paralleled from the old ways of the Winnebago. The songs, the drawings, the mound 2, the cross, the use of the regalia are all old. They are used in old ways for new purposes, and sometimes with new interpretations.

2 It is the old sacred mound of the Buffalo Dance.

In order that we may realise how completely this is the case let us turn to Radin's analysis of the "relation of the peyote cult to the old cultural background."

He points out first that Rave, as a prominent member of the Bear clan, had participated in almost all of the old ceremonies, and was intimately acquainted with the Winnebago ritualistic and organisation units. Consequently as the new cultural pattern developed, it did so wholly on a basis of the old ceremonial practices. We need not suppose however that they were consciously uppermost in Rave's mind. His construction of the new was largely a continuation, or application, of the old, but it did not appear so to him. In the same way

Rave's extension to the peyote of all the associations grouped around the medicinal herbs was unconscious and instantaneous. The only really new thing he brought back to the Winnebago for further assimilation was the peyote itself, its ceremonial eating, and its effects 1.

Round this one new feature gathered gradually many of the old observances and customs a ceremonial circuit of the lodge; two sacred peyote, one male the other female; the old sacred mound of the buffalo-dance; crossed lines drawn on the earth; the association of the peyote with the hearing of voices, a visit to the home of God, the gift of song, the fore-telling of events, and so on. Yet certain interpretations representing new Christian beliefs came in also: the mound was interpreted as Mount Sinai; "the crossed lines as the cross with Christ upon it, the ceremonial crook as the shepherd's crook, or as the rod with which Moses smote the rock 2." These new interpretations, however, varied from person to person, as the old ones never did.

1 Op. cit. p. 20. 2 Op. cit. p. 21.

In some instances it is difficult to tell whether there was real substitution or merely re-interpretation in terms of the old culture:

Dipping one's hand in water and drawing lines on the forehead of an individual sounds like the real Christian baptism, to be sure. Yet we know that painting the patient's face was a prominent feature in the shaman's treatment of disease; and that Rave speaks of it in connexion with the conversion of his own wife. Are we then to regard the baptism here as a re-interpretation of the old Winnebago custom, or as a real substitution of Christian baptism? And if the latter alternative is accepted, what influence are we to ascribe to the older Winnebago belief in suggesting Christian baptism? 1

Precisely the same question arises in regard to the crook, the practice of public testimony, and certain of the stories which have become attached to the peyote ceremonies. There is no doubt that with regard to every one of these the Winnebago already possessed elements in many respects similar. Such borrowing as took place was, as Radin says, selective, and was determined "by the specific possessions of the recipient's background 2." Once the peyote cult began to make headway among the tribe, specific additions were inevitably made by different individual converts. These cannot be traced in detail. But the important point is that they were all distinctively Winnebago. The new cult, that is, became more and more established within "the emotional and cultural setting of the old pagan background 3." Hensley, himself, who appears to have been more radical in his innovations than anybody else concerned, "felt 1 Op. cit. p. 21. a Op. cit. p. 22.

9 Op. cit. p. 15.

it necessary to introduce an origin myth 1." This myth was borrowed from a southern tribe, but in Hensley's narrative it had already assumed all the characteristics of a Winnebago fasting experience and ritualistic myth, similar to those connected with the founders of the old Winnebago cult societies 2.

Thus the whole peyote cult became subject to the influence of the old Winnebago practices, and in it they persisted with new expressions.

From Radin's account we can see clearly how two different attitudes were involved. First we have that of the older and more conservative converts. They tended to interpret the new in terms of the old. Thus "to one, the eating of the peyote gave the same magical powers as were formerly associated with membership in the Medicine Dance 3." To another: "faithfulness to the teachings of the peyote cult became associated with a certainty of reaching God, of being able to take the right road in the journey to the spirit land 4." Rave's own attitude towards the Bible is another illustration of the same tendency.

In the second place there is the attitude of the younger, and less conservative converts, especially of such as had been trained in the East, and brought directly under the influence of Christian teaching. These, on the whole, precisely reversed the conservatives' point of view, and tended to interpret the old in terms of the new. Their influence comes out most clearly of all in the use which they made of some of the old folk tales and myths.

"The old people," they said, "often spoke of the Trickster, but we never knew what they meant. They 1 Op. tit. p. 16. 2 Op. tit. p. 16.

8 Op. tit. p. 15. Op. tit. p. 15.

told us how he wrapped a coon-skin blanket around himself, and went to a place where all the people were dancing. There he danced until evening, and then he stopped and turned around. No one was to be seen anywhere, and then he realised that he had mistaken for people dancing the noise made by the wind blowing through the reeds.

So do we Winnebagos act. We dance and make a lot of noise, but in the end we accomplish nothing 1."

And again:

"The Trickster was walking around with a pack on his back. As he walked along, Some one called to him. Say! we want you to sing." " All right," said he, "I am carrying songs in my pack, and if you wish to dance, build a large lodge for me, with a small hole at the end for an entrance." When it was finished, they all went in, and the Trickster followed them. Those who had spoken to him were birds. He told them that while dancing they were not to open their eyes, for if they did so their eyes would become red. Whenever a fat bird passed the Trickster he would choke it to death, and if it cried out he would say, "That's it, that's it! Give a whoop!"

After a while one of the birds got somewhat suspicious, and opened its eyes just the least little bit. He saw that the Trickster was choking all the birds. "He is killing us all," said the bird. "Let all who can run for their lives." Then he flew out through the top of the house. The Trickster took the birds he had killed, and roasted them; but he did not get a chance to eat them. For they were taken away from him by somebody.

So are we Winnebago. We like all that is forbidden. We say that we like the Medicine Dance; we say that it is good; and yet we keep it secret and forbid people to witness it. We tell members of the dance not to speak about it until the world shall come to an end. They are afraid to speak of it. We, the Winnebago, are the birds, and the Trickster is Satan 1."

In this way the old tales were pointed with new morals, very much as is done every Sunday in countless places of worship in our own times and community.

Two further points must be added, and we shall then have all the main features of this interesting case of borrowing before us. The actual dissemination of the cult among the Winnebago followed family lines. A convert at once set to work upon the other members of his family. His mode was to make a strong appeal to family ties and personal affection. He showed unusual courtesy, showered innumerable favours upon relatives he was anxious to convert, and thereby earned the gratitude of the recipient, who at some critical moment, let us say, such as illness or mental depression, showed it by partaking of the peyote 2.

If the convert's attention passed beyond the bounds of his family, his method of propaganda remained the same, and consisted in a sustained attempt to establish very friendly relations with the person whom he was anxious to influence.

Finally, as the cult spread, as a certain amount of delegation of leadership became necessary, and as the immediate personal ascendancy of Rave consequently declined, the stronger and the more definite became the influence of the old Winnebago culture.

We must now try to see how an analysis of the facts of the illustration that is before us, may bring out some of the psychological processes of transmission of culture by borrowing. We began our study of "contact" from the primitive instinctive social relationship forms. We 1 Op. tit. pp. ie-7. 2 Op. tit. p. 13.

must begin our study of borrowing by a consideration of individual instincts or of individual interests. Whether, as in our present illustration, the borrowing is effected directly through a given individual, or whether we have borrowing as a result of the continued intercommunication of two peoples, without a change of place of residence on the part of either, the process starts definitely from what an individual notices and responds to in the new environment. Now all the available evidence shows us that in Rave's case we have a man whose interests from an early age centre about ceremonial practices. It was not merely that he knew that there were these practices. Every Winnebago would know that. It was not merely that he knew what they were. It was that he had, as Radin says, "participated actively in all the prominent ceremonies," and had a definite bias in this direction 1. As to whether there are sufficient reasons for assuming a distinct religious instinct or not, we need not now inquire. But that there is a "religious interest, or bent," original so far as the individual is concerned, stimulated by early training, but not wholly derived from this, and taking specific forms of development in different instances, seems to me indisputable. Rave, and I think also Hensley, show distinct evidence of the possession of such interest. Its possession forms the first condition of the borrowing of the peyote as central in a ceremonial pattern, of the songs, of the origin myth, of the Bible, and, in part, at least, of the public testimony. Apart from this the borrowed elements of alien culture would not have attracted more than a mere 1 I may be allowed to point out here that Dr Radin has seen this interpretation of Rave's character, and has expressed his entire agreement.

passing notice, would not have been interpreted, would not have been remembered; and, most important of all, the stimulus to overcome the conservatism of the old home, and to introduce the new elements there would have been lacking.

This demand for a prior operation of individual interest, or instinct, may be made for all instances of transmission by borrowing. What are the kinds of detail which have most frequently been introduced into new settings in this way? Articles of food and of dress, weapons of warfare, stories and myths, practices connected with material arts, ceremonial observances, religious beliefs, details of play. They are all of them characters about which special individual interests often gather, or towards which individual responses are directed. Here at the very root of the process of borrowing is a reason why, in any particular instance, some elements of culture should be affected and not others. Here is a basis, in borrowing, for the definite "lifting" of cultural elements out of one setting and into another. We may say broadly, with regard to any element of culture whatsoever which excites a lively individual interest, that this detail may be removed to a new home, although associated cultural elements are not transmitted.

Perhaps, in the end, this means that there is practically no element which may not be treated as a unit for the purposes of transmission. It will, however, be noticed that in the list which I have given of the details most often transmitted by borrowing, no place is given to important changes of social organisation. There is no doubt that certain methods of social organisation, particularly as they affect relatively small groups in a community, are borrowed by individuals at a high stage of development. Thus peculiar college organisation and practices are frequently carried by individuals from one group to another. But at a primitive level it almost seems as if this does not occur, and as if radical changes of social organisation can be effected only by contact, and never by borrowing. This may be partly due to the fact that modes of social organisation are so built into the group structure that it is by an effort of abstraction possible only at an advanced stage of development, or to persons of very exceptional character, that an individual is able to make them objects of interested attention. They represent on the whole social impulses proper, called into operation essentially by life in society, and they are very largely of a specific social character, requiring not only a social stimulus, but the stimulus of a special social grouping, to bring them into play. Thus fundamental modes of social organisation are cultural characters which are likely to be carried about with a body of culture, by a whole group, and are less likely to be borrowed by individuals, and so "lifted" from their general cultural setting.

Further, details of culture may gain a footing in a community very gradually, owing to their repeated practice by an individual. But changes in social organisation, to be effective, demand the simultaneous co-operation of a considerable number of members of the group.

Though this distinction is broadly true, there is perhaps one feature of social organisation, and this a feature of enormous interest, which may constitute an exception. It has been pointed out by many writers, that names of kin commonly tend to outlast the social institutions by which they were originally produced.

Thus ethnologists have frequently argued that the presence of kinship names may be used as evidence for the earlier existence of institutions now defunct. May we assume that where two groups having different systems of social organisation live near enough one to the other to allow of a fair amount of inter-communication, kinship terms can be transmitted as units? Suppose the sections of the group which bear the common name, possess also ceremonial functions, the latter being common in the two groups, or similar in both. It then seems possible that the names may either have spread from one group to the other as units, or else have been taken over with some feature of ceremonial only. Perhaps such a process is unlikely, but if it ever has occurred the presence of certain kinship names need not mean that a particular type of social organisation, with which they are generally found, must have existed wherever the names are used. For the names in this case would represent u lifted" elements, and not integral parts of a whole body of associated culture.

However this may be and I do not wish to suggest that we have here more than a bare possibility the beginning of the individual borrowing, with its interest basis, is obviously only a very small part of the whole process. The next of our factors to come into play are the group difference tendencies. Whatever the instinct or the interest aroused, the individual in whom it is aroused can never free himself from the effects of his special social training. In fact it is precisely in reference to his predominant instinct and interest tendencies that the individual is most responsive to his native social environment. Within his own community, just as in an alien community, the customs, beliefs and material that ifte in line with a man's original tendencies are those which most effectively claim attention. This is simply to say that the very same influences that lead to borrowing, also make the borrowed material peculiarly likely to be assimilated to old practices, ways of thinking, and modes of feeling. Once the individual tendencies have prompted the borrowing, the group difference tendencies enter and determine what shall become of the borrowed material.

In the last chapter I put forward the view that many of the "compromise formations" arising from the contact of cultures, as a result of which there is some introduction of the new together with much preservation of the old, involve a tendency towards constructiveness which requires a social setting for its practical application. We have now to pursue the idea of constructiveness somewhat further. The essential considerations are that the new is not merely accepted, and the old is not merely preserved, but that new and old are woven into a practical working system which is expressed in the community, and changes the lives of the members of the group in more or less important ways.

We have seen the mechanism at work in the case of John Rave. That very interest in ceremonial or religion which prompted him to take over the peyote, also put the peyote into its place in relation to the old Winne-bago customs. The point that I want particularly to stress is that the process, definitely constructive as it was though only to a small degree, since, at first at least, it did little more than weave a new element into an old culture pattern was not consciously so. We may return to Radin's description of how Rave produced his ceremonial.

What relation did his old knowledge bear to thI new cult he founded? Was there, for instance, a conscious substitution of the type of ceremonial organisation, and of the ritualistic unit of the older ceremonies; or was there a sub-conscious continuation of the same? I think that we are probably dealing with the latter, and that none of the units of the ceremonial complex really arose into his consciousness. It is (as Radin goes on) rather important to bear this in mind; for it has a fundamental bearing on the question of the older cultural units playing the role of conscious patterns 1.

This view is wholly in line with the trend of modern psychological thought. Constructiveness, whether it is expressed in social organisation, in artistic invention, or in mechanical contrivance, has been in the past far too closely identified with conscious purpose. My contention is that there is a special form of constructive-ness which has to do with social organisation. Except in its latest and highest developments it will be found that never wholly, and rarely to any large extent, is the construction effected the outcome of a conscious purpose in which its details and their relations come before attention. What happens is in part what we have seen in this case of John Rave. A special interest prompts the acceptance of a cultural trait as one which is to be practised. The same interest has been developed in a particular social environment, and is consequently expressed in a number of specialised tendencies which form individualising features of the particular social group. The old special tendencies operate upon the new material, and in the result we get either a new practical pattern, or else the former patterns reappear in the new material. There is social re-organisation, a true effort 1 Op. dt. p. 20.

of constructiveness has taken place. But the change is no search for an ideal foreseen, conscious manipulation of cultural elements has little or no part to play.

The effects of the constructive tendency, as they are seen in social life, are practically never due to one person only. The next of our general factors to be considered are the tendencies arising directly from the presence of a social group, and affecting the innovating individual. They exert an influence which displays a very remarkable consistency in large numbers of cases. The present example provides an excellent and a typical illustration of their operation.

We have seen how when Rave first endeavoured to introduce the peyote among the Winnebago his attitude towards the old ceremonial practices was passive, acquiescent and conservative. He was at this time reacting mainly as a member of the old community, and it is most significant that, throughout the history of this case of borrowing, wherever the influence of the community is uppermost, the conserving tendencies are predominant. But Rave's attitude changed. As the cult gained a certain amount of acceptance he became definitely a ceremonial leader. The more conservative elements of the community were ranged against him, while the few adherents of the peyote cult looked upon him as having cut himself away from the older practices, and as having introduced something distinctively new. From both sides came social influences arising directly from the group of his contemporaries, which together determined a change in Rave's attitude. He now began to emphasise the difference between the new cult and the old practices, and to be definitely hostile to the past.

His behaviour is in no respect peculiar. The passage from acquiescence to hostility is made by practically all reformers who attempt to introduce borrowed elements of culture into their native environment. Precisely how the hostility is expressed will depend upon the community, the borrower, and the sphere of culture concerned. But the process is one which belongs entirely to the realm of social psychology, and its broad results, which are the same in all instances, are of peculiar interest.

There seems no doubt whatever that it was Rave's growing hostility to the old Winnebago life which prompted his ready acceptance of Hensley. Of course it was not this alone. Rave was a man of outstanding influence and character, but all the facts suggest that his leadership was of the comradeship type. That is to say, he was very readily responsive to movements initiated by others, and able to assimilate them for the advancement of that in which he was interested. Hensley was a younger man. He was in many ways a more daring innovator. He had been educated in the East, and was more subject to alien Christian influence. What followed throws, I believe, fresh light upon the way in which the social constructive tendencies operate.

New elements came into the peyote cult. And not only do we find new elements, but there are new interpretations also. The testimony, apparently in the first instance adopted merely to make the medicine work, now tends to be looked upon as a genuine confession of sin. Even after Hensley has disappeared from the cult some of his additions remain. The Bible is there, though only as one element of the regalia, the cross is present as a Christian symbol, the mound is called Mount Sinai. The cultural pattern has gained in distinctness and individuality. It is more completely organised. It represents a structure in which the old persists, but the new has gained an established position.

Again, we find that this pattern, this new construction, and the resulting social organisation never were definitely planned by any person. They were not the product of Rave's foresight, or of Hensley's, or of any other individual member of the peyote cult. The first step was the introduction of a new element by Rave. Then followed the work of the group difference tendencies of the Winnebago which set the new element into an old ceremonial frame. Then came the inevitable operation upon Rave of socially initiated influences as a result of which he became growingly hostile to the old ways of life. Then the more violent innovator appeared. Hensley's and Rave's contributions mingled, were dealt with by the peyote groups, and in the end a pattern evolved which was undoubtedly a social construction, but which no person in the whole community can be said to have foreseen.

This is, at any rate in part, the story of all the cultural patterns that have ever been elaborated. The final constructions, with the details and their modes of relation, are never fully foreseen. The constructive tendencies which make new patterns of organisation within the community, are at work in the individual and in certain groups as inevitably and as universally as the conserving tendencies. But there is no reason for supposing that either the conserving or the organising tendencies must operate in the full consciousness of any given individual. In their social expressions they practically never do.

We must now turn our attention to the mode of dissemination of the peyote cult. And here we come upon those fundamental forms of social relationship which proved to be of the first importance when we were dealing with contact. How borrowed elements are diffused throughout a group clearly depends upon a number of different factors. Suppose the elements to be introduced by an individual, as in the case which we are now considering. Much will then depend on the type of leader which this individual makes. If he is of the domineering or aggressive type, the dissemination is the less likely to follow old lines of social organisation, and the material disseminated is the more likely to retain its novel character. But if he is of the acquiescent or comradeship type it is the more probable that the material will be disseminated along the lines of existing social institutions, and also that the novelty of the new material will be somewhat worn away in the process. This should make it clear that a considerable influence in dissemination may be exerted directly by the characteristic mode of social organisation which holds good when the new materials are introduced into the community. Finally there is no doubt that we ought to take into account also the nature of the new cultural material itself. New games are not likely to spread in exactly the same ways as new weapons, new ceremonial, or new beliefs.

Now John Rave, as we have seen, appears to have been an acquiescent or comradeship type of leader 1. The real unit of social organisation of the Winnebago is the family, in the narrow sense of that term. The family is on the whole, in spite of the predominant position of the elders, a fellowship group. Already I 1 As I have pointed out in an earlier footnote (p. 175) Dr Radin admits that his observations agree with this view.

have urged several times that a "comradeship" group makes naturally for conservatism. The dissemination of the peyote cult followed the lines of the family. Practically all the influence of the real Winnebago converts was towards the more and more complete merging of the new practices into the old cultural patterns. The moment Rave's personal influence was withdrawn these tendencies became yet more strongly marked. Thus we may say that what becomes eventually of the borrowed material depends largely upon the social relationship that holds between the people among whom it is disseminated. And the more this approximates to the comradeship type the more is the borrowed material likely to lose its characteristic features and to become merged in an old culture.

It now becomes more evident than before that the problem of determining, in a given instance, whether a certain element of alien culture has been "lifted," or whether it must have been transmitted together with associated elements, is almost always a difficult one. For even supposing that a mass of associated cultural traits are originally taken over, provided they find a home in a group exhibiting relations of social harmony, they will be bound to undergo much modification, as a result of which most, though not all, of the peculiar features may disappear. This problem, however, more properly forms a part of the study of the assimilation of borrowed material.

A final principle emerges from our discussion. Whenever, in this or in the preceding chapter, our attention has been turned to constructiveness, or to the development of social organisation, it has been in connexion with a conflict of tendencies. We were reminded of construction in the last chapter when we considered compromise formations, and in this chapter when we considered how newly accepted practices may be confronted by old group difference tendencies, or how the recently borrowed practices accepted by one individual, may have to be reconciled with others accepted by a different person. The fact is that it is only where tendencies, persons, or groups are not wholly in harmony that construction, either within the individual mental life or in the community, is possible. The most highly organised groups are always groups which have contained discordant elements or sections. But the working out of this principle also belongs to the study of changes produced within a community itself when alien material or practices have once been introduced.

The peyote cult seemed in the end to divide into two groups, though there was no open break between them. By the one group the new was interpreted in terms of the old. This was the Winnebago group proper, the converted conservatives. By the other group the old tended to be thought of in terms of the new. On the whole this was the group of younger people, with an Eastern education. A similar grouping tends to arise in reference to nearly all borrowed material in every community. Such groups show the parts played in the whole process of borrowing by the two social instinct tendencies of conservation and construction. But our illustration indicates very clearly that there need be no mere opposition between the two tendencies. Both groups accept new elements, and while to the one the new is something to be interpreted, to the other the new furnishes an interpretation. It is the inter-play between these two groups which mainly determines the destiny of borrowed material, or custom. But to this inter-play we must turn in the next chapter.

I have thought it well to make the whole of my discussion of borrowing revolve about this one example. But I hope it will be clear that the principles which it illustrates apply far beyond the bounds of the Winnebago community. Allowing for differences in the character of the reformers, in the nature of the materials borrowed, and in the social organisation of the community concerned, the same psychological processes operate in all cases. The point to which I would again draw attention is that the same conditions have been discussed alike in borrowing and in contact. But the order of their appearance has been changed. With contact the most fundamental factors were the primitive social relationship forms; with borrowing, individual instincts and differences occupy the first place. How the individual interests, which are at the basis of the first step in transmission by borrowing, are reinforced by socially expressed needs, desires, and tendencies in determining the process and effects of dissemination, we shall have to study in more detail in the next chapter.

I may now summarise the main results of the discussion on borrowing.

1. By borrowing we mean the transmission of elements of culture through some important individual or individuals.

2. Our study has centred around the story of the introduction of the peyote cult among the Winnebago Indians, by two individuals.

,8. At the basis of all such transmission is the operation of individual instincts or individual interests.

4. These, however, work in conjunction with the group difference tendencies of the community of the innovator. The latter tendencies play a greater or a less important part according as the individual is of a comradeship or dominant type of leader. The new and the old tendencies coming both into play may produce a new cultural pattern, or may bring new material into the old patterns. Such constructive efforts do not demand conscious foresight of details on the part of the individuals chiefly concerned.

5. Once an innovating individual attempts to introduce new elements of culture into his old community influences arise, both from groups accepting his introductions, and from groups rejecting them, which play upon him and tend to excite his hostility to the established culture.

6. It then frequently happens that he joins yet more radical individuals than himself, the resulting further constructive developments of culture being again by no means necessarily foreseen by any member of the group in which they develop.

7. The mode of dissemination of the borrowed elements depends partly upon the personality of the reformer, particularly as expressed in his relationship to the group immediately concerned; partly on the pre-existing social organisation of the community: and partly on the branch of culture affected.

8. In general, the more the dissemination takes place along the lines of groups displaying the primitive comradeship reaction the more conservative the borr wing is likely to be, and the more the new is assimilated to the old.

9. While contact proper on the whole favours the transmission of cultural elements en masse, borrowing often means the "lifting" of specific cultural traits, other associated traits being ignored. But the subsequent loss or the assimilation of particular

elements which may take place as a result of dissemination makes it very difficult to say in a given case whether or not the "lifting" of elements has occurred.

10. The constructive tendency, as it is brought into operation in the development of social organisation, always demands conflicting impulses or competing groups. The constructions effected are never wholly, and rarely mainly, the expression of a consciously formed ideal.

CHAPTER VII
PSYCHOLOGICAL FACTORS IN THE DIFFUSION OF CULTURE

The Argument: At the basis of the diffusion of new culture throughout a group jis the fact that the elements introduced must be attached to a demand which is widely spread throughout the community concerned that is, either to an instinctive response, to specific tendencies peculiar to the people affected, or else to some practically useful end which has already received recognition in the existing culture of the community. This holds good whatever may be the details of the particular mechanism of diffusion which is brought into play; and it has much to do with the fact that while material culture is often adopted as a whole, ceremonial culture is, on the contrary, more frequently split up into details in its passage from group to group.

Once any element or mass of culture has gained a footing in a community, the first step in its dissemination is usually the growth of a special social group which acts as its custodian. Upon this group are brought to bear influences from outside itself which then function in determining the subsequent modification of the new cultural possessions. There is pressure from those members of the community who do not belong to the social group. Suppose it is a question of the possession of some secret of material art, then members of the community who do not possess the secret may strive to obtain it, and so the special group may find its boundaries enlarging and its peculiar position in the community in danger of disappearing. The natural answer to this is the further elaboration of the cultural secrets possessed. If the special group is formed about

THE DIFFUSION OF CULTURE 191 ceremonial elements, then, in general, there is less likelihood that the boundaries of the group will be broken by newcomers; but the group must maintain its prestige by remaining in close practical touch with the lives of the various members of the community. Here also is a basis for the further elaboration of culture. Thus the modifications of culture which accompany diffusion are, in general, the direct outcome of group responses to pressure exerted by sections of the community who are outside the group.

This is the mechanism by which cultural patterns are produced. In studying the development of cultural patterns it is a mistake to concentrate attention upon variations of individual attitude. What we must chiefly consider are: first, the position and functions of special groups within the community; secondly, the position within a special group of the outstanding individuals; and thirdly, the relationship forms that are brought into play as between group and group, and as between individual and group.

Broadly speaking we may maintain that the most characteristic situation for the elaboration of culture is where a special group occupies a position of moderate dominance and is at the same time in close working relations with the rest of the community.

The simplification of culture in general follows either the complete isolation of a thoroughly dominant group, or the breaking down of a group's boundaries through the admission of more and more members from without.

Simplification by isolation tends rather to belong to religious and ceremonial culture, while simplification through popularisation has its sphere on the side of the material arts. Concerning the details of both, however, much further consideration is necessary.

When any element of culture, or any group of cultural elements, finds a new home, either through contact or through borrowing, this is usually but the beginning of its series of adventures. For the new elements may become diffused throughout the whole of the community which has accepted them; and they often persist within this community. Both through their diffusion and in the course of their persistence they are bound to suffer modification. We have considered some of the main conditions of transmission by contact and by borrowing. We must now study the conditions of the changes of culture which are brought about by influences arising within a group after it has accepted the new element of culture. And first of all let us consider a fact lying at the basis of all of the main mechanisms of diffusion a fact of direct psychological significance.

When we considered transmission by borrowing, we found that the process began by an appeal to individual instincts and interests. The individual who roams afield notices in alien cultures only those features which stimulate already formed tendencies within his own mental life. It is such features alone which he will adopt into his own life, and so transmit to others. Yet experience shows that an individual may notice, remember, and, so far as his own practice goes, adopt foreign customs or beliefs, without making any attempt to spread these customs among the members of his native community when he returns to them. This is indeed a common occurrence at a fairly advanced stage of cultural development, where individual freedom is more clearly defined, and individual interests are more widely diversified. At this stage transmission through the influence of important individuals seems usually to demand some further impetus, and hence to afford a good illustration of the reinforcement of tendencies. A special interest has prompted the initial borrowing, and now, super-

THE DIFFUSION OF CULTURE 198 imposed upon that, comes some form or other of " public spirit," as it is called, some group of tendencies directly stimulating propaganda and proselytising.

But we have again to remind ourselves that the nearer we approach to a primitive level, the more do outstanding individual interests attach themselves to immediately practical ends. We have seen how this is exemplified in the case of contact of peoples, where superiority in material arts is probably the most powerful agent in transmission of cultures. And very often it is by the same means that dissemination or diffusion of individually borrowed cultural elements is secured. Or again the individual interest is made to centre about some common instinct, and hence gains an immediately widened appeal. We have seen how safeguard from danger is apt to take a prominent place in the development of primitive ceremonial. It is by association with this uniting the instinctive fear response with an end of immediate practical usefulness that borrowed ceremonial detail is often disseminated.

Of the peyote, for example, we are told that its first and foremost virtue was said to be its curative power. Rave gives a number of instances in which hopeless venereal diseases and consumption were cured by its use; and this to the present day is the first thing one hears about it. In the early days of the peyote cult it appears that Rave relied principally for new converts upon the knowledge of this great curative virtue of the peyote. The main point apparently was to induce people to try it, and I hardly believe that any amount of preaching of its direct effects, such as the hyper-stimulation induced, the glorious visions, and the feeling of relaxation following, would ever have induced prominent members of the medicine-bands to do so. For that reason, it is highly significant that all the older members of the peyote speak of the diseases of which it cured them. Along this line lay unquestionably its appeal for the first converts 1.

We may say definitely that the first step in a process of the diffusion of borrowed culture throughout a community is the attaching of the borrowed elements to some common or some widely shared tendency either to an instinct response, or else to some practically useful end already sought after in practices recognised by the existing culture of the community concerned.

An interesting fact sometimes noticed with regard to the diffusion of material culture, as contrasted with that of ceremonial, seems to me to point in the same direction. In the case of material culture there appears to be a strong compulsion to take over whole complexes, in all their detail. The influence of the horse upon the culture of the Plains Indians supplies a good illustration.

The horse (says Wissler) reached most if not all of the typical Plains tribes from 300-200 years before they lost their cultural independence. In its diffusion over the area a large number of associated traits were carried along as a whole, or as a cultural complex 2.

In part, no doubt, this immediate diffusion of the cultural complex as a unit was due to the fact that in certain of the affected regions a fairly well developed dog-traction culture already existed. But this only serves to point the illustration. The material culture moved readily and as a whole because, without modification, it was fitted to secure certain practical ends 1 Radin, "The Peyote Cult of the Winnebago," Amer. Jour. of Religious Psychol vn, p. 12.

2 "The Influence of the Horse in Plains Culture," Amer. Anthrop. N. S. 16, 1914, pp. 1-25.

that appealed at once to the inhabitants of the areas into which it was introduced. In general, says the same writer, It appears that the tendency in material culture is not so much to profit by borrowed ideas as to take over specific complexes: to take over one specific technological complex after the other, and not to catch up from here and there disparate ideas, to be fitted into one or two unifying conceptions. This is rather in contrast to the conditions observed in the diffusion of ceremonial aspects of culture 1.

It thus certainly seems to be a fact that where material culture makes headway, this is because, as a whole, and with little or no distortion, it fits already existing practical demands common to all the members of the new community. This is less true of alien ceremonial, and so the latter spreads, in the first place, either as an addendum to a welcome material culture, or else because a part of it becomes attached to a practical or an instinctive response.

Once again let me call to remembrance at this point that I am attempting to deal only with conditions which have a very direct significance for social psychology. Beyond doubt the mechanisms for diffusion of culture are many and varied, but in one way or another they all seem to involve something of the kind I have indicated. The point is worth developing more fully, and I will give illustrations from the paper by R. H. Lowie on "Ceremonialism in North America 2." In this paper Lowie cites a considerable number of instances of 1 "Material Culture," Amer. Anthrop. N. S. 16, 1914, pp. 447-505.

2 Amer. Anthrop. N. S. 16, pp. 602-631.

13-2 196 PSYCHOLOGICAL FACTORS IN undoubted diffusion of ceremonial practices, covering practically the whole of North America:

The fact of diffusion (he says) must be regarded as established; and the very great extent to which ceremonials have travelled from tribe to tribe, coupled with the undoubted diffusion of other cultural elements in North America, indicates that, while the process has been greatly accelerated by improved methods of transportation and other circumstances promoting intertribal intercourse, it must have been active prior to these modern conditions due to white influence.

He then turns to a consideration of the mechanisms of diffusion, and points out that (1) "ceremonial regalia were often carried in war, and might readily be imitated, or snatched away from the enemy, and thus become a ceremonial feature of a new tribe"; (2) "during meetings of friendly tribes, dances were sometimes performed for the entertainment of the visitors, who might thus learn a new ceremony"; and (3) " whenever a ceremony was considered (as frequently happened) a form of property, the right to perform it was naturally transferable to an alien who paid the customary amount of goods."

In all of these cases, however, as Lowie points out, we have to distinguish between the transmission of the external features of the ceremonial and that of the ceremonial itself of which the external features may be regarded as symbols. His instance is a good one.

The Matilpe a tribe of the Kwakiutl Indians of the North Pacific area had not been permitted by the other tribes to secure the Cannibal performer's regalia. At one time this village was approached by a party of men and women from the northern tribes, one of the men wearing the badge of the Cannibal order. Two Matilpe youths killed the strangers, and one of them assumed the

Cannibals' cedar-bark ornaments, and at once began to utter the characteristic Cannibal cry "for now he had the right to use the dance owned by the man whom he had killed." It is (says Lowie) clear that the knowledge preceded the acquisition of the badge. In the native mind, to be sure the Cannibal Dance was a form of property that could be acquired by killing the owner; and before its acquisition it did not, from the native point of view, form payt of the Matilpe culture. But in reality, of course, it did form part of that culture; for otherwise the attitude of the Matilpe, both before and after tke murder would be impossible 1.

This is to say that mere conquest by war, apart from the assumption of prior tendencies and in many cases of prior cultural acquisitions, is not a mechanism by which culture is disseminated. And to some extent precisely the same is true if we consider the two other means of diffusion here suggested, diffusion by friendly intercourse and by purchase. In both cases the disseminated elements are transmitted, not merely by being brought into contact with their new cultural environment, but because they do actually appear as satisfying tendencies whether of a religious, artistic or directly practical character present in the lives of those who now accept them. " The Winnebago chant Sauk songs during their Medicine Dance; and the music of songs is readily passed on from tribe to tribe, as in the case of the Grass Dance 2." This is not merely because one tribe visiting another hears the songs during a period of friendly intercourse. It is because the songs do actually appeal to aesthetic, or practical, or ceremonial tendencies already developed in a special manner among the tribe which takes them over. The same is true of elements which 1 Op. cit. p. 615. a Lowie, op. cit. p. 616.

spread, not as the result of a kind of collective friendly witnessing of ceremonial performances, but by passage from one individual to another. The capability of satisfying pre-existing instinctive tendencies, or widely shared practical needs, is essential in all cases of diffusion, whatever the other mechanisms may be.

All that can be accomplished by the means which we have so far considered, however, is to give to the transmitted elements a footing in their new community. Once this culture has acquired its appeal, the precise manner in which it is thereafter disseminated commonly brings a great variety of conditions into operation. But all the instances are alike in certain respects. In the first place, all such dissemination speedily involves the formation of special groups within the community; and in the second place, the social relationship forms subsisting within these groups, and between the groups and the rest of the community, have a very important bearing upon subsequent changes in the transmitted material.

In the early stages of a process of diffusion, when dissemination is being pushed forward through the formation of groups, there is no doubt that pre-existing social arrangements play a very important part. With the peyote it was the family group that provided the first medium of dissemination. But it may be a warrior group, or a craftsman group, or a story-telling group, according to the nature of the elements introduced, and the pre-existing social organisation. The point that does seem of some importance is that diffusion of alien elements within a community practically always demands the utilisation of existing groups, or the formation of new groups who may act, first as centres of dispersion, and, secondly, as custodians of the introduced elements.

THE DIFFUSION OF CULTURE 199

We may take the case of the introduction of some new material art. In one sense we have here a cultural element which is very speedily diffused throughout a whole community. The new art makes as a rule an immediate practical appeal. All the members of the community can share the material advantages which it confers; but in almost every case its special technology becomes the possession of a few. The results of the art, but not the actual practices of the art, are disseminated. A good illustration may be taken from the life of the Ibo.

The life of an Ibo lad (it is said) is greatly influenced by the locality in which he lives. His fellow-townsmen may follow an acknowledged profession, or they may be simple farmers, fishers or traders. The men of Awka, for example, are renowned throughout the Ibo country as clever blacksmiths, and they traverse the country from end to end plying this craft. These men make extended itinerations annually, a large number of towns being visited. Again the men of Nri are the priests whose presence is essential for valid celebration of the ceremonial rites in connexion with the coronation of kings, and they travel far and wide in the performance of their priestly functions 1

We have, that is, a large number of groups possessing special cultural secrets, or having special functions. By means of these groups materials or ideas are diffused throughout the whole community; but the production of the material, or the communication of the ideas, is the function of the special group. When new culture is introduced it gains its position and is disseminated through the development of new groups, or through the adoption by the old groups of the new cultural elements, 1 Basden, G. T., Among the Ibos of Nigeria, London, 1921, p. 78.

The study of the disposition and structure of groups serving the purposes of dissemination is of very great interest, but too complex to enter upon here. Looked at from without the centres developed for the diffusion of material culture within a community often appear to h ve an almost exclusively local or geographical basis. But this is never more than a part of the story. It may be that owing to the presence of certain natural products, culture connected, say, with the preparation of food becomes localised. But once this step has been taken, other than geographical factors, facts belonging to the realms of sociology and social psychology, tend to keep the practice of the culture within its localised group. As Wissler remarks: a group having once worked out a process like the use of acorns, its practice tends to find its way over the contiguous acorn area, and where established to persist. The successful adjustment to a given locality of one tribe is utilised by neighbours to the extension of the type and the inhibition of new inventions or adjustments 1.

When we turn to the branches of culture which have to do with ceremonial, religious, artistic or linguistic developments, we again find that introduction into a new community is practically always followed by the formation of special groups for diffusion and preservation. But in this case it seems that pre-existing social structure nearly always plays the chief part. Artistic and linguistic forms tend, even at a stage of fairly high development of culture, to become the special concern of existing ceremonial or religious groups, and their diffusion is apt to be strictly limited to certain members 1 "Material Culture," p. 485.

THE DIFFUSION OF CULTURE 201 of the community only. Ceremonial and religious innovations are likely to be taken up either by special sections of existing ceremonial groups, or else by groups having an intimate relationship, such as the family group of the Winnebago.

The point, however, upon which I wish to direct special attention is that once these groups are formed there is brought to bear upon their members precisely the same socially initiated influences that we have already seen affecting the individual innovator. The man who is the centre of attention in a group at once becomes subject to new conditions of behaviour. He responds to these, in most instances, in such ways as to increase his prestige within the group. We saw these tendencies at work moulding the form and matter of the folk tale. We saw them producing hostility to old ceremonial ways in the religious reformer. We considered how they might stimulate constructive tendencies, and the elaboration of new cultural patterns. We must now try to trace their effect upon special groups in determining changes of culture that are produced from within a community.

Here again we shall have to keep in mind the difference between material and artistic culture, and ceremonial and religious practices. In real life these two groups are very closely intermingled. Secrets of material culture are held side by side with special ceremonial functions. The manufacture of war weapons, or of canoes, the preparation of various forms of food, are very often indeed the peculiar craft of groups having closely associated ritual functions. But, at the same time, the attitude of outsiders towards the material culture is broadly different from their attitude towards the ritual. And on the whole we may say that a group is likely to become more isolated, more distinctively differentiated from the rest of the community in the practice of its religious and ceremonial functions than in its pursuit of the material arts. In both cases the predominant effect of the outside social influences arising within the same community is to accentuate those differences which characterise the specially formed groups. While this process is apt to be long continued in the case of the ceremonial group, it is far more prone to suffer check in the case of the group with the secrets of material culture.

Probably the chief reason for this difference between the treatment of ceremonial and material culture is that at the primitive level, ceremonial grows largely out of fear. The ritual practices are not so much desired for themselves 1, as cultural elements which it is dangerous to omit, and at the same time dangerous to indulge in, except with proper safeguards. The group whose prerogative it is to practise them is thus playing with dangerous toys, it loses no chance of increasing its prestige by its assumption of an aloof attitude, and by emphasising the fearful nature of its secrets. To a greater or a less degree the ceremonial group at all levels tends to occupy a marked, if not an isolated position, and this is partly in consequence of its natural response to that 1 This, of course, is not by any means always admitted. Lowie, for example, urges that there is no point in attempting to find a psychological formulation for a ceremony. "Consider the ceremony not as a primitive religion, or as a primitive attempt to coerce the forces of nature, but as a free show, and then it is seen that ceremonialism exists for ceremonialism's sake." No doubt something may be said for such a view, but it covers only a part of the facts.

THE DIFFUSION OF CULTURE 208 fear which its practices inspire in the rest of the community.

But this consideration does not in the least apply to the group in its function as practising material arts. Very often the members of such groups intermix freely with the rest of their community, and practise their culture far and wide. What they produce immediately satisfies common needs in the most straightforward manner. The group gains its prestige, not through fear, but through its positive value in the everyday life of the community. As a group it will endeavour to maintain its integrity, and to increase its authority. But its social relationship to the rest of the community is different from that of the ritual group, and the methods by which it endeavours to maintain and improve its position are correspondingly different. On the one side we have, in general, tendencies towards the isolation of groups, on the other we have constant broadening of the basis of groups. The former leads to an initial elaboration followed by the decay of culture, while the latter results in simplification and perhaps in the disappearance of the arts, unless they are rejuvenated by alien influences. These effects must now be considered in greater detail.

There are, broadly speaking, two general conditions of a psychological nature for the development of elaborate culture within a special group. The first of these conditions is that membership of the group should carry with it a position of prestige in the eyes of those who remain outside, and the second is that, in spite of this superiority the special group should not be too strictly cut off from influences coming to it from beyond its own limits. The elaboration of culture within a com- munity, that is, appears to demand a social group which is seeking dominance, but is not in fact immediately and overwhelmingly dominant. On the one hand absence of organisation favours the simplification of culture, and on the other hand a strict organisation which gives a group unquestioned dominance, so that it ceases to respond to the influences arising from other groups in the community, also tends to produce a decayed and simplified form of culture.

Dr Haddon, in his study of the decorative art of New Guinea, points out that in the Torres Straits and Daudai, representations of animals are common, but they are not as a rule elaborated into pictures or scenes. They remain disjointed fragments. And this, he believes, may be due to a general lack of social organisation in the districts concerned, and to a wholly democratic social state 1. If, on the other hand, we take the enormous elaboration of ritual which took place among the Jews after the Exile, with the establishment in a position of unchallenged superiority of a priestly group, and compare it with the degeneration of that ritual which later took place, we seem to have simplification due, not to the absence of organisation, but to the over-organisation of a particular social group. Again, speaking in a very broad sense, I should maintain that the first type of simplification is the commoner in respect to the material arts, and the second type in regard to ceremonial and religious practices.

Supposing that this view is both correct and significant, it should follow that, as a general rule, ritual simplification and disintegration are preceded by a period of elaboration of ceremonial. We will therefore 1 Roy. Irish Academy, Cunningham Memoirs, No. x, p. 66.

THE DIFFUSION OF CULTURE 205 consider some of the conditions which favour development of elaborate ceremonial within a community. Here, as elsewhere, our analysis cannot hope to cope with the complexity of the facts. The result which we are studying, the elaboration of ceremonial culture, is obviously the outcome of a large number of conditions, by no means all of which are of direct psychological interest.

The first thing that we must do is to distinguish as sharply as may be, between the reception of culture into a new home, and the weaving of the newly accepted culture into more and more elaborate patterns. The elements to be elaborated come, as has been illustrated in the last two chapters, from without the community concerned, as a rule, and in any case from outside the ceremonial group which is immediately involved. But the arrangement of these elements is the work of the ceremonial group, and is mainly a matter of the interplay of this group with others in the community.

The complexity of Australian ceremonial culture as contrasted with the unusual poverty of their material arts has often been commented upon. Now many of the elements of their culture certainly seem to have been introduced from an alien environment. But the communities which adopted them already contained a strong ceremonial group consisting of the elders. Whether the functions of this group were in any way transferred to the immigrants, or the possessions of the immigrants became a part of the ceremonialism of the already existing groups of old men, the ritual group was a strong one, and at the same time was in constant and many-sided contact with the rest of the community. It is a part of the social responses of a dominant group in intimate relations with the rest of the community 206 PSYCHOLOGICAL FACTORS IN to strive to increase its prestige. The group will react in this manner as inevitably as does the individual leader of the normal type whenever he is both in close touch with, and in authority over, his followers. Consequently any new ceremonial elements that are introduced, if they are accepted, will be added to the old patterns, and used by the group as a kind of additional property for impressing outsiders. In this way the new elements, so long as they can be retained together with the old ceremonial, contribute to the group's enhanced fame and reputation. Thereupon, while the new will to some extent modify the old, the old will far more strongly influence the new, forcing it into a conventionalised form. This elaboration process is particularly likely to occur at a primitive level, because there is hardly any daily activity of life which may not acquire its characteristic ceremonial, and hence the ceremonial group is usually in the closest working relationship with the rest of the people.

It will be seen that my way of approaching this subject is different from that which psychologists have usually adopted. When the elaborate character of primitive ritual is brought in question, it is perhaps most natural for the psychologist to attempt an explanation solely in terms of the individual attitude. The member of a primitive community is supposed to think by different rules from ourselves. He is supposed to revel in contradictions, and to show no impatience with the irrelevant. Whenever he sees one thing follow another he is supposed to believe that the first has caused the second.

Sometimes he is right, and at others wrong. He is unable because of lack of adequate technique to dis-
THE DIFFUSION OF CULTURE 207 tinguish that which is essential from that which is merely incidental, or that which is social from that which is physical. He believes that the order and success of his world depend upon the accuracy with which he is able to reproduce that which tradition teaches him to be the cause. The slightest variation in the prescribed method is believed to be disastrous. Thus rain will not follow upon the performance of the rain ceremony unless all the traditional minutiae have been carefully and literally carried out. This lack of logical analysis is one of the most potent factors in the development of the most elaborate rituals, often extending

over days and sometimes over weeks and months. When at a time of crisis a new element is added, the old remains with but slight modifications 1.

Such an account as the one I have just quoted seems to me to show admirably how futile psychological discussions concerning problems of primitive culture often have been. It slurs over the all-important question of how new elements enter an old ceremonial by speaking of them merely as incidental to "a time of crisis 2," and it turns far too much upon the illogicality of the primitive man. It is perhaps comforting to imagine that the member of a primitive group works with different 1 Henke, The Psychology of Ritualism, p. 59.

2 It should be stated here that Henke does discuss what he regards as the main conditions of the development of ritual, pp. 60-62 and ch. vn. He distinguishes three stages. The first is the one characterised in the quotation. The second is when the group learns to distinguish between what will and will not produce certain practical results (pp. 60-61). The third is " when the group has added the conception of a completely socialised God and the ideal of a completely socialised humanity to the principle of autonomy and to the scientific attitude which culls away any attempt to attain physical results from the ritual." The whole analysis, to my mind, turns far too much upon the conception of changes due to conscious modifications of highly intellectual individual attitudes.

208 PSYCHOLOGICAL FACTORS IN categories from our own. But there is exceedingly little evidence to support such a view. It is not that the primitive man's categories are at fault, but that the material with which he works is on the whole different from ours. The new elements that are involved in ceremonial elaboration come from contact and borrowing. Their assimilation to the old, so far from being a witness of the individual's willingness to accept the irrelevant, affords the strongest evidence of the deep-seated nature of the tendency to make the new relevant. The new cultural elements go into the old cultural pattern, and if they persist within that pattern they do not remain as mere unrelated accretions. They change, are conventionalised, the culture is elaborated, and we have a further illustration of the operation of social constructive processes, the result of which is never actually envisaged by any given individual.

If I am right, the psychology of the elaboration of culture ought to lay chief emphasis, not on any mainly negative or uncritical attitude upon the part of the individual, but on the positive effects upon a moderately dominant group of socially initiated impulses. It is the group's answer to the challenge which operates upon all such groups, the challenge to maintain and if possible to increase prestige, or else to disappear.

We have now taken three steps in our study of the psychological basis of the processes of diffusion. First, transmitted cultural elements gain a footing in a new community by being attached to some instinctive response, or to some very widely shared tendency, or to some practical end which has an immediate and a common appeal. In the second place, they are diffused, and may be preserved, through the formation of special

THE DIFFUSION OF CULTURE 209 social groups, or by becoming the special concern of already existing groups. In the third place, their further elaboration or simplification is in the main the group response to impulses coming to it from members of the community who are outside the group.

The processes involved in this third stage are mainly responsible for the development, through specific groups, of cultural patterns. Already several times we have been reminded of the influence of these patterns in determining the final form of modification of incoming materials or practices. And in the general scheme of treatment which I have adopted throughout this book, cultural patterns are seen in the expression, within distinct groups, of what I have called group difference tendencies. So far we have been concerned mainly with some of the effects of such tendencies. But should we be able to trace the actual growth of cultural patterns we should be concerned, not with the specific results of the operation of the group difference tendencies, but with their development, and with their general functions.

Perhaps it is in the field of ceremonial culture that the fact of cultural patterns has been most clearly shown. Here we may turn again to Lowie's treatment of the North American ceremonial. The Tlingit and the Haida are two closely related tribes belonging to the North Pacific Coast area. Both of them possess important feast ceremonial, generally known as "potlatches."

There can be no doubt (says Lowie) that the Tlingit and the Haida potlatches represent a single cultural phenomenon. Nevertheless there is remarkable disparity between the associations of the great potlatches of these tribes. Among the Haida, the main festival was conducted by a chief on behalf of his own moiety, and was intended only to enhance his social standing. The Tlingit performed a potlatch for the benefit of the complementary moiety and for the sole avowed purpose of showing respect for the dead.

A single cultural trait, that is to say, finding its way into two different, though in many ways nearly related communities, develops in each case distinctive associations, and a characteristic form. Similarly

All important bundle ceremonies of the Blackfeet require a sweat-lodge performance; in nearly all rituals the songs are sung by sevens; for almost every bundle some vegetable is burned on a special altar; and every ritual consists essentially in a narrative of its origin, one or more songs, the opening of the bundle, and dancing, praying and singing over its contents 1.

The same thing is true not only of ceremonial, but of artistic and material culture too. Wissler has demonstrated the occurrence of a number of "design areas" in reference to the decorative art of the American Indian. By concentrating attention upon broad likenesses and differences of design we can, he maintains, " consistently differentiate a few centres of development and influence. These prove also to be centres of specialisation in industrial art." And consequently the design areas are in part conditioned by the geographic and material environment factors which influence the distribution of material art. Not only do we get these broad design areas, but each small territory presents its own particular characteristics. " Art, too, has everywhere strong individualities which tend to obscure the common elements 2."

Our question is as to whether we can give any account, 1 Lowie, op. cit. p. 617.

2 The American Indian, New York, 1917, ch. v.

in psychological terms, of the formation of these culture patterns. Lowie strongly maintains that we can not. Whenever an idea having an alien origin gains acceptance within a tribe, he argues, "it tends to assume the character of a norm which determines and restricts subsequent thought and conduct." Now the notion which underlies this norm may vary indefinitely from case to case. And in every case it originates, not as an idea of a norm, but "like all other thoughts that arise in individual consciousness; its adoption by other members of the social group is what creates the pattern." Never can we tell what ideas are thus going to develop into patterns. In one community some particular concept or practice may "assimilate an alien introduction." In another community, very similar to the first, what appears as the same concept or the same practice, may exercise no influence upon this foreign element which offers itself for possible acceptance. "All that we can say is that patterns exist, and are one of the most active forces in shaping specific cultures 1."

I do not think that the psychologist need accept this conclusion. In the first place we certainly can say one thing more than that "patterns exist." We can see how it is that they come to be formed. And here it is that factors belonging distinctively to social psychology come into play. The evolution of such patterns is an integral part of the dissemination of culture through the formation of groups. A group can act powerfully as the guardian and transmitter of culture, only so far as it gives the culture its own peculiar stamp. Should it fail to accomplish this it will disintegrate, be invaded by members of the community not possessing its own 1 Op. cit. pp. 619, 620, 621.

14-2 212 PSYCHOLOGICAL FACTORS IN secrets, or be merged in some other group. The formation of cultural patterns is in part the answer of a group to forces which are pressing upon it from outside. It is a way the group has of preserving itself. This, as will be seen, is to put in another form our contention that the elaboration of culture, the weaving into characteristic forms of elements drawn from different sources, follows upon the presence of a group in a community which is in close touch with it, and is constantly threatening to break into its bounds from without.

This is psychology; but it gives no answer to the problem propounded by Lowie. It shows that from the point of view of social psychology the determination of cultural patterns need not be regarded as an ultimate fact. But it does not in any way demonstrate what particular ideas will, in a given case, become central in a pattern. This also, however, does not appear to me to be either a futile or a hopeless problem, though it has hardly been seriously attacked as yet. The treatment really belongs to the social psychology of specific groups. There is a precisely analogous, though naturally less complex, problem in individual psychology. Supposing a new idea, or a novel mode of conduct, is presented to two different individuals. Whether they will receive it or not, and what, if they receive it, they will make of it, depend upon their mental equipment and particular state at the time when the idea or the act comes to their notice. But, should they accept it, each will deal with it in his characteristic way. He will have his " patterns " which assimilate the novel. If we know the individual differences of the person in question: the relations of his instinctive tendencies one to another, to the interest,

THE DIFFUSION OF CULTURE 218 or bias, tendencies with which he came into life; and the ways in which these have conflicted or combined in the formation of new modes of response, we can give a fair account of what will happen. What is needed is an intimate knowledge of the individual.

Similarly in the study of the formation of ceremonial patterns what is needed is an intimate knowledge of the group: in particular of its characteristic internal organisation, and of the nature of its social relationship to the rest of the community. The point that I especially wish to emphasise is that our attention should be concentrated not upon the exact nature of the individual attitude what the individual feels or thinks of when he sees or takes part in a given custom but upon the interplay of tendencies in a group having a specific organisation, and between this group and others in accord with the social relationship involved.

The examination of the mode of organisation of the specific group would, I think, throw much light upon the part that is played by the individual both in the elaboration and simplification of culture forms. Here again I must insist that our concern should be, not that the individual thinks or feels so and so in reference to some particular culture trait, but first of all as to his position within the group. Is he a leader, and if so, is he of the assertive, or of the comradeship type? Once this fact has been ascertained it is probable that much of the peculiar development of specific culture patterns within a group the individualistic art designs and technological peculiarities in particular, and to a less degree religious and ceremonial features could be traced to the work of outstanding individuals. But such influence demands a group whose boundaries are restricted, and is on the whole most likely to be effective at a fairly high level of development.

I have spoken throughout this chapter as if we had always to deal with an element, or a group of elements, coming from without, gaining a footing and eventually being assimilated into an existing culture. This is obviously a great simplification of the facts in many instances. In all cases of true contact there is usually a certain amount of interchange of elements. In some directions a group of elements belonging to one of the cultures concerned takes the leading place, and in other directions cultural traits from the other side are uppermost. Let us briefly consider one such instance.

The decorative art of the central district of British New Guinea is characterised by a striking absence of the delineation of human or animal forms, although both of the latter abound to the north-west and the south-east. In the district in question there is definite evidence of important foreign influence. Dr Haddon, in discussing this case, takes the view that the art of the central district is proper to the original Papuan inhabitants. But, he says, a difficulty arises when we come to the tattoo patterns, they being precisely similar to the designs burnt on bamboo pipes and lime gourds. Did the immigrants adopt the patterns from the natives, or vice versa! I certainly incline towards the former alternative. The immigrants do not appear to be at all an artistic people. On the other hand their women are far more richly and universally tattooed than those of the inland tribes; in fact it appears as if the practice had spread from the former to the latter. The only suggestions I can offer on this head are that the immigrants were a tattooed people, and that when they arrived their men exceeded

THE DIFFUSION OF CULTURE 215 their women in number, and consequently they had to intermarry with the original inhabitants. The influence of the energetic strangers was prepotent, and the custom of tattooing spread not only among their native wives, but also among their kindfolk; and finally the designs brought by the travellers were swamped by the local art, and, as in religion and magic, so in art, the conquerors had to yield to the psychological influences of the conquered 1.

If we accept Dr Haddon's explanation, we shall find that it will fit readily into the scheme put forward in this chapter. The conquering immigrants form a dominant group. Whether the actual practice of tattooing may be undertaken by any of them, or whether it is the special concern of a particular organisation within their community, it gives an already existing interest tendency in design. Tattooing remains as a part of the culture of the dominant group, and, owing mainly to intermarriage, is extended to the indigenous people. But the position is markedly one in which a good deal of pressure from without is likely to be exerted on the group who perform the art of tattooing. This is apparently what Haddon means when he speaks of "psychological influences"; we have, for example, the situation in which the kinsmen of the women who have married the strangers are attempting to enter the dominant group and to learn its arts. The group, then, by taking over the original superior designs, increases its prestige in the community as a whole by applying them in new directions. The resulting culture gives us the new material art tattooing together with the old cross-inscribed panel designs, the art coming from one party and the designs from the other, but both 1 Op. cit. pp. 178 ff.

alike, as they are united, serving to exalt and stabilise the position of a particular group in the community.

That the new designs brought by the travellers should be entirely swamped by the local art, is a matter of much interest. Such replacement may perhaps be regarded as a kind of disintegration of culture, but its further discussion may be postponed for the present.

I have here attempted to treat in a somewhat general fashion certain of the psychological conditions which mould cultures in the process of their dissemination. But it is interesting to inquire in greater detail precisely how elaboration and simplification are secured. To that we will turn in the next chapter.

We must now summarise our discussion of the psychological factors involved in the diffusion of culture.

1. Cultural elements find a footing in an alien society by being attached to tendencies already operative within the society. Such tendencies may be instinctive, as they often are when ceremonial is concerned; immediately practical, as they usually are when material arts are concerned; or they may be specific tendencies peculiar to the culture of the particular people affected.

2. Within their new community such elements are disseminated and preserved by special groups, and in the formation of such groups pre-existing social organisation plays the chief part.

3. Once such groups are formed pressure is exerted upon them from outside, as a result of which the normal group response takes the form of elaboration of culture in such a way as to enhance the group prestige.

4. Such elaboration expresses itself mainly in the weaving of the various elements concerted into cultural patterns, rather than in any addition of really novel elements, all such additions coming mainly, if not wholly, from sources outside the group itself.

THE DIFFUSION OF CULTURE 217 5. In a broad sense we may say that the characteristic condition for the elaboration of culture is to have a special group, moderately dominant, in close relation to other elements in the community. In an equally broad sense we may say that the characteristic condition for the simplification of culture is either to have a thoroughly dominant group, cut off from much contact with the rest of the community; or else to have a group whose boundaries are continually breaking down through the admission of more and more members from without. Again speaking very generally, the first condition of simplification seems to belong rather to religious and ceremonial culture, and the second to the degeneration of material arts; but concerning both much further consideration is necessary.

CHAPTER VIII

SPECIAL DEVICES IN THE ELABORATION AND SIMPLIFICATION OF CULTURE

The Argument: Elements of culture as a general rule travel much more rapidly than their significance, which is often attached to them after they have been accepted within a new community.

We must distinguish between the problems of how peculiar interpretations arise within a group, and how they become diffused throughout the group. The first is in general the work of the individual, the second is in the main a question of the position of that individual in relation to his fellow members. Since the individual is necessarily limited in his interpretations by his own past experience, it frequently happens that cultural units having a different origin are assigned very much the same meaning, and this is another of the factors which contribute to the formation of cultural patterns.

Not only are elements of diverse origin thus woven together, but a very common device at the primitive level is elaboration of culture by reduplication. Since repetition may take many different forms, by its means great apparent complications of culture may be produced, although all the time what is being achieved are new arrangements, and not new material to be arranged.

In some instances we have definite evidence of elaboration produced by conscious effort of analysis. The effects of conscious analysis may be distinguished from those in which the analytical effort is unwitting, for in the second case what we find is a tendency for certain elements to swamp all the others, whereas in the first the elements analysed are able to enter into varied combinations with other elements, all the details concerned maintaining their integrity.

THE ELABORATION OF CULTURE 219

Simplification of culture may mean the processes of the introduction of order and law into cultural possessions which were originally of a chaotic nature; or it may mean the actual loss of details. The first does not necessarily lead to decay, but the second usually does. The second only is considered here.

The main special processes involved are: (a) decay through that dominance of particular features which may follow upon unwitting analysis; (6) decay following directly from the fact that cultural elements move more rapidly than particular interpretations; (c) simplifications due to the clash of tendencies, or to the shifting of interests within a group; (d) decay consequent upon the merging of groups; (e) disintegration due to the over-organisation of groups and their isolation from the rest of the community. A matter of special interest is the study of devices that have been adopted in different communities to guard against simplifications arising under any or all of these various heads.

In the last chapter I attempted to picture the general conditions under which, with dissemination of elements of culture, processes of elaboration and simplification are liable to occur. But the devices actually adopted in elaboration, and the exact manner in which the processes of simplification are carried out, must be further considered. Attention must be directed upon the underlying psychological tendencies which are gaining expression, and not merely upon the character of the elaborations and simplifications themselves. It is a matter of no small importance to attempt to set forth the various special forms according to which the development of culture proceeds, and to understand their conditions, in so far as the latter can be expressed in terms of human response.

A brief study of certain forms of ceremonial develop- ment will form an excellent introduction to the problems with which we have now to deal. Here it is natural to turn first to the ritual performances of the Australian natives, for they represent a very long continued process of ceremonial development in groups which have for extended periods been cut off from outside influences. In commenting upon certain decorative designs of the native tribes of Central Australia, Spencer and Gillen point out that these differ remarkably from those of tribes to the east and the west.

Whence the Central natives derived a style of decoration of their sacred objects which is so entirely different from that of the tribes living both on the east coast and to the west of them, it is difficult to understand. One thing is certain and that is that wherever they derived it from they have had it for long ages, as it is associated with their oldest traditions. The entirely different scheme of ornamentation found amongst the tribes of the eastern and south-eastern coasts, of the centre and of the west, points to the fact that these three large groups, each of which consists of many tribes, must have diverged from one another at an early date, and that each one has since pursued its own path of development practically uninfluenced by the others 1.

Even if it is agreed that foreign influences have taken a greater share in the shaping of Australian culture than would at one time have been admitted a view which, as we have seen, the complexity of certain of their ceremonial practices renders highly probable still nobody can doubt that these communities have, for long periods, been mainly self-contained. Study of the characteristics. of their culture ought therefore to teach us something as to the nature of the developments which are possible within the limits of a group. 1 The Native Tribes of Central Australia, London, 1899, p. 151.

THE ELABORATION OF CULTURE 221

One very important point arises immediately. The initiation ceremonies of the north-west Central Queensland aborigines 1 are very similar to those of the Central tribes. They follow much the same course, and contain many identical elements. Also, as Spencer and Gillen point out, certain of the bull roarers of the former tribes "are identical in form and ornamentation with those of the latter, and are used in connection with initiation ceremonies and as love charms, and may not be seen by women 2." Yet at the same time the "significance attached to them" in the two communities appears to differ.

This is no isolated case. Cultural materials in general show far less variety than do the interpretations attached to them. Ceremonial features may be common over a wide area, containing a large number of groups, and yet, from group to group, the accepted significance of the features may change considerably.

The same fact is true of other cultural materials besides the ceremonial. For example there is no doubt that a very great amount of early decorative art has a representative significance. But the associations between forms and their interpretation vary very much in different communities. Among the North American Indians 3, for example, "flying goose" designs are used by "the Tlingit, Thompson, Pit River, Maidu, Wintun, and Yurok, but we fail to find these designs identical or even similar." Again "The Porno quail tip design is found elsewhere under the names bushes, pine cones, mountains, squirrel foot and foot." No doubt it is 1 See Roth, W. L., Ethnological Studies among the North-West Central Queensland Aborigines London, 1897, chs. vm and xm. a Op. cit. p. 152. 8 Wissler, The American Indian, pp. 96-7.

possible that these may be merely descriptive names, indicative of the signs, but not actually expressing their meaning. Even so, the names are interpretations of the signs, and what are to outward appearance the same signs may have different interpretations, or what seem to be the same interpretation may be attached to different signs in one group as contrasted with another.

There is no need to emphasise this fact here, since it has already been widely accepted. But it is important to remember that while ceremonial practices, details and products of material art, artistic designs, songs, and linguistic peculiarities may very often come to a group from without, it is frequently the case that the significance which is attached to the elements of culture grows up from within. Symbolism is apt to be peculiarly esoteric, and hence its study is beset with special difficulties 1.

The first problem, then, is as to how peculiar interpretations can grow up within a community and become current therein. This is a question, in the first place, of the psychology of the development of meanings, and, in the second place, of the transmission of meanings by one person to another. Probably the assignment of meaning is first due in all instances to the individual, who may then, perhaps, communicate the meaning assigned to others. Now what meaning may be assigned to any material whatsoever by an individual is a matter of his instinctive tendencies, their arrangement, and their relation to his individual aptitudes and to his education. But the influence which his assigned inter- 1 Cf. Mallery's "Picture Writing of the American Indians," Rep. Ann. Bur. Eth. 1888-9, pp. 133, etc.; or DAlviella's Migrations of Symbols, London, 1894.

pretations may have upon other members of his group depends upon his position in relation to them within the group. Assuming the group to display on the whole the relationship of primitive comradeship, and the individual in question to be more or less in the position of a leader, his interpretations will spread rapidly. The more homogeneous the group the more probable is it that his interpretations will satisfy tendencies shared by his fellow-members, and hence find ready acceptance. The interpretations which gain currency in a particular group are, however, always liable to be affected by influences coming from special individual training or observation, and as they spread they are likely to be further modified by social tendencies representing the existing group organisation. Thus, both by virtue of the original individual assignment of meaning, and by its chances of further modification, differences of interpretation grow up in different groups.

We have seen already how the mechanism by which culture is transmitted often renders it impossible that the original significance, whether it is to be regarded as symbolic or not, should at the same time pass over to a new home. The outward observances are carried but not the inward interpretation. Thus, for example, there is a definite mechanism by which the Churinga 1 belonging to one tribe of Central Australian natives may be lent 1 "Churinga is the name given by the Arunta natives to certain sacred objects which, on penalty of death or very severe punish-iaent, such as blinding by means of a fire-stick, are never allowed to be seen by women or uninitiated men. The term is applied. to various objects. but of these the greater number belong to that class of rounded, oval or elongate, flattened stones and slabs of wood of many various sizes, to the smaller ones of which the name of bull-roarer is commonly applied." Spencer and Gillen, op. cit. p. 128.

to another. Spencer and Gillen describe in detail the various ceremonial practices which were observed " when. an Erlia, or emu totem group, living in the Strangway Range, lent some of its Churinga to another Erlia group which lives about twelve miles to the east of Alice Springs 1 On the return of the borrowing party, the Churinga which had been received were taken by the old men, carefully examined and hidden away. "There then followed a corrobboree, in which those who took part introduced a Strangway Range performance 2."

In all such cases chants, words, dances, actual movements and sacred objects may be borrowed, and become familiar to a new group. But often the original significance of these is not known, since that would require far more intimate personal relations than have in fact occurred.

It is, however, psychologically impossible that the borrowed material should remain and be used, or practised, in a community without being given some significance. Moreover its common use or practice by a relatively homogeneous group always tends to give such significance or some details of it general currency throughout the group. This spread of a common significance is aided by the fact that, in its original individual determination, instinctive and widely shared tendencies almost always play a part. Still there remains a chance, which rapidly increases as development proceeds and further elements are received from without, for the growth of peculiar interpretations. Thus cultural elements usually come from without by contact or by borrowing, but cultural interpretations may readily, and very often indeed do, grow up from within by 1 Op. til. p. 159. a Op. oil. p. 162.

THE ELABORATION OF CULTURE 225 individual initiation, and transmission from member to member of a group.

The growth of peculiar interpretations of cultural details within a community, constitutes another of the means by which cultural elements, all of them, perhaps, drawn from a foreign source, are associated in new forms within a given group. Originally distinct units, coming, it may be, from various sources, are associated by dint of some individual interpretation which assigns the same significance to them all, and, this interpretation spreading, they may grow into a complex cultural form.

In the last chapter we discussed how new incoming elements have often been added to existing practices, and have taken their places in a general form already achieved. Thus the Blackfeet Beaver Bundle became a model. for all other sacred bundles within the tribe, and even absorbed the originally distinct Sun Dance and Tobacco ceremonies 1. This final absorption is, however, not a case of association of different elements through some individual interpretation, but of the assimilation of different characteristics through the dominance within a community of certain ceremonial practices. It must be continually borne in mind that all of these processes, while they help to clear up the psychological mechanisms underlying the development of complex cultural forms within a community, still leave the material which is worked into the characteristic forms to be contributed from without. ""Although a community which is cut off from outside influences shows but little sign of a power to invent really new material, there is one mode of elaboration which is obviously open to it. The old may be repeated.

1 Quoted by Lowie from Wissler, op. cit. p. 626. B. 15

Reduplication is beyond all doubt the most common mode of elaboration at the primitive level. And this has an added interest from the fact that it is exactly what happens over and over again in the mental life of the individual, and is the more likely according as the individual is responding without full conscious control. Materials given to be perceived are multiplied in number in their reproductions. Actions to be performed are repeated over and over again in the same way. We have commented already on the frequency with which expressions or ideas in the popular story are reiterated. All these represent modes of elaboration which are found to occur within the limits of the single individual life, or of the single group.

Reduplication is one of the most striking features of the Australian ceremonies, and no small amount of their complexity consists in doing or saying the same things over and over again with but slight variations. The dancing and the singing which accompany most of the practices are monotonous. Among the North-West Central Queensland natives the dancing of the males "consists in the main of a stamping movement of the feet, raised alternately and rhythmically to the time beaten on the boomerangs etc., by the audience." The singing "in its simplest form consists of the repetition, over and over again somewhat after the manner of a chant, of some simple statement or assertion." As for the music, that also displays the same character of repetition, and is apt to appear as "a sort of wail commencing with a sudden rise and ending with a slow prolonged fall 1."

If we turn to the apparently elaborate Intichiuma 1 Roth, op. cit. pp. 119-20.

THE ELABORATION OF CULTURE 227 ceremonies of the Central Australians we find abundant evidence of this tendency to elaborate by reduplication.

The name Intichiuma is applied to certain sacred ceremonies associated with the totems, and the object of which is to secure the increase of the animal or plant which gives its name to the totem 1.

Take for example the Intichiuma of the emu totem as described by Spencer and Gillen 2. This began by the drawing upon specially prepared ground of a somewhat conventionalised representation of an emu. The drawing was covered by boughs which were removed at the beginning of the ceremony. First came "a monotonous chant," lasting for half-an-hour, during the course of which the parts of the drawing were explained by the chief leader. The drawing was then covered up again and u the men returned to the original meeting-place, where, for the rest of the night, they chanted, sitting round the Churinga." During the night three large Churinga were specially decorated and prepared, and three of the elder men and a number of the younger men were chosen to act as far-back ancestors of the emu totem, and descendants of these respectively. At daybreak certain of the younger men were sent off to the women's camp, and the rest" assembled at and sang round the drawing." At sunrise the party left their camping ground and proceeded to a specially selected ceremonial ground. Meanwhile the women and children had been driven from the (glBip, and arrived at one end of the ceremonial ground soon after the arrival of the main body of men. In the middle of the ground stood the three elders, the decorated Churinga on their heads, and these elders, 1 Native Tribes of Central Australia, p. 167.

2 Ibid. pp. 179-183.

without moving their feet imitated the aimless gazing about of the emu, each man holding a bunch of twigs in his hands, the Churinga on the head with its tuft of feathers being intended to represent the long neck and small head of the bird.

The women watched intently.

Then, with a curious gliding movement the performers moved in the direction of the women who thereupon uttered cries of alarm. Once more the three men stood quietly, moving only their heads, and then again ran for a few yards. Upon this the women turned and fled towards their camp.

The men then returned to the camping place and the Churinga were set upright in the ground as before. About mid-day certain of the Churinga were once more examined and rubbed with red ochre by the chief leader and all the older men, "to the accompaniment of continuous chanting on the part of the other men who sat around." Again they all gathered round the drawing of the emu the meaning of which was once more explained by the head elder. Singing continued at intervals during the day, and just before dusk three newly appointed emu-ancestors were decorated and their supposed descendants "again drove the women and children from their camp to the ceremonial ground, and the performance of the early morning was repeated. 55 The next day exactly the same procedure was repeated and after this "the three Churinga were divested of their decorations, the Ilpintira (i. e. the sacred drawing) was very carefully obliterated. and the ceremony came to an end."

The description from which I have just quoted shows that a strong tendency is found for the repetition of certain of the ceremonial features. The same character-

THE ELABORATION OF CULTURE 229 istic appears in other ceremonies of the same people 1, while the detailed account of a particular set of cor-robboree performances by Roth shows the reduplicating influence at work almost as strongly 2. The Australian natives are not alone in their tendency to repeat. Elaborate ceremonial almost everywhere shows the same features of abundant reduplication.

If we turn to the development of art forms the device of repetition seems to have gained a stronger position than ever. Indeed Haddon speaks of reduplication as "a characteristic device of the decorative mind." In Papuan ornamentation, curved lines, reduplicating the angle of a mouth, as in fish designs, are often met with. We have to remember that here we are dealing with an art which is in all probability dominantly realistic. Thus In some cases (says Haddon) as in undoubted fish these lines are certainly intended for gill-slits; in others for example in crocodiles whatever they are intended for, they certainly are not gill-slits. In the latter cases they may be merely the expansion of that tendency to reduplicate the lost motive or design which appears to be characteristic of the decorative mind; on the other hand it may be an example "of a transference of features or attributes which often occurs in the art of savages 3.

A glance at the illustrations given in Haddon's memoir, or for that matter, in practically any book dealing with the characteristics of primitive art, will show the ten-d ncy towards reduplication coming out strongly. This tendency probably falls into that general movement towards the elaboration of culture which, as I tried to show in the last chapter, may in part represent the 1 Cf. Spencer and Gillen, op. tit. ch. vn, etc.

natural reaction of a group to the social influences coming to it from the rest of a community.

The repetition may of course take a number of different forms. Similar actions may be repeated in different places, or at different times in the course of the same ceremony, or in connexion with the same artistic effort. The repetitions may be performed in order by different participants or for different ends. The device of reduplication may, in fact, appear to add considerably to the elaborateness of culture, while it does not involve the reproduction of any new elements beyond what naturally and unwittingly occur whenever an attempt is made to do the same things over and over again.

It is a question of the very greatest interest, and difficulty, how far elaboration of culture is to be accounted for in terms of actual conscious invention. Certainly such invention cannot be wholly ruled out. But it appears to demand a group whose practices have already gained a firm position in the community. The members, and particularly the leaders, of the group may then cease to be mainly pre-occupied with gaining a certain position in relation to other groups, or with the practical end of their peculiar cultural possessions. They may turn their attentive interest upon the actual performances or arts themselves of which they possess the secret, or in regard to which they hold some special right. Here, if anywhere, we get the stage at which ceremonial is regarded in the light of a free show of interest solely for itselt. But this demands, if it is to proceed to any extent, a fair amount of development, and somewhat settled conditions of life. One process that may occur under these circumstances is that leader-members of a group

THE ELABORATION OF CULTURE 231 may actually attempt to analyse the group culture into its simpler components, and to evaluate the different parts in different ways. This at once immediately increases the probability of transference of like or of different elements from one setting to another, and may suggest modifications of elements which soon come to have every appearance of being wholly novel.

It must not be forgotten, however, that other processes, besides that of conscious analysis, may give rise to novel combinations through the transfer of elements from one setting to another. No small amount of apparent novelty is, as we have seen already in this chapter, due to similar interpretations becoming current for elements having diverse sources; or to the same attitude being adopted towards objects which originally belonged to different systems. Much of it may be traced to those wholly unwitting processes of condensation which are always apt to accompany efforts to repeat ceremonial or other practices which have been heard of or seen. Nevertheless conscious analysis of the structural elements of culture does appear to occur, and may have important effects, both as regards elaboration, and as regards simplification.

We get, for instance, some striking illustrations of this in the Maya systems of hieroglyphics. Although the Maya people cannot be regarded as primitive except in the sense that they flourished very long ago, it is worth " r hile turning to the writing for a few moments.

The Maya were a lowland people inhabiting the Atlantic coast plains of southern Mexico, and northern Central America. They developed a very highly complex aboriginal civilisation. They appear to have " emerged from barbarism" during the first or second century of the Christian era, though undoubtedly a long period of development had preceded this.

It is certain (says Morley 1) that a long interval must have elapsed from the first crude and unrelated scratches of savagery to the elaborate and involved hieroglyphics found on the earliest monuments, which represent not only the work of highly skilled sculptors, but also the thought of intensively developed minds 2.

An extraordinary period of development followed, and this again was succeeded by various phases of decline and recovery into the details of which we need not enter.

Unfortunately there is no means of tracing the long and gradual development of the hieroglyphics. But the point which is of particular interest to us at present may be stated at once.

A brief examination of any Maya text (we are told 3). reveals the presence of certain elements which occur repeatedly but in varying combinations. The apparent multiplicity of these combinations leads at first to the conclusion that a great number of signs were employed in Maya writing, but closer study will show that, as compared with the composite characters or glyphs proper the simple elements are few in number.

Now each Maya glyph is complete in itself. The various parts of it consequently undergo very considerable modifications, partly in order that the complete character may appear as a balanced and harmonious design and partly that it may exactly fill its allotted space. A single example may be given: In a and b we have the normal or regular forms of this element. In c, however, the upper arm has been omitted 1 "Introduction to the Study of Maya Hieroglyphics." Bull 57, Bur. of Amer. Eth.

2 Op. cit. p. 2. 8 Op. cit. p. 23.

THE ELABORATION OF CULTURE 233 for the sake of symmetry in a composite glyph, while in d the lower arm has been left out for want of space. Finally in e both arms have disappeared and the element is reduced to the sign, which, we may conclude, therefore, is the essential characteristic of this glyph particularly since there is no regularity in the treatment of the arms of the normal forms 1.

(Reproduced from Morley op. cit. Fig. 10, p. 23.)

Now: it is true that, apart from any effort of conscious analysis, certain features always tend to stand out as central from artistic designs, and from ceremonial or other customs. What then seems to happen is that the central feature tends to become dominant, swamping the others. There is a kind of unwitting analysis, but its results are by no means those of the conscious determination of structural elements such as we have exemplified in the Maya writings. For the Maya elements may enter into all manner of combinations with the other parts of a composite glyph. They need not appear specially prominent. They need not swamp the other, and accessory, elements in the least. They can be taken from setting to setting and made to form almost v udless novel constructions, as anybody who cares to glance through the reproductions in Morley's interesting book or any other volume dealing with the same subject may readily see.

The teaching of writing was in the hands of the priests. The priests appear to have been in the closest contact with the political and social life of the various communities involved. Moreover the priests taught the secret of the writing only to those of the highest degree. That is to say, we have that very situation closely organised groups possessing important secrets, and intimately in touch with the rest of the community which, as I urged in the last chapter, gives us the typical social situation for the elaboration of culture. In this case the elaboration was rendered enormously more effective by conscious analysis which, by adopting certain elements as essential, opened the way for great wealth of construction with underlying relative simplicity of interpretation. Once again, however, what we have is elaboration, not by the invention of novel materials, so much as by the production of novel combinations.

There can be no doubt that similar processes of purposeful analysis may often have participated in the development of elaborate culture. Among the Porno and Dakota Indians for example, there is a great elaboration of designs for basket work. These tribes constitute what Wissler calls "centres" of areas of design. Here, he says, designs have been analysed into their structural elements and names given to the same. Further, when definite composite designs have been established, the names of the separate design elements in the complex are compounded into a single term. In other words we have an intense systematisation of design composition, with a corresponding terminology 1.

1 The American Indian, p. 96.

THE ELABORATION OF CULTURE 285

Moreover the same process may be observed in its less advanced stages. The Maidu and Arapaho Indian possess less specialised systems of decorative art, and at the same time a longer set of design names. These, it is claimed, turn out u to be the result of a less elaborate classification and a failure to comprehend the advantages of design analysis 1." In fact there seems every reason to believe that we might pass in stages of very gradually increasing definiteness from the wholly unwitting first step of analysis which gives us some one or more central feature, this feature then proceeding to dominate and absorb all the others with which it is associated, to the definite and conscious efforts at analysis which give us genuine structural elements available for ever new combinations in different settings. At the one end we get material such as that of the Alaskan pictographs of which it is pointed out that:

However rude the outline there are for some animals certain conventional signs that clearly indicate to the initiated what figure is meant. With the brown bear it is the protruding tongue; with the beaver and wolf it is the character of the teeth; with the orca the fin; with the raven the sharp beak, with the eagle the curved beak 2.

At the other end we get such definite conscious analysis as has already been illustrated from the Mayan hieroglyphics.

The elaboration which is produced by conscious analysis must always, I believe, witness to the direct power of the individual in the group, whereas the mainly unwitting selection of central features, certainly need 1 Op. cit. p. 97.

2 "Picture Writing of the American Indians" (quoted from Niblack), p. 47.

not do so. That such selection, entirely unnoticed at the time by the individual who performs it, frequently does occur, may be shown by experiment. Let any material of a relatively complex nature be presented to a subject's observation, and thereafter, at lengthening intervals, let this subject be asked to effect reproductions of the material. It will commonly happen, under such conditions, that certain features gradually come to assume a very prominent position in the whole. To these features all others may tend to be subordinated, until in the end the former dominate the whole reproduction. Yet all the while the individual concerned has made no conscious selection, and may even be unaware that he has changed the character of the original. If, instead of repeated reproductions from one person, a chain of attempts is secured in which a number of persons take part, the same process can readily be observed. And what can thus be secured to-day by experiment, has occurred over and over again, in the course of cultural development, by means of ordinary social intercommunication. Indeed, since the voluntary subject of a psychological experiment is commonly far more careful and on his guard, than is the individual in ordinary social life, processes of unconscious selection are more likely to occur in the latter case.

At the same time, and with all possible allowance made for the process of unwitting selection, it can hardly be doubted that, even from the earliest stages in the organisation of society, the individual may have been able to make his power felt, and very often in the direction of an elaboration of culture. The difficulty is not so much to see that this is so, as to realise what are the limits of individual accomplishment in this direction.

THE ELABORATION OF CULTURE 237

The remarks which Spencer and Gillen direct to this point are well worthy of our consideration.

As amongst all savage tribes (they say) the Australian native is bound hand and foot by custom. What his fathers did before him, that he must do. If during the performance of a ceremony his ancestors painted a white line across the forehead, that line he must paint. Any infringement of custom, within certain limitations, is visited with sure and often severe punishment. At the same time, rigidly conservative as the native is, it is yet possible for changes to be introduced. We have already pointed out that there are certain men who are especially respected for their ability, and, after watching large numbers of the tribe, at a time when they were assembled together for months to perform certain of their most sacred ceremonies, we have come to the conclusion that at a time such as this, when the older and more powerful men from various groups are met together, and when day by day and night by night around their camp fires they discuss matters of tribal interest it is quite possible for changes of custom to be introduced. Every now and then a man arises of superior ability to his fellows. When large numbers of the tribe are gathered together at least it was so on the special occasion to which we allude one or two of the older men are at once seen to wield a special influence over the others.

This is all perfectly clear, and the further picture which the writers go on to draw; the meeting of local groups; the suggestion of innovations by a head-man who " stands pre-eminent by reason of superior ability"; the consequent adoption of the innovations throughout a particular locality; the larger meeting of the tribe, with head-men from a still wider area; the discussion of the local change; its further recommendation by its author; the backing of this recommendation by other head-men from the affected district; and finally the spread of the innovation over the whole tribe the whole process appears admirably clear and probable. But then on the top of all this we have to remember that the authors are perfectly frank as to their inability to give definite illustration. "It must, however, be understood," they say, "that we have no definite proof to bring forward of the actual introduction by this means of any fundamental change of custom 1."

It is not, in fact, difficult to see how the individual might introduce radical changes which should then become current in his community; but, as a matter of psychological fact, the possibilities of the individual in this direction are very much limited. He may analyse; he may be the source of much reduplication; he may make new patterns of the old material; he may introduce peculiar interpretations; but in the actual invention of new detail he is practically helpless, unless he has access to communities outside his own and of a different culture. It is this, beyond anything else, which, as we saw in the discussion on borrowing, acts as the spur to those constructive processes as a result of which new forms of social organisation may be achieved; new cultural material produced; and radical changes brought into being. Perhaps for the psychologist the most interesting consideration is that, whether as an effect of contact and the resultant inter-play of social forces in which no one individual can be observed to take the leading part, or as an effect of definite individual borrowing, the radical constructive processes in social life always appear to involve factors whose operation is wholly unwitting.

1 Native Tribes of Central Australia, pp. 11-15.

THE ELABORATION OF CULTURE 239

Our study of the conditions and modes of elaboration is far from complete; we must, however, now pass on to consider the apparently opposite processes of simplification. Here we are at once met by a great difficulty in deciding on the exact application of the term. There is a simplification which consists in producing the appearance of order in a set of customs, or beliefs, that formerly seemed to be full of warring elements. In that sense some of the most elaborate of products may at the same time rightly be called simple. For example, the Maya hieroglyphics seem structurally to be exceedingly elaborate, and in fact are so. But once we have understood how they all display an order of certain essential elements, we can see that as a system they are simpler by far than the more straightforward method of. the pictograph.

There is, however, a simplicity which definitely involves the loss of elements, and which appears, at least within its own realm, to mark a disintegration of culture. Here we may perhaps make a valid distinction between the effects of that" dominance " which unwitting analysis may produce, and the effects of analysis which is consciously performed in the service of some end. The former tends to produce an assimilation of all elements to one form, the latter preserves many forms, and leads to their combination in new ways. In the Dresden Museum, for example, there is, says Haddon, a fine spatula from DEntrecastreaux the handle of wliich is carved to represent a mantis. It is interesting to note that the ends of the first pair of limbs are turned into birds' heads, such a hold has this latter idea obtained over this people 1.

The bringing together of elements from different sources may, in fact, give rise to a genuinely complex form, or it may yield a result in which certain of the elements are wholly lost, being swamped by the rest. It appears on the whole to be probable that the latter is likely to be the case whenever a "dominant" motive, or "pattern idea," or the like is arrived at mainly by unwitting analysis.

Another important source of simplification is the fact that cultural products, or materials, travel more readily than actual interpretations. For this means that elements which are received into a community and copied therein, are reproduced by mere rote and in course of time practically always lose some of their features. Many illustrations of this are given in Dr Haddon's work on the decorative art of New Guinea. He has, for example, collected together a number of instances of a bird and crocodile design carved on paddle handles from the Massim district of New Guinea. In its full form the bird has a neck and body, and the crocodile has an open mouth with tongue and teeth. The bird loses its body, and then its neck until the eye alone is left, this being in some cases reduplicated. The teeth of the crocodile disappear, then its tongue, and finally both bird and crocodile are entirely lost. In some instances the artist, knowing that a bird ought to be present, has, even in the late forms, introduced one, but generally this is not typical in character. The processes of simplification and disintegration due to the simple copying of material whose significance is ill-understood are constant and wholly unwitting, and may in course of time produce results of the greatest importance.

Here it would be interesting to attempt some study THE ELABORATION OF CULTURE 241 of the various means that have been adopted to guard against decadence of this character. Sometimes groups are set apart whose peculiar duty it is to preserve material or customs against disintegration. Special devices again are often adopted to preserve an order of sequence correctly, such preservation frequently being regarded as a matter of considerable importance. The basis of these devices seems to be that there are, in fact, certain types of material which are psychologically more suited to preserve accurate reproduction than are others. But it is by no means maintained that these are purposely selected. Many devices are discovered." and used in everyday life, although their psychological nature and significance remain unknown.

Every society, probably, could furnish us with examples of survivals. The mechanisms by which these are produced may vary considerably, although all survivals afford illustrations of the simplification of culture. Sometimes, as we were reminded when we discussed the social consequences of the violent clash of tendencies, survivals represent earlier arrangements or beliefs which have been driven underground. Such customs and beliefs may persist for very long periods indeed, and are liable, under certain conditions, to break out in almost their original form, though normally they either seem completely to have disappeared, or to show but the merest vestiges of their original complexity. Sometimes survivals seem rather to be due to a shifting of interest which may take place within the community through, let us say, the growth into prominence of new individual interpretations. Perhaps a process of this sort accounted for the apparent change of attitude which has taken place among some of the Australian tribes in regard to the knocking out of teeth.

The custom is probably to be regarded as one which was at some distant time prevalent amongst the common ancestors of the central and eastern coastal tribes, but which has undergone changes as the tribes became separated from one another, and developed, so far as their customs are concerned, along different lines. In some it has retained its old significance, or may even have acquired still greater importance as an initiatory rite, but in others, as, for example, all those inhabiting the central area, it has lost its old meaning, its place has been tak n by other rites, and now it is merely what may be called a rudimentary custom 1.

What we find here holds good in all societies. There is this constant moving about of elements, and simplification in one direction very frequently means elaboration in another. Undoubtedly this factor of shifting of social interests is, however, a very complex one, which itself calls for detailed and special study.

A further point seems to me worthy of particular investigation. As I suggested in the last chapter, any group holding a secret regarded as important by the rest of the community at once tends to be subjected to outside pressure. There will be many who will aspire to membership, and sometimes membership may actually be acquired, by purchase, or other means 2. Now though crafts, for example, or ceremonial practices, may be preserved with considerable faithfulness by a small group, particularly when, being in close touch with Ihe rest of its community, the group is striving to maintain its position, the matter is different if the boundaries of the group are enlarged. With increased membership 1 Native Tribes of Central Australia, pp. 218-14.

2 Cf. Basden, op. cit. pp. 79-80.

THE ELABORATION OF CULTURE 243 comes greater and greater chance of the degeneration due to unskilful or careless copying. Also secrets widely known are very apt to be less sedulously guarded, and the position of the group may decline in consequence, a result which, in its turn, is bound to affect the culture which it possesses and practises.

Finally, over-organisation of a group may also lead to disintegration of culture. For the group now has secured a position of dominance, and needs to make no further marked effort. It consequently tends to lose touch with the rest of the community. This robs it of its most lively stimulus to further achievement, and there is a danger that its own apparent security may lead to simplification and disintegration through mere indolence. But this is a type of simplification which is more apt to affect special groups in a highly developed community than it is to disturb society at a primitive level.

I have dealt in a summary manner with certain of the conditions of elaboration and simplification. There is need for additional research, and all the suggestions put forward require further scrutiny. I have merely indicated a few of the conditions which have psychological interest: there are others. And yet others again such as the disintegration which follows barbarian invasion and conquest are not specifically psychological, though their importance is not to be doubted. In the investigation of the special processes of elaboration and simplification, as indeed is the case everywhere else in the field of the study of primitive culture, the great work of the psychologist lies yet before him.

The main suggestions of the present chapter may now be summarised: 1. Elaboration of culture is often produced by the 244 THE ELABORATION OF CULTURE growth within a community of characteristic symbolism, and modes of interpretation. These, arrived at by the individual, may yet express common tendencies and become current throughout a group. Thus elements of culture having different sources may be attracted together and form complex patterns.

2. A common mode of elaboration is by reduplication of elements.

3. Conscious inventions, and the analysis of cultural elements, may facilitate the transference of elements from one setting to another and so favour elaboration.

4. All of these modes contribute to the production of new complexities of pattern rather than to the acquirement of new materials. The new material, in practically every case, must come from without the group immediately affected.

5. Simplification, in the sense of loss of cultural elements, may come through the growth of some dominant idea, belief or practice by unwitting analysis, the dominant element tending to absorb others, 6. Another mode of simplification is by the unwitting loss of elements through uninstructed copying, it being a common characteristic that elements of culture travel more readily than do the interpretations of such elements.

7. All survivals give us instances of simplification, and may be produced, among other ways, by the violent clash of opposed tendencies, or by a shifting of points of interest within a community.

8. Disintegration may follow if for any reason a group which holds cultural secrets considerably enlarges its boundaries.

9. Over-organisation, as a result of which a special group which has attained an apparently stable position of dominance, is cut off from contact with the rest of the community, may also lead to processes of the simplification of culture. But this is apt to mark rather an advanced than a primitive stage of social development.

CHAPTER IX

THE INTENSIVE STUDY OF THE SPECIAL GROUP

The Argument: When we consider the present condition of psychology, one of the most noticeable facts is the increased attention which, on all sides, is being given to the detailed study of individual differences. In the most general sense this is due to a widespread attempt to set the broad principles of psychology into working relation to the concrete affairs of life.

Turning to our own discussion, we find that it has been in the main pre-occupied with somewhat general principles. Whenever we have attempted to apply these to the actual life of man in the group, the class of factors which have at once advanced into a prominent position has been that of the group difference tendencies.

These are to the group just what individual difference tendencies are to the person. And, in fact, social and general psychology follow closely parallel lines of growth. This suggests that the most important need for the further development of the psychological study of society is to be found in a thoroughgoing intensive analysis of the responses of the special group at particular periods.

This applies equally to the construction of a social psychology adequate to modern needs. For a very striking characteristic of modern, as contrasted with pritnitive, society is the multiplication of groups which marks the former, together with an improvement in those means of communication which keep diverse groups in effective contact. Thus a study, for example, of what is sometimes called "collective bargaining," and of the breaking of contracts entered into by

"representative men" from different groups, shows how great an influence in modern life may be exerted upon an individual directly by virtue of his membership of a group.

Again, an individual who belongs to many different groups, all of which are in effective contact, usually gains greater freedom and improved status. It follows from this that the social constructive tendencies have a wider opportunity and a more unfettered expression in modern life, and the contemporary group may thus gain a more decisively marked individuality.

Both of these considerations indicate that, as we turn our attention from primitive to modern culture, we are called upon to change, not our mode of approach, but rather our points of emphasis.

Practically all the discussions attempted in this survey are introductory in character and of necessity incomplete; we have made but a beginning of the psychological study of our problems. This is only in part due to the great complexity of the subject-matter. More important is the fact that the next step in advance demands the adoption of a mode of approach somewhat different from that hitherto attempted in the present book. We cannot now take this step, but we can certainly indicate in what direction it should be taken. I propose therefore to devote this chapter to a discussion of the main requirements that must be satisfied, if further progress in a genuinely psychological study of society is to be made.

Let us first turn to a brief consideration of the present position of psychology in general. Current psychological discussion tends more and more to be concerned with a study of individual differences. Towards this significant development a number of reasons have contributed. In part it is due to a pre-occupation with problems of a pathological nature; in part to the great recent advances in applied psychology; and in part to the fact that all psychology now tends to be less an affair principally of the study, and more at grips with the life and behaviour of the work-a-day world.

The student of abnormal behaviour finds constantly that in order to understand the causation of the reactions in which he is interested, he must not only analyse their nature, but carefully trace their history in the individual manifestations which come before his notice. A great amount of the study of the psycho-pathologist is occupied with case histories, and his constant attempt is to understand the individual patient. There is no doubt that abnormalities in behaviour are, in general, merely exaggerations of certain of the factors which operate in normal life. Both the results and the methods of psycho-pathology, therefore, are of the greatest significance to psychology in general.

We find, for instance, that recent psychological literature concerning the abnormal contains frequent references to symbolism. It is interest in the pathological which has forced the study of symbols into the prominent place it occupies in contemporary discussion. There is, however, no branch of psychological interpretation more liable to wild and generalised speculation than this branch of the interpretation of symbols. Beyond doubt the greatest source of confusion is the neglect of specific historical study. As I have urged efsewhere 1, a person may receive a symbol, may retain it, may even himself employ it as a symbol; and yet the signification which he attaches to it may be very different from that given to it by the person who passed it on. 1 Folk Lore, vol. xxxi, Dec. 1920, pp. 264-93.

In fact any explanation which turns upon symbolic representation can be accepted as valid only in so far as it keeps clearly to the principle that a symbol must be interpreted strictly by reference to the mental life and personal history of the individual who uses the symbol, or to the characteristic responses of the group to whom the symbol may be said to belong 1. That is to say, the success of the attempt to treat the significance of symbols as matter for scientific investigation depends to a large degree upon the study of individual and group differences.

In the varied fields of applied psychology, exactly the same holds good. The student whose aim it is to apply psychology to the problems of everyday life is forced into a careful study of individual differences. It is, for example, a very simple hypothesis that in the performance of any task of manual work, there is one set of motions, and one set alone, which can be regarded as the best set for the elimination of fatigue and the efficiency of production. It is an equally simple deduction that all workers at this particular task should be taught to employ this special set of motions. The hypothesis was framed and the deduction made in the early stages of the development of what is generally called "motion study 2." But whether the hypothesis is true or not, the deduction is certainly faulty.

It is psychologically improbable that any one good method or style can ever be the best for all persons, and it remains for psychological research to determine the relation between individual physical and mental 1 See also Folk Lore, vol. xxxn, March 1922.

2 E. g. by F. W. Taylor and F. B. Gilbreth. An excellent brief account of their work is given by E. Farmer in the 14A Report of the Industrial Fatigue Research Board, London, 1921, entitled "Time and Motion Study."

differences and the different methods needed to satisfy these differences 1.

There is no need, however, to dwell upon this point. What has been found essential in abnormal and in applied study, is of equal importance over the whole field of psychology. We begin by the determination and statement of a number of simple laws and general principles. But the very moment we proceed to elaboration, or try to detect our laws actually in operation, that moment are we forced to take into our serious consideration individual character and individual history. The case as regards general psychological study admits of no dispute.

Several times, in the course of this discussion, an analogy has been drawn between general and social psychology. The same sort of problems, and, what is even more important, the same general plan of treatment and type of solution, are common to both. Here, once more, in their joint need for a study of the different tendencies, general and social psychology fall wholly into line one with the other.

In the present series of studies a scheme has been laid down for the psychological examination of primitive culture, and the scheme has been applied to the treatment of a few problems of outstanding interest. Whatever the problem, the same factors have been found to be at work, uniting in different ways, and producing varied results. We have traced in different fields the operation of the fundamental social relationship forms, the social instincts, the individual instincts in their social expressions, the influences arising directly from membership of a group, the group difference tendencies, 1 Myers, C. S., Mind and Work, London, 1920, p. 22.

and, in some cases, the characteristics of important individuals. But it is necessary to proceed beyond the mere knowledge that these are the factors that come into play, and beyond the knowledge of what, in a general sense, they accomplish. The task before us is to discover exactly how they work in this or that specific community, and in reference to this or that specific sort of material. All our illustrations have involved some attempt to carry out this further study. But in the main they have been used to justify belief in our scheme as an instrument with which to approach the problems of social behaviour. The impressive thing is that as soon as we have tried to see our scheme at work in real life, the class of factors which has at once sprung into particular prominence has been that of the group difference tendencies.

Our position, then, is exactly analogous to that of the student of normal individual mental life. He begins his study with an accepted list of mental processes sensing, perceiving, imaging, remembering, judging, reasoning, various forms of feeling, and of acting, and so on which are found in all people. He formulates the laws governing the relations of these processes, and states the general results of these relations. He learns how one process helps or checks another, how they become associated according to a few broad rules, and how, as a result of their interactions, new and more complicated processes are produced. But as soon as he attempts to observe the precise manner in which these broad aricl basic responses work together in his own or another's actual mental life, he has to recognise the importance of the tendencies and combinations that differentiate one mental life from another.

At the very beginning of our study 1 it was pointed out that the group difference tendencies are to the group precisely what the individual difference tendencies are to the single personality. To concentrate solely upon the common features of individual behaviour, and upon the simple laws of the relation of these common features, is merely to take the first step in general psychology. In absolutely the same manner, the scheme outlined in this present book, which is chiefly occupied with a study of the relations of the broader features of social behaviour, is intended as no more than a first step in social psychology. We have prepared our instrument, but if we would use it we must pass into new fields of exploration.

Further progress depends mainly upon a thoroughgoing intensive study of the group difference tendencies, as they are to be found at work in specific communities. So far, the social psychologist has shown himself somewhat impatient of this task. Having exerted his powers of analysis to arrive at a general scheme, he has attempted to apply this scheme at once to the solution of problems which affect society as a whole. Such a procedure appears the more easy in proportion as the general scheme proposed gives but small consideration to the place occupied in social life by the group difference tendencies.

To some extent, for example, Professor Macdougalps work undoubtedly lies open to this criticism. On the whole it is fair to say that his Introduction to Social Psychology is mainly pre-occupied with a study of those deep-lying instinctive reactions which unite all people, some of which are found as much outside as within the 1 See pp. 3; 47-8.

social group. It is true that the sentiments, particularly what is called the "self regarding" sentiment, and the relation of these to volition, receive fairly detailed study, and that sentiments often act as differentiating factors between person and person. So far as this book goes, however, the whole of the treatment is admittedly and designedly but an introduction to the definite psychological study of society. And as soon as Macdougall applies his "Introduction" to concrete problems of group behaviour we find him embarking immediately upon a discussion of the very widest and most general problems of society considered as a whole 1. The part taken by the group difference tendencies, by virtue of which much of the almost infinite diversity of social structure and development is secured, cannot be entirely ignored, and there is therefore some discussion of certain types of groups. But his types are very broad types the crowd, the army, the nation and only their general differences come under consideration. We are invited very speedily to deal in the most sweeping manner with wide problems: what is a nation? what are its mind and its will? how do ideas act upon national life? what are the general factors in the development of the nation-group? and what are the main broadly distinguishable periods of racial development? These, undoubtedly, are all questions which must be asked. They are not simple questions, however; and they cannot be answered in one way only. To search for simple answers to these enormously complex problems is to step into the realm of social philosophy rather than that of psychology, with its dominantly realistic bent. Wherever any such simple explanation is advanced in respect to 1 See The Group Mind, Cambridge, 1920.

the actual life of any real group, it requires modification, and the main reason for this is to be found in the fact that, operating within every group, are certain differentiating tendencies which, from the psychological point of view, form that group's distinguishing characteristics. It is thus a matter of the greatest importance, for the further development of a sound psychology of primitive culture or indeed of any kind of culture that what Lowie calls the "monographic attitude" should be adopted.

Some students (says Lowie) fix their gaze upon a single people at a single epoch of its existence, and endeavour to describe this one culture with the utmost fidelity. In the higher reaches of this type of work the ethnographer becomes an artist who sympathetically penetrates into the latent spirit of his culture and creates a picture after the fashion of Gobineau's Renaissance 1.

Lowie has no difficulty in showing the dangers of this kind of research, should it be taken to be complete in itself. "Science cannot rest content with this aesthetic immersion in distinct manifestations of human society." The reactions of the single group or people, within the given epoch, must be shown to have their place in a scheme which embraces other peoples, and extends beyond the limits of any set time. But while, perhaps, investigators whose ethnographical interests have been uppermost may possibly have tended rather to ignore the importance of the general scheme, the psychologist has on the whole been more apt to fall into the opposite mistake, and to suppose that the single scheme, reached by an analysis of "Society," is alone important.

It must have been noticed that, as a general rule, 1 Primitive Society, New York, 1920, pp. 2-3.

throughout this book, I have taken most of my illustra tions from a small number of studies, and have drawn upon the same sources over and over again. I have done this of set purpose, because I wished by implication, to insist throughout upon the psychological value of intensive monographical study. The researches of Spencer and Gillen into the social behaviour of the Australian aboriginal tribes 1 9 those of Smith and Dale on the Ba-ila; the studies by Boas of the North Pacific peoples; and Hutton's book upon the Nagas all these are outstanding examples of the type of work to which the psychologist must go if he is to put into order, and develop in any detail, his account of the causation of primitive human responses. First hand intensive studies, written from the definitely psychological point of view, such as Mr Deane's account of the Fijians, are particularly important at the present stage of development of the psychological treatment of social life.

There already exists a supply of material; but the psychologist is needed to work out its significance. In order to accomplish his task, he must, it seems to me, have some general scheme such as I have elaborated in the present discussion in his mind. He must then proceed to display the factors already indicated in their varied concrete applications. Consider a question upon which we have merely been able to glance in our discussions of the social mechanisms of the diffusion of culture. The commonest instruments of diffusion are, we found, special groups, or groups with special funfc-tions. The formation and functions of such groups always involve a historical setting. It has been shown that 1 Though here no doubt the area covered is very wide, and could with great advantage be split up into smaller fields.

the lines of their organisation, and the general character of their achievements, are largely settled by pre-existing social arrangements. These differ from time to time and from community to community. In order to discover with what variety of formation and function social groups act as centres of the diffusion of culture, we are bound to enter upon a most careful study of the influences of group difference tendencies in this and in that community.

Again, we have displayed one or two of the commonest devices, and a few of the broadest principles, involved in the elaboration and simplification of cultural materials. But it is clear that these processes bring into play very widely differing tendencies according to the social setting in which they proceed. Here also, then, we find that further advance demands an intimate knowledge of the particular communities concerned.

Yet once more it is an undoubted fact that whether materials are accepted from without, and what, if they are accepted, is done with them, depend very largely indeed upon "cultural patterns." If such patterns are ever to be more than merely accepted facts, if they are to be considered analytically, their development traced, and the manner of their causation elucidated, the main thing required will be thorough-going intensive psychological studies of the groups who possess such " patterns."

In fact the same requirement faces us whatever the concrete problem to which we turn. It is the detailed iavestigation of the responses of particular communities, carried out from a psychological point of view, that is chiefly needed.

Suppose we substitute the study of modern for that of primitive culture. We shall find that exactly the same contention holds good, and, if anything, is of an even greater importance. This is more than a merely interesting fact; it is, as I shall endeavour to show, a matter of real significance in relation to one of our leading problems.

So frequently that it may now be regarded as a commonplace, the remark has been made that the main difference between life in the primitive and life in the modern community lies, probably, in the superior complexity of the latter. This certainly does not mean, as we have had plenty of reason to see, that early social life is simple. Indeed the view that as we approach the study of modern conditions we come from complexity to yet greater complexity, may appear somewhat disheartening to a student who wishes to construct a social psychology adequate to contemporary social life. But, when we try to find in what the superior complexity of civilised life consists, we discover that it lies mainly in the multiplication and division of specific groups, together with immense improvements in the mechanisms of inter-communication. The importance of the latter is that it brings a very much greater variety of groups into effective contact one with another, and also that the same individual may be called upon to act as a member of a larger number of groups. Among the constantly recurrent factors of our general scheme have been those tendencies arising directly from membership of a group. Some of these were found to be very wide-spread and general, and we have dealt especially with those ccfti-nected with the production of laughter, the creation of astonishment, and the fixation and exaggeration, under certain circumstances, of the individual peculiarities of leading men. Some of them have a much narrower

reference, and spring from the peculiar constitution and activities of the group immediately concerned. The latter class displays once more to the influence of the group difference tendencies. As groups split up and become more numerous and diversified the parts played by these become more and more manifest and pervasive.

The general conclusion is precisely the same. If the social psychology of contemporary society is to develop further it must continually take account of the group difference tendencies which form the most direct expression of the influence of certain groups, of their traditions, and of their purposes or functions.

This consideration leads immediately to a question which has been held in abeyance since the beginning of the book. I then suggested 1 that the main difference between the psychological treatment of the problems of primitive and of contemporary society lies, not in the nature of the reactions involved, but in the relative importance of certain responses at different stages. We are now in a position to see one of the implications of this statement. As we proceed from primitive to modern, the influences which come directly from membership of a group, and particularly the group difference tendencies, become more and more important determinants of human behaviour in society. That this is so is in the main due directly to the increasing differentiation of groups, and, to an even greater extent, to that development of means of communication which places the social individual in a considerable number of different groups all, or many, of which may be in close working relationship.

A full discussion of this would lead us far beyond the 1 See pp. 17-24, limits of the present work, but it seems important that at least one illustration of what is meant should be given in some detail, and for this purpose I shall choose a problem which has a direct bearing upon present-day political and industrial organisation.

With the increasing differentiation of social structure consequent upon growing civilisation, many groups having different modes of organisation and varying functions, are occupied with the same practical problems and situations. They all seek to influence the trend of affairs in reference to these problems, although the modes of dealing with them which they adopt may be exceedingly diverse. Thus there has grown up, as an outstanding characteristic of much of our political and economic activities, the device of the "representative man."

The very presence and operation of this device gives us an interesting problem in social psychology. In all probability, by far the greater number of the implications involved in the choice of a man to represent a group for bargaining or for executive purposes were never clearly thought out by those persons who used the device. Yet the plan has been put into actual practice under a large variety of conditions, and may be said to have all the appearance of a practical " notion," or idea, which has been thoroughly worked out by minds interested in social reform. The "notion" of the representative man affords, in fact, a good example of how an idea may act as a kind of nucleus of a constructive device in society, although it is not, and perhaps never has been, a definitely conscious construction fully present in the mind of any person who has made use of it.

The "representative" man is one whose purpose it is to stand for the group in the effective conduct of practical affairs. He meets representative men from other, and usually from differently constituted groups, and with these he discusses what policy ought to be adopted in face of a situation which affects all the groups concerned. It is understood that any decision arrived at by the group of representatives will be regarded as binding upon all the groups for which they stand.

The problem which I propose briefly to discuss is one which has been in increasing evidence of recent years, that of the breaking of agreements entered into by representatives. The elected representatives meet, they conclude a contract, the groups concerned apparently accept the agreement, and then, soon afterwards, some group is found to have repudiated the settlement, and broken the contract. There follows much acrimonious dispute, the honesty of the parties concerned is assailed, and in all likelihood the representative is charged with deceit.

This group violation of contracts is usually regarded from an ethical point of view and condemned. But it can be regarded from a psychological point of view and explained. The most important factor in the explanation is the influence arising immediately from membership of a group. As a member of the electing group the representative is subject to its traditions, to its differentiating tendencies, to its distinctive modes of response. The more strongly differentiated is the group, the more profound and distinctive are the influences. Coming from these he enters a new group, the group of representatives, the discussing group. Just as an individual, put to work upon a new task in a laboratory, may be 17-2 observed to acquire new "sets" or habits with extraordinary rapidity, and thereafter to fall into these with great readiness, so people forming a new group in contemporary society very speedily acquire the distinguishing stamp of special tendencies which soon exert an influence almost like that of long standing traditions. That this is the case must have been observed by anyone who has served upon a new body elected for some particular purpose. The members of the new group meet together, and, almost at once, there spring up tendencies moulding their responses which, it may be in obvious or it may be in subtle ways, distinguish that group, and are found at work within it, but nowhere else. Thus the behaviour of the representative man in the group which concludes the bargain, and his behaviour in the group which has elected him, are conditioned by different sets of factors. He may be equally honest and well-meaning in both, and yet a comparison of his behaviour in the two cases, might appear to afford the strongest ground for charging him with inconsistency.

The representative man is in the position of a leader in the group which elects him. But we have already seen how this may intensify the influence of the group difference tendencies 1. The members of the group look upon him as in some way expressing their own outstanding wishes, emotions, and ways of regarding things. Upon him are focussed all the differentiating influences which give to the group a peculiar position in society. The more he approximates to the comradeship, diplomatic type of leader, the more he is likely to be swayed by these influences. The same character renders him all the more likely to be influenced by the peculiarities of the 1 See pp. 174-5; 178-9.

new group. Thus he may accept an agreement within one group, and then, when he has to put the contract before another group may, without any conscious intent whatsoever, say or do things which are prejudicial to its acceptance.

It goes without saying that this is not the whole story of broken contracts, but it is a part, and an important part, of the social psychology of the matter; and it marks a danger inherent in the device of the "representative man." The psychology of the politician's broken promises is undoubtedly in part the very same tale. Perhaps it is fair to remark that political organisation, particularly in modern times, by its very nature tends to favour the diplomatic type of leader, the man who expresses his group rather than impresses it. This being so it is no matter for wonder that broken agreements are commonest of all in the political world.

Whether we are dealing with economic struggles, or with political bargaining, the occurrence of broken contracts witnesses strongly to the need in the social psychology of contemporary society for a detailed study of those tendencies which mark out one group from another.

There is another way in which change of emphasis must occur as we pass from the study of a primitive to that of a modern group. And since this change is very closely connected with that necessity for the intensive study of the special community which has occupied our attention in this chapter, it may well be mentioned now. The very fact that in contemporary society an individual almost always belongs to a number of different groups which are nevertheless in effective contact, tends to give him a more independent status.

It is with the social individual very much as it is with a unit of mental content such as an idea. So long as the unit is found in one context only it is "tied," but in proportion as apparently the same element of mental content is found to have diverse accompaniments at different times, so it gains freedom, and can be used to take part in various trains of constructive thinking.

The same line of development which makes the group difference tendencies of particular importance in reference to the social psychology of the more highly advanced community, also frequently sets the individual in a position to become a more effective agent in the moulding of social behaviour. It is at no point in the process of social development possible wholly to eliminate the influence of outstanding individuals. Probably, in the past, the scope and power of this influence have often been underrated. Yet there appears to be little doubt that as society increases in complexity, so the influence of the individual is apt to become greater and more far-reaching. And it may, I think, be fairly maintained that the results of this influence are to be seen chiefly in the fact that, as the social order advances, so does the increasing diversity of social organisation which arises show more and more definitely the operation of the social constructive tendencies. For these, as we saw in a previous chapter, frequently witness immediately to the power of the individual in a group 1.

This, however, is not the place in which to attempt to develop fully the demands of a satisfactory social psychology. All that I wish to do at present is to suggest how, in the light of the preceding discussions, we may interpret the position that there is no gulf separating 1 See chapter vi.

the psychological study of primitive from that of modern culture, and to state what is the general nature of the relation between the two. If I am right, the plan of approach must remain substantially the same in both cases; and further, because of its relative simplicity, the study of the primitive group is probably the best introduction to the construction of a social psychology adequate to modern needs. The underlying plan of treatment must remain the same as we pass from the one to the other, but the transition demands a shifting of stress. I have merely indicated two of the places at which the shifting of emphasis must be most marked.

One task remains to be completed within the limits of the present book. Now that we have concluded our discussion of a number of the concrete problems set us in the study of primitive culture, some attempt must be made to re-state the plan of treatment with which we set out, to consider what this plan can accomplish, how it may be further developed, and where its limitations are to be placed. To this general summing up of the whole of our treatment the final chapter will be devoted.

Meanwhile our present discussion may be summarised as follows: 1. Further advance in the application of the scheme proposed in the present work to the problems of primitive culture must depend mainly upon an intensive psychological study of particular communities.

2. This means that the line of development of social psychology is similar to that of individual psychology, for as the latter tends to place greater and greater emphasis upon a study of individual differences, so the former must recognise more and more the importance of those tendencies which are differentiating features of a social group.

3. As we pass from the consideration of primitive to that of modern culture, we find that the psychological factors remain in general the same, but that, largely in consequence of the multiplication of groups, together with great improvements

in means of communication, the influences arising directly from membership of a group tend to acquire a greater significance. For the same general reasons, the direct influence of important individuals is apt to take a higher place as a determining factor in later social history.

CHAPTER X CONCLUSIONS

The Argument: Our attempt throughout has been to study the main underlying conditions of human behaviour in primitive society, in so far as such conditions can be regarded as wholly or partly mental, or as having a direct relation to mental conditions. All of the factors thus dealt with may operate together with considerable divergences of individual feeling, action and thought, and we have not regarded it as necessary to attempt a detailed analysis of such individual experiences.

Each of the conditions specified in our general scheme has been considered as an active agency leading to some form of behaviour, though never as the sole condition of such behaviour. In the present chapter an attempt is made to render the notion of tendency more definite, and to show that explanation by tendencies is not open to the charge of being a mere vicious circle.

Having obtained our general scheme of underlying conditions of behaviour, the next step is to apply the scheme to concrete problems of social life. Such application shows that the most important thing to bear in mind is not the number of root tendencies, but the fact that in actual life they operate together; and that we have always to consider the order of their arrangement, and which of them is dominant at a given time. It shows also that the generalised conditions with which we begin, working together with the facts of external environment, continually lead on to more and more diversified forms of response. These have to be studied in their turn, and in the end we may be able to connect the group reaction with diversities of individual experience and show how the former grows out of the latter.

Whether we deal with primitive or with modern culture, the general nature, both of the problems and of the factors used in their solution, remains the same, though the order of their arrangement and their complexity may vary in important respects. This being so, our present studies may be regarded as introductory to further discussions of the psychological characteristics of modern social life.

We have now completed such discussion of concrete problems as will be attempted in the present book, and must turn to consider precisely what has been accomplished, and how much promise this accomplishment holds in regard to future development. I propose to devote this chapter, therefore, to a re-examination of the plan of treatment with which we set out, to a statement of the points which seem to be of particular importance, and to a further estimate of the line of advance along which our present studies should lead us.

We set out definitely with the idea, not of analysing the exact nature of mental processes as they may occur at a primitive level of society, but of arriving at a knowledge of the determinants of human behaviour in the primitive group, in so far as such determinants are wholly or partly mental, or have a direct relationship to mental conditions. This attitude has been maintained throughout, and it is, I believe, absolutely fundamental to any genuinely scientific discussion of the problems of social life.

Yet it leads directly to a line of treatment, the essentially psychological character of which may appekr to stand in need of justification. Psychological discussion usually turns upon the analysis and description of the nature of individual wishes, desires, feeling, percepts, images, memories, beliefs, and the like. It is concerned chiefly, that is, with analyses of individual attitudes, and of specific mental processes in their individual expression. But reference to such factors as these has, on the whole, been conspicuously absent from the preceding discussions. We have throughout studied the agencies leading to response, and not to any great degree the description and analysis of the responses themselves. This can be seen to be true of every one of the factors of our scheme of treatment. Of all of them it can be said that they are conditions determining behaviour, and that we have been interested in them mainly on that account. The operation of any one of these conditions within a group is consistent with a great variety of individual feelings, tendencies to action, and knowledge, and in dealing with its general place in a scheme of social psychology these individual differentiations need not be taken specially into account.

Suppose, for example, we consider that fundamental social relationship form which I have called " primitive comradeship." This has frequently been treated definitely as a determinant of the attitude of one individual to others within a social group, and consequently as a direct condition of the individual response in society. It may, however, be applied to an attitude adopted towards ideas, or emotions, or actual modes of bodily behaviour. And although as a result of its operation a group may appear to behave uniformly or harmoniously, the individual attitudes and experiences accompanying this behaviour may differ widely. The very ready diffusion throughout a community of certain ideas, or of certain social mechanisms, which may occur as a consequence of the operation of primitive comradeship, clearly does not mean that in all respects the individual emotions, beliefs and general attitudes towards that which is diffused must be taken to be identical.

Or again, as we have seen, "dominance" may compel certain forms of social response; may, for example, be an extremely important psychological condition determining the effects of the contact of different groups. But it would be absurd to urge that, in every case in which dominance comes into play, the attitudes of the different individuals in a group towards the dominant leader, or set, are in every respect identical. One person believes in the leader and likes him, another doubts, a third disbelieves and dislikes, a fourth is relatively indifferent, and so on. Any attempt to deal separately with the individuals would involve us in the seemingly endless task of analysing attitudes and responses differing by all sorts of subtle shades. All the persons in the group are, however, subject to the dominant tendency exerted by the leader or by the set which is in the ascendant, and socially their responses are rightly taken to belong to the same order.

The case is in no way different when we turn to the other factors of our general scheme. The instinctive tendencies, whether they are specifically social, in the sense that they are not found at all outside of the group, or whether they are individual instincts in their social expression, may be accompanied by diversities of individual attitude of very considerable magnitude. The impulses which arise directly from membership of a group clearly do not demand an identical attitude dh the part of the members of the group towards the person, or persons, affected. And so with the other factors until, of course, we come to our definite study of the individual: it is as conditions of social response, capable of being discussed objectively, and not as final terms in an analysis of individual experience, that they come within the scope of our investigation.

This means that the first step necessary in the development of an adequate social psychology is the adoption of a definitely objective method of approach. We ask, that is, what are the conditions of behaviour, not what does an individual think, or feel, or desire when he behaves. Indeed it might almost be said that what I am proposing is a form of behaviourism. Behaviourism as a method in psychology means that the student restricts himself to an elucidation of the conditions of observable human responses. As a theory or, it could perhaps be maintained, as a cult it has come to carry the further implication that the conditions considered belong to one class only, those wholly capable of expression in terms of physical or organic change. I do not argue for the adoption of this further view. No one of the general conditions of human behaviour in the group which we have dealt with can, it seems to me, be reduced without remainder to contractions of muscles, secretions of glands, and the passage of nerve impulses. But they certainly can be treated objectively as general conditions affecting the life of man in the community, mingling, and so giving rise to new agencies or conditions of behaviour, and operative side by side with large variations of individual attitude. What makes the treatment genuinely psychological is that the conditions (fealt with are considered throughout solely as they affect the lives of human members of society.

But now a further misgiving may arise. Every one of the broad conditions of social behaviour which has found a place in the scheme I have proposed, has been treated as a definite agency contributing towards the production of certain results. The commonest of all the terms which have been used to describe these conditions is "tendency." Although this is a convenient word, however, it is very apt to have a vague and floating significance in psychological discussion. It is the easiest thing possible to set up all kinds of tendencies, for various purposes, and to use them as explanatory factors in very much the same way as the old "faculties" were employed. It is desirable, therefore, to examine more carefully the significance of this term, as it has been applied in our present discussion.

A very good method of approach is to observe the responses of any person who is set to work upon some new experiment in a psychological laboratory. There is now a mass of evidence, obtained under experimental conditions, which shows that among the most important of the determining factors of performance in such cases is what is frequently called "consciousness of the task." The phrase undoubtedly covers a number of conditions. There is, for example, all that may be involved in the understanding of instructions given, in the subject's own conclusions with regard to the purpose of the experiment, and in the affective accompaniment of his responses. Beyond these intellectual and affective characters, however, consciousness of the task appears in all cases to involve what must be described as an active prompting, contributed by the subject himself, in the direction of this or that type of response. This fe what, in everyday terms, is meant by gaining a subject's "good will," or by whether or not a subject is disposed to "play the game." Anyone who has had any experience whatever in the setting and marking of mental tests will at once recognise how great a difference this active co-operation of the subject may make. The difference is not due, so far as can be ascertained, to perfect or imperfect understanding. It is not due to the pleasure or unpleasure with which the new task is approached. It is to be referred rather to some preformed bias, or urge, or tendency on the part of the subject, which acts as a real condition, though never as the sole condition of his behaviour.

Again and again, in setting tests of various kinds before a class, I have been struck with the great difference between individuals precisely in these factors of "playing the game." Some persons approach the whole situation in a listless and lazy frame of mind. Others are critical, scoffing, and take their tasks as useless trivialities. Others abide by the rules, co-operate, and, to use another common phrase, u come half-way to meet you" in their readiness to do as they are told. The differences are most markedly not differences in capability of understanding, but they are invariably reflected in the performances of different subjects.

The next point is one of great importance for the general scheme of treatment that has been put forward in this book. Watch any person gradually learning a new and fairly complicated task. As I have already said his early performances are in part conditioned by certain active promptings towards responses of some kind which have to be regarded as contributed by his own mental character. These combining with the specific demands of the new task, produce a new mode of behaviour. But at first this behaviour, whether as watched from without or as experienced from within, is apt to seem hesitating, confused, and perhaps frequently in error. At this early stage the subject may, at many points of his series of responses, have to fall back, not only upon what he has learned in other settings, but upon some bent, or prompting, towards a particular type of performance which has to be regarded as formed before he set to work upon this particular task. The task, that is, is now carried out, not for its own sake, but because it is related to some already existing tendency in the life of the subject: it may be to the dominance exercised by the experimentalist; to a general docility on the part of the subject; to a regard for rules of any kind, or to a number of other ways in which an observer may, so to speak, "rise to meet" the claims of an experiment.

As the new task is performed over and over again, the points at which recourse is had to these generalised promptings become fewer. To outward observation the behaviour runs more smoothly, and the subject himself is far less conscious of checks. Hesitation, confusion, the shock of not being able to pass on to the next stage, all drop out. What has happened is no mere omission of features which have now become superfluous. It is the actual acquisition, through the combination of the old, more general tendencies with the new external conditions of the task set, of a novel and very much more specialised tendency. The observer, when he now enters the laboratory and is confronted by the specific conditions of the experiment, immediately and unfalteringly performs the required task. For his appreciation of the external conditions put before him is new directly re-inforced by a bias, which is at least temporarily a part of his mental character, to perform precisely that series of responses which are demanded. This new and derived "set" or tendency towards a special series of responses may persist but a short time. With disuse, or with a turning aside to other tasks, it may cease to have an independent status, so that should the experimental situation be presented anew, the observer again has recourse to more generalised promptings. But so long as it does persist the tendency, specialised as it is, acts as a real condition and may even be said although it seems impossible to furnish absolute proof to possess an independent "drive 1."

There is another point of importance. Take the ideal subject of a set of mental tests. His performance, according to the view just put forward, is not merely a matter of his understanding of the situations set before him, but of a loyal and effective acceptance of the rules of the game. To that extent it is true to say that he behaves in the manner described because his tendency to accept and act in accordance with the spirit of a given procedure is awakened. Yet, even while he is obeying it, this tendency need be by no means prominently before him. Usually it is not. The tendency is not less effective because the person who expresses it is unaware of the fact. As a rule all such tendencies, however general or however specific they may be, operate in a wholly unwitting manner.

By tendency, then, I mean an active prompting towards a given mode of response whether cognitive, affective, or expressed in definite bodily movement which arises when an individual is brought into touch wfth a situation and attends to it. The tendency must have material to work upon, there must be some definite situation apprehended; while for its part the material 1 Cf. Wordworth, R. S. Dynamic Psychology, New York, 1918, pp. 36-37.

must be met by a tendency if it is to provoke response. The tendency is to be regarded definitely as a mental factor, but it by no means follows that it is a conscious factor. Generally indeed the subject is wholly unaware, at the time at which he makes them, of the part which it is playing in his adjustments. It is a factor which he himself must be regarded as contributing, while the specific situation to which response is made must be regarded as something supplied from without. Consequently tendencies, though mental in their character, can, as I have already urged, be treated in a perfectly objective manner if we so please. Just as we say that a given series of responses was conditioned by a definite set of external conditions, in precisely the same sense we may say that it was also conditioned by a given set of tendencies.

I desire to emphasise one further point. The notion of tendency, as it may be arrived at by an analysis of a subject's experimental responses in a laboratory, is always of something in operation. That is, it requires, as a correlative notion, the idea of a situation which is in some way being attended and reacted to. We may undoubtedly speculate about what happens to a tendency when no such situation is present, when, that is, the tendency is not in actual operation, and the prompting activity ceases to prompt. But there is no real need to raise the question, at any rate so far as the present work is concerned. Properly speaking a tendency not in operation, whatever it may be, is not a tendency. We may perhaps believe that for every tendency there is some corresponding permanent mental structure. But if this is the case we know at present strikingly little about the matter. Moreover, such a structure, even if it could be shown to exist, could itself never be used as an explanatory condition of any form of behaviour. At the most it would be a hypothesis which might conceivably account for the persistence of tendencies, but which certainly could not account for any actual series of responses adopted by any individual in the face of a given situation.

The tendencies which have been made use of in our way of dealing with primitive culture fall into four fairly well-marked classes. First there are those such as the social relationship forms and the instinctive types of response which have the widest possible social application. The situations which they arise to meet are such as may be found wherever there is social grouping at any time or in any place. Second, there are the individual interest tendencies which, like the instinctive tendencies, display a remarkable degree of persistence, but unlike them serve to differentiate one person from others. These come into our scheme whenever we try to deal with the case in which important individuals sway or affect a whole group. Third, there are certain derived tendencies, such as were to some extent dealt with when we discussed the effects of the reinforcement and conflict of the widest impulses. These demand somewhat more specific situations before they come to expression, but still apply to an exceedingly wide range of social grouping. And finally there are what I have called the group difference tendencies which apply to particular grtnips, at particular periods, very much as in our laboratory illustration the special experimental situation seems to come to provoke a narrowly defined tendency to a particular series of responses. The tendencies belonging to this class also are obviously derived. It i8-a appears probable that, once they have become thoroughly established and stabilised in the form of social conventions and institutions, they act as determining factors of behaviour in just as direct and simple a manner as the most fundamental instinctive responses. For example, the tendency to perform certain dance movements which helps to explain the behaviour of the women at a Ba-ila funeral seems undoubtedly to have grown out of far wider sexual, submissive, fear, and grief tendencies. But, by dint of its frequent social repetition, it gains a direct and simple actuating power. The wider tendencies upon which a derived tendency is in part based need not themselves appear in the operation of the more specialised forms. The latter seem always to develop in the direction of gaining independent status, though whether they ever wholly succeed in attaining this position must at present be regarded as doubtful.

All through I have treated tendencies as explanatory factors. But it should now be clear that in no single case whether the tendency be original or derived are they regarded as the sole explanation. The behaviour which we set out to explain is only partially conditioned by the tendency. Always, as well, there is the situation, the perception, imagination, or conception of which gives to the tendency its material to work upon. That is to say, behaviour and tendency are never identical; and to employ the latter as an explanatory factor, is not to revolve in a useless circle.

Our first step, then, in the search for the psychb-logical conditions of primitive human responses, is to elaborate a basic scheme of the main tendencies that are operative in helping to shape the course of behaviour in the group, and to see how, in general, such tendencies are related one to another. Our next step is to apply this scheme, so as to discover how it actually works in reference to this or that type of concrete material or problem.

The second step I have taken, in the present series of discussions, in regard to a few of the questions affecting the interests of men in the primitive group. Enough has been done, I hope, to indicate how the study of social psychology, beginning with an objectively considered scheme of certain general conditions of human behaviour in the group, must develop its main lines of research.

In this light the preceding discussion of the maintenance of elements of culture within a community, and their consequent elaboration and simplification, may be considered. The whole of the inquiry consisted in an application of the general scheme to special problems. It was found that maintenance always demands the operation of certain pre-existing tendencies, instinctive or specialised, in a community; that in general it is secured by the rise and development of special social groups, and that from these groups influences speedily arise which are specific to the constitution and purpose of the group concerned. Some of the ways in which elaboration and simplification arc secured were discussed. The effect and, at least in part, the social mechanism of the growth of symbolism, the operation of a tendency towards reduplication, and the growing part played by conscious invention were considered. Tfie progress of simplification through unwitting analysis; through uninstructed copying; through the clash of tendencies and the shifting of points of interest in a community; and both through the merging of groups and through their isolation was traced.

All the time the use of our general scheme was developing in two main directions. First we were learning how important a matter it is to trace the implications of the inter-relations of those conditions of behaviour which found a place in the scheme. And secondly we were seeing how, in their actual operation, these generalised conditions give rise to numbers of more specific influences.

The first point is one which has often been mentioned; but it is so important that in this reconsideration of our line of approach to the study of social psychology, it must be emphasised yet again. As soon as we try to trace the general conditions of our underlying scheme actually at work in specific fields, the most important thing to realise is that in all cases our general conditions work together, and that their results depend very largely upon how they are arranged, and which of them is dominant. It is with the realisation of this that we begin to cope with the complexity of actual social life. And it is to a large extent this consideration which justifies our view that the general conditions from which we start may equally well stand as our introduction to the psychological study of contemporary society.

Indeed I think it is possible to go farther, and to maintain that a steady realisation of the significance of the inter-relation of the conditions with which we begin, is of greater importance than the mere number of such conditions itself. The number of responses which have by various writers been regarded as fundamental for social psychology has been considerable, and there has, on the whole, been far more dispute concerning the status of such responses than attempt to discover how they are related one to another in real life. Perhaps no one list ever will be accepted as complete and final, but it may well be the case that a study of the ways in which those conditions that are, by a given writer, considered to be fundamental work together, and of the consequences of their inter-relation, would lead to a wider agreement as to the psychological conditions of social behaviour. The same conditions would be found to have places in varied schemes, although they might occupy different positions in different discussions.

The second point, that in the application of the general scheme to different fields we see its broad conditions of behaviour conflicting or combining, and so giving rise of more specialised influences, shows, as I have already urged, exactly the line of development which the social psychologist must pursue. That this is the case can perhaps be seen more clearly if, reversing the order of treatment adopted in the present discussion, we make an attempt to consider the group responses first of all as they are constructed out of varying individual attitudes and experiences. There is no doubt whatever that behaviour in the group has its distinctive forms. This is true, however small is the group. Everybody must have noticed the precarious character of the inference from a knowledge of how individuals react separately to what they will do when they come together. Our studies have shown us the main reason why this is so. It is because the mere fact of the grouping itself contributes some of the determining conditions of Behaviour within the community. What is the precise nature of the relation between individual subtleties of attitude and those determining factors of social behaviour which are drawn directly from group characteristics is, I think, not the first, but the last question of social psychology. We begin with the general scheme. We apply the scheme to relatively special problems which still are broad enough to affect large numbers of different groups, as we have done in our present discussions. We then take the more specialised responses which this application shows us in operation the particular modes and mechanisms of the transmission and maintenance of culture, for instance and trace these at work in the special group at a particular period, or in reference to special departments of culture. This again yields us yet more particularised responses, current within the given group during a known period, or in regard to a special type of material.

At this stage, provided the group concerned is sufficiently open to direct observation, we may legitimately attempt to go farther. We may now try to trace what are the variations of individual attitude in regard to the specialised social responses, and their results, with which our study has now acquainted us. For example, if we take the disintegration of culture which is apt to follow from the over-organisation of a group, and consider its main modes, we may, provided the over-organised group is sufficiently under observation, try to connect these modes of disintegration directly with the thoughts, feelings and actions of the individuals within the isolated group. If we can do this successfully for all of our problems we have taken the final step in the development of a complete social psychology. For we have now effected a union between that study ov the individual as such which is the concern of general psychological investigation, and that account of the psychical conditions of behaviour in the group which social psychology sets itself to pursue.

Thus our line of development is from the most general determining conditions to the most particular, and our final step is to show the relation between the two. Throughout the whole of our study, our procedure is strictly psychological, since, from first to last, we are concerned with a scrutiny of conditions that are of interest to us in that they come into operation as determining human behaviour in the group.

In the very first chapter of this book I tried to make it clear that I consider the psychological study of primitive culture and that of modern social life to be by no means so different as is often supposed. They both, I believe, have to deal with like problems, and both to employ the same methods. Further, both can best be developed on a basis of the same fundamental scheme, and many of the factors to be used are identical in the two cases. That is to say that the whole line of treatment adopted in the present book ought to be regarded, not merely as a contribution to the psychological study of primitive culture, but in a wider sense also, as a presentation of the way in which social psychology must in any case be developed.

Many of the remarks which have been made in the course of our discussion of special problems were put forward partly in justification of this view. But now that a final summing-up of what has been accomplished is being attempted, the contention that we have not two distinct studies, one of primitive and one of modern cfulture, but one consistent method of study, capable of application alike to early and late social life, calls for further comment. For it is probably much more commonly supposed that the psychology of primitive peoples differs radically from that of the modern world, and represents a kind of mystical, pre-logical, lawless phase of mental development which sets the early man at a very far distance indeed from ourselves.

Fully to examine such a position would demand a careful analysis of many concrete illustrations of primitive thinking and behaviour. But that it may be erroneous in important ways can be shown readily enough. Probably the most complete, and the most forcible, expression of the view just characterised is that of Levy-Bruhl in his two very well-known works 1 on the mental processes of primitive man. I choose for brief critical consideration the position which he adopts in the second, and, on the whole, less extreme, of the two books.

To begin with, it is perfectly clear that Levy-Bruhl is proposing an analysis of primitive mental processes, and not primarily a consideration of their main conditions. This proposal probably contains some implication that such processes are to be distinguished as belonging to a very different class from our own. He protests strongly, for example, against the method of studying primitive mentality by attempting to put oneself in the place of the early member of society. Such a procedure, he says, is bound to produce hypotheses which, though they may be plausible, are in fact nearly always false.

Instead of doing this, let us, on the contrary, be on our guard against our own natural modes of mental process, and let us try to discover those of primitive people by an analysis of the ideas which appear to be current within their own groups, and of the ways in which such ideas are connected 2.

1 Les Fonctions Mentales dans les Soei6U Infmeures, Paris, 1910, and La Mentalite Primitive, Paris, 1922.

2 La Mentalm Primitive, p. 15.

Now if we attempt to follow out this exhortation we may very well find ourselves confusing two different questions. There is the question of how primitive man reacts, and the further question of what he reacts to. As I urged in the first chapter, and have illustrated throughout, responses possessing broadly the same character may be made to materials which differ widely. Suppose we analyse primitive ideas and their connexions, we are then primarily concerned with what the primitive man attends to, and not chiefly with how he attends. If, then, we find great and striking differences in the content of attention, we may be tempted to suppose that in some way the process of attending must be equally different.

And this is what Levy-Bruhl does appear to suppose. He is just as strongly prejudiced against the view that primitive man reacts much as we do, as others have been prejudiced in favour of this view. Let us consider the course of his treatment in his book on Primitive Mentality. He deals here, in the main, with the idea of causation. We get multitudes of travellers' stories, all intended to show, in various different realms, what things are by the primitive man connected with what other things. Levy-Bruhl, naturally, has no difficulty in showing that the things directly causally related by the primitive man are not identical with those that are so connected by the modern man of science. In particular the mind of the savage shows a great lack of concern with "secondary causes," with intermediate links of a chain of events. Led away by his strong belief in the operation of mystic and powerful agencies which have a direct contact with daily affairs, he wholly ignores the lessons of ordinary experience. "Causal links," says

Levy-Bruhl, " which are for us of the very essence of nature, the foundation of its reality and its stability, have no interest 1 " for the primitive man: he is swayed by a "kind of a priori over which experience exerts no influence 2."

It is first to be observed that Levy-Bruhts antithesis is not between the primitive man and the ordinary member of a modern social group, but between the former and the scientific expert at work within his own field. This ignoring of "secondary" causes, this direct relating of surprising and sudden events to remote and recondite agencies, is a common enough response, to be observed by anybody who cares to look for it in modern life almost any day he wishes. The error here, as in much recent social and abnormal psychology, is not that the primitive or the abnormal are wrongly observed, but that the modern and normal are hardly observed at all.

In the second place it certainly ought to be pointed out that this ignoring by the savage of the intermediate links given in his daily experience varies very greatly according to the general department of life concerned. Even in the realms chiefly dealt with by Levy-Bruhl those of death, disease, dreams, omens, wounds, war, desire and the like it is not absolute 3. While if we care to turn our attention to the practical inventiveness of primitive man in regard to the search for food, the provision of dwellings, and the development of material arts, it appears that he is as capable of learning from 1 Op. cit. p. 19. 2 Op. cit. p. 21.

3 L6vy-Bruhps own illustrations on pp. 10, 21, 38, etc. seem to show that the savage may be less indifferent to the parts played by intermediate steps in a train of events than he tends to suggest.

experience as the most cultivated of our contemporaries. Moreover, within these realms he learns from experience in exactly the same ways as we do.

We come back, that is, to the position maintained at the very outset of our discussions, and developed in the last chapter. The main difference between primitive and modern is in the arrangement of tendencies; in the determination of which tendencies are dominant at a particular stage; and especially in the operation, in modern and more complicated social life, of numerous derived and specialised tendencies which have been developed in the ways suggested at different points of our treatment. The savage attempts explanations, rationalisations, as we do. More than that he proceeds in the same way, by connecting specific events with something else, and generally with something wider than that which he desires to account for. Not only at the primitive, but at every level, whenever directly practical tendencies are uppermost the procuring of food, shelter, clothing, the guarding of life itself against danger daily experience may count for much, and modes of explanation be adopted which set up chains of causal sequence depending upon minute observation. But again at all levels, though more readily in earlier periods, once times of unusual stress appear the observational explanation may be lost, and rationalisations may be advanced which transcend the findings of ordinary observation.

Thus in different realms and at different times we find events and things differently related, and it may seem to us that primitive and modern mentality are widely diverse. But the difference is partly, as was said at the beginning, due to the great changes of material environment which obtain from place to place or from time to time, and partly to the arrangement of tendencies with which that environment is confronted. The root tendencies connect the years, and though we may acquire new forms of response the old that persist have still the same character and general functions as they ever possessed. A tendency to seek explanations for their own sake, for example, was formerly apt to be dominated and swept along by the imperious demands of the necessities of bare existence, so that it was placed in a subordinate position to other tendencies. It was often checked by fear, and in this way at once connected with forms of religious ceremonial. Such a state of affairs no longer holds good to anything like the same degree. On the contrary the tendency to explain by using the materials of patient observation has grown so strong that it often rules the very tendencies by which it was formerly dominated, and though at all stages it operates in the same way, by seeking the connexions of things, it now works out those connexions in a more leisurely, thorough, and, as we should say, inductive manner.

There is (Dr Rivers has asserted) no greater hindrance to progress in our attempts to understand the mind of men of lowly culture than the belief so widely held that his actions are determined by motives having that vague and lawless character ascribed by many to the thought of savage man. I believe there is no single department of social life in which it cannot be shown that this view is false 1.

I conclude therefore as I began. There is no need to 1 Fitzpatrick Lectures of "Magic, Medicine and Religion," Lancet, 1916, vol. i, p. 123. See also Rivers's essay on "The Primitive Conception of Death," Hibbert Journal, 1912, pp. 393-407.

cut off the study of primitive culture from that of contemporary social life. Both fields display the same tendencies, though these vary considerably in their relations one to another, at different times. And since in modern times the root tendencies may be checked, controlled, and constantly directed in their sphere of operation by derived impulses having a specific character, it is well to begin with the problems afforded by primitive culture. The latter are not essentially different, but they are less complicated.

It will now be clear that these studies in the application of psychology to certain problems of primitive culture are to be regarded as introductory to further studies in the psychological treatment of problems of modern culture. I have already shown that such further research must for some time to come be mainly occupied by an investigation of the particular psychological characteristics manifested by specific groups during set periods of their existence. And I have already given general indications of the main directions in which our future studies are likely to differ from those which we have now concluded.

The main general results of the present discussions may now be summed up: 1. The first step in the development of a social psychology, whether of primitive or of modern culture, should be the formulation of a general scheme of basic conditions of human behaviour in the group, together with a con-sjderation of how the psychological characters which form the scheme are related to the facts of material environment.

2. It is more important to consider the inter-relations of the responses thus taken to be fundamental than to discuss at great length the precise status of such responses.

3. The basic responses are to be considered as the expression of tendencies which are capable of objective treatment, and must be regarded as part determinants of behaviour together with facts which belong to the material and social environment. They are truly psychological in the sense that they are contributions to the determination of behaviour coming from within the life of the person or group whose behaviour is being f studied, and also in the sense that they are considered throughout in their connexion with the actual life of man in society. They are, however, never regarded as the sole conditions of behaviour, and thus cannot be said to be identical with that which they are called in to help to explain.

4. The underlying scheme of fundamental responses put forward in this book applies alike to primitive and to modern social organisation, though changes in relative emphasis and increase in complexity mark the transition from earlier to later stages.

5. The line of development of social psychology must be from a study of the broad and generalised responses of our fundamental scheme to that of the particular and individual institutions and tendencies of the specific group; the last step of all being to effect a contact with general psychology by showing how, upon a basis of the diversities of individual response, the peculiar features of group behaviour may be shown to be constructed.

6. Our discussions concerning the relation of psychology and primitive culture are thus preliminary to investigations into the psychological characteristics of modern group life.

CAMBRIDGE: PRINTED BY w. LEWIS AT THE UNIVERSITY PRESS

Lightning Source UK Ltd.
Milton Keynes UK
UKOW040037211112

202509UK00003B/77/P